The NORTH END ITALIAN Cookbook

The
NORTH END
ITALIAN
COOKBOOK

THE BESTSELLING CLASSIC FEATURING
EVEN MORE AUTHENTIC FAMILY RECIPES

MARGUERITE DIMINO BUONOPANE

LYONS PRESS
Guilford, Connecticut
An imprint of Globe Pequot Press

TO MY HUSBAND, ANGELO; MY GRANDCHILDREN SAVANNAH,
TESSA, JULIANNA, AND SIERRA; AND THE LATE ACTRESS,
JANE RUSSELL, MY BEST SOUS-CHEF AND FRIEND

To buy books in quantity for corporate use
or incentives, call **(800) 962–0973**
or e-mail **premiums@GlobePequot.com.**

Lyons Press is an imprint of Globe Pequot Press.

Photos Credits: Pages ii (bottom) and 99 by Janet Knott. Pages vi, xii, 38, 53, 60, 74, 138, 192, 237, 293, and 304 courtesy of the author. Pages 23, 26, 47, 70, 118, 140, 157, 165, 209, 229, 256, 270, 296, 321, 339 by Ben Lipson. Photos pages ii (top left), iix, 41, 58, 104, and 355 by Jazz Martin, courtesy of *Scene* Magazine; Photos pages ii (top right), 7, 35, 64, 81, 92, 111, 124, 127, 143, 149, 185, 189, 191, 211, 221, 272-273, 295, 311, 323, 332-333, 345 © Adam Mastoon; all others licensed by Shutterstock.com

Project editor: David Legere
Text design and layout: Nancy Freeborn

Library of Congress Cataloging-in-Publication Data is available on file.
ISBN 978-0-7627-8190-4

Printed in the United States of America
Sixth Edition, First Printing
10 9 8 7 6 5 4 3 2 1

CONTENTS

ACKNOWLEDGMENTS

I thank the many friends, seniors, neighbors, and restaurateurs upon whom these recipes have been tried and urged me to write this compilation. I have to sincerely thank the wonderful chefs from our popular restaurants. They took the time to help me with some of the translations and spelling.

I heartily thank the friends whose recipes I have used here and have found delightful. I must say, however, with an apology, that I have often made some changes, additions, or deletions after trial. I give thanks to my neighborhood for having every kind of restaurant, a fruit and vegetable walk-in, specialty shops, meat stores, a grocery store, freshly made pasta and baked bread, an old and famous unique specialty shop where you can find all kinds of herbs, beans, ground coffee, nuts, garlic, and all other spices. A liquor store provides us with the special wines needed in these recipes.

A big thank you to all the senior citizens in my neighborhood that were proud to share their specially guarded recipes, and patiently helped me understand all the scribbled notes. Our ancestors deserve a special mention for their years of peasant cooking and handing them down to the next generation.

My special thanks to all those writers who have, quite unknowingly, given me hours of pleasurable reading. No one person writes a book. I hope I have brought you a greater appreciation for the pleasure of preparing and serving many home-style Italian meals in the comfort of home and family.

INTRODUCTION

When I stop to think of it, my world is full of a number of things, including recipes. They are everywhere: in newspapers, magazines, and all over TV. What do we talk about to friends when we get together? Recipes! And what is taking up whole shelves in our kitchens? More recipes! Recipes are wonderful aids to happy living. We will never have time to try them all, which doesn't dampen my collecting enthusiasm in the least. Recipe collecting is a good hobby for every cook. Whether experienced or not, you can always learn something new, or just learn!

Cookbook collecting has certainly come into its own in the past few years. The irony is that those who love to collect them often don't even use them. They point out that using a cookbook damages it with splattered food and torn pages. Perhaps you will feel that way about this hardcover edition, filing it away, but I hope you instead choose to use it!

In collecting these recipes I have made many friends, both by meeting people interested in cooking who have invited me into their homes and by correspondence. Cooks, I have discovered, are friendly people. I have found a few who refuse to part with an age-old recipe or even one they especially treasure. Sometimes guarding these recipes is not a refusal to hand over something precious but an actual inability to do so. Family recipes are so often without exact measurements. It is always a pinch of this or that, other ingredients and a smile. My mother did it this way and so did my grandmother and her mother before her. When you recall your childhood, don't you always think of something your mother used to make, and wish it had been written down?

In Italian kitchens, cooking has always been looked upon as a pleasure, not as a chore. Do not be frightened off by seemingly complicated dishes. Many can be prepared ahead of time and reheated before serving.

The basis of the most colorful Italian dishes are tomatoes, garlic, and olive oil. Yet it is not at all unusual to find an Italian who likes neither tomato sauce nor garlic. He probably has his spaghetti with a butter and cheese sauce and a melon and prosciutto for an ordinary antipasto.

But there's more to a cookbook than its recipes. There's always something that gets me thinking about food. I love to eat, and therefore I learned early on I had better cook. Do not expect this volume will magically transform you into an Italian cook! But if you wish to approximate the ideas inherent in Italian cuisine, I think this book can, as much as possible, transform you into an Italian family member.

Although Italian food is often delicious beyond belief, some aspects are a matter of preference. For example, the enormous diversity in cooking and serving spaghetti sauces alone is not surprising, since in Italy the recipes vary from region to region. Some people like to mix the sauce and the spaghetti before serving, and when this is done, there is usually an extra bowl of sauce for those who desire more.

The compiling of this book has revived nostalgic memories of my youth. By this time I had already developed a philosophy that in order to prepare good food, one has to be able to recognize good food. Once the recipe is known, the fundamentals of food preparation are all the same. No cook can possibly remember all the ingredients and the exact amounts that go into all the recipes involved in food preparation. Good cooks make mistakes all the time. But the journey is what a recipe is all about. Cookbooks should teach us how to cook, not just follow instructions. The point of a recipe should be to help us find our own way.

I cannot always give the exact number of people each recipe will feed, as appetites vary enormously, but I think most cooks can tell by a swift glance at the ingredients. Most of these recipes I would say are for an average family with average appetites.

Before you begin cooking, look up the required recipe, read it through, and think it out. Note the materials and quantities required. Success in cooking depends on careful attention to every detail, from start to finish. I have tried to make it easier for you by describing the pan size to use, when to cover or uncover the foods, when to raise or lower the heat, and other pointers. A highly developed shopping sense is important, especially knowing which foods are in season. The essential element is the amount of time you linger over the food that will lovingly nurture family and friends. Bear in mind, good cooking is honest, simple, and sincere. Food is an expression of caring and compassion, a way of saying "You're special in my life."

The dishes found here have been tested by time. If cooking is an art, as we like to think it is, this book should appeal to the tastes of all people.

I am sure that readers will find in this cookbook some old and familiar Italian peasant food recipes. I hope they will become favorite reminders of days gone by, spent with all kinds of wonderful foods in early Italian homes where Ma and Dad and grandparents spent more time proving who cooked best than appreciating each other's expertise.

Note: Many recipes in this volume suggest that homemade pasta be used as its base. If that is not practical for you, take some time to research the shops in your area. Most towns have a place where a freshly made product can be purchased, still soft, moist, and made for cooking the same day. The texture and flavor of freshly made pasta is a true delight.

NOTE TO THE READER

The same book with a new look! The recipes in *The North End Italian Cookbook* are basically the same as when the first edition was published thirty-seven years—and a quarter of a million copies—ago. But since the original publication, other methods of preparation have been suggested for several of the dishes. The best of these I am sharing with you, as I gather all of my favorite family recipes together in this expanded edition with hopes it will bring you many hours of pleasant reading and joyful cooking.

ANTIPASTO, SALADS, AND APPETIZERS

ANTIPASTO SALAD PLATTER

SERVES 8–10

I serve antipasto as a way of keeping my guests happily eating while I'm in the kitchen putting the finishing touches on the other courses. Antipasto can be simple and inexpensive or elaborate, and it usually comes in four categories—meat, fish, vegetable, and cheese. You may use all or any of the following ingredients and still obtain a delicious presentation.

SALAD

1 head romaine or red lettuce, washed and drained

1 red bell pepper, thinly sliced

1 green bell pepper, thinly sliced

4 large mushrooms, wiped clean and quartered

Slices of the finest prosciutto rolled around cantaloupe slices

¼ pound provolone cheese, cut in chunks

¼ pound Genoa salami, thinly sliced

4 hard-boiled eggs, each sliced in half

1 (16-ounce) can chickpeas, drained

2 pepperoni sticks, sliced thick

Huge cooked shrimp, shelled and deveined

Fresh figs, quartered

Cauliflower or broccoli florets

½ cup small black pitted olives

Several cherry tomatoes

1 purple onion, sliced in medium-thick rings

Drape a very large decorative platter with lettuce leaves. Delicately and evenly arrange the antipasto ingredients on top.

SALAD DRESSING

1 cup extra-virgin olive oil

¼ cup red wine vinegar

¼ cup lemon juice

Salt and freshly ground pepper to taste

2 garlic cloves, crushed

1 (2-ounce) can flat anchovies, drained (optional)

1. Combine the dressing ingredients in a jar with a tightly fitting lid. Shake well until blended.

2. Evenly pour the dressing onto the antipasto ingredients. Using two spoons, gently lift the lettuce underneath so the dressing falls slightly and coats the antipasto.

3. Adjust seasonings before serving.

This dressing is good on any garden salad and will keep indefinitely in the refrigerator.

CAPONATA

YIELD: 3–4 CUPS

This Italian appetizer is expanding its horizons. Besides being served on a tray with other wonderful goodies like prosciutto, olives, and provolone, caponata is now being used as a topping on hot dogs and hamburgers, ham and cheese sandwiches, etc.

½ cup extra-virgin olive oil

1 medium eggplant, unpeeled and cut in 1-inch cubes

2 celery stalks, chopped

6 large stuffed green olives, sliced

1 medium onion, minced

1 garlic clove, crushed

1 tablespoon small capers

¼ cup tomato paste

1 cup water

¼ cup red wine vinegar

½ tablespoon sugar

Salt and pepper to taste

Pinch of oregano

Pinch of dried red pepper flakes (optional)

1. Heat oil in large skillet and fry eggplant cubes, tossing with a wooden spoon, until lightly browned.

2. Add celery, olives, onion, and garlic. Cook until vegetables are crisp-tender (at this point you may add an additional small amount of oil if needed). Set aside.

3. In a small bowl combine capers, tomato paste, water, vinegar, sugar, and salt and pepper.

4. Pour caper mixture into the skillet with the vegetables, stir lightly, and simmer 1 minute. Remove from heat. Sprinkle with oregano and red pepper, if using.

5. Cool and place in covered container in refrigerator until thoroughly chilled. Serve on lettuce leaves, if desired.

COLD STUFFED EGGPLANT

SERVES 6

This makes a wonderful appetizer, lunch, or light dinner, served with a salad and garlic bread. It is a very unusual and hard-to-come-by dish. I once made this on television, and the cast devoured it in no time. Serve warm or cold.

3 firm medium eggplants

Olive oil

1 cup chopped onions

2 garlic cloves, mashed

3 ounces canned tomato paste (or slightly more)

¼ cup chopped fresh parsley

3 anchovy fillets, chopped

1½ tablespoons dried oregano

Pinch of dried red pepper flakes

Salt and freshly ground pepper to taste

Drop of Tabasco (optional)

1 pound ground beef

¾ cup freshly grated Romano or Pecorino cheese

1 cup or more fresh bread crumbs

1. Wipe eggplants with a paper towel and cut in half, lengthwise. Scoop out the pulp, reserving a ½-inch shell. Chop the pulp into small cubes. Turn the pulp onto paper towels and drain for 30 minutes.

2. Heat ¼ inch of olive oil in a large skillet. Sauté the chopped onions and mashed garlic until soft.

3. Add the chopped eggplant pulp and cook for a few minutes.

4. Put the mixture in a large bowl. Add the tomato paste (you may need more to achieve a rich color), parsley, anchovies, oregano, red pepper flakes, salt, pepper, and Tabasco. Toss the mixture until well blended.

5. Brown the meat in any remaining juices in the skillet. Drain and discard all fat. Season the meat with salt and pepper.

6. Combine the meat with the eggplant mixture, grated cheese, and enough bread crumbs to hold the mixture together. Put the filling into the eggplant shells.

7. Place the filled shells in a baking pan and pour in water or stock to slightly cover the bottom of the pan. Cover the pan tightly with aluminum foil.

8. Set the pan on the middle rack of a pre-heated 375°F oven. Bake for 1 hour, then remove the foil and bake 10 more minutes on the top rack.

9. Serve at room temperature or refrigerate for a couple of days. Cut into thick slices just prior to eating.

FRESH FIGS WITH PROSCIUTTO

SERVES 4

This colorful, fresh salad is delicious at any time of the year. It is very attractive and makes an impressive, refined appetizer.

1½ ounces arugula, rinsed and dried

4 fresh figs

4 slices Parma prosciutto

¼ cup olive oil

1 tablespoon fresh orange juice

1 tablespoon clear honey

1. Tear the arugula into fairly small pieces and arrange on 4 serving plates.

2. Using a sharp knife, cut each of the figs into quarters and place them on top of the arugula.

3. Cut the prosciutto into strips and scatter over the arugula and figs.

4. Place the olive oil, orange juice, and honey in a screw-top jar. Shake the jar vigorously until the mixture blends and forms a thick dressing.

5. Drizzle the dressing over the prosciutto, arugula, and figs, tossing to mix well. Serve the salad immediately.

WARM GREEN BEANS AND POTATOES INSALATA

SERVES 4–6

When fresh beans are available, my guests always enjoy this simple peasant salad, which is delicious warm or cold. Serve it for lunch with leftovers or as a side dish at dinner.

1 pound fresh green beans, tips removed and snapped in half

½ pound small potatoes, unpeeled

⅓ cup olive oil

3 tablespoons red wine vinegar

2–3 garlic cloves, chopped

1 tablespoon or more dried oregano

1 tablespoon chopped fresh parsley

Pinch of dried red pepper flakes (optional)

Salt and freshly ground black pepper to taste

1. Steam the beans for 8–10 minutes, until tender. Drain and place on a serving platter.

2. Boil the potatoes until tender. Drain (do not rinse), let cool, and then cube, leaving the skin on. Add to the green beans.

3. Using a large spoon, gently toss the beans and potatoes with the remaining ingredients.

4. Serve the salad at room temperature or refrigerate for a marinated flavor.

ARUGULA AND RADICCHIO SALAD

SERVES 6

Arugula has to be my favorite of all lettuce. Add other vegetables, if desired, or just serve with this delicious dressing. The dressing is on the rich side, so use only as much as needed and reserve the rest for another day.

SALAD

2 bunches arugula

2 small heads radicchio

1. Rinse and trim the arugula.

2. Cut the cores from the radicchio, rinse, and tear the leaves into bite-size pieces.

3. Dry arugula and radicchio. Wrap in paper towels, place in a plastic bag, and refrigerate until cold, about 30 minutes.

CREAMY GARLIC DRESSING

1 large egg yolk

Juice of ½ lemon

1 tablespoon red wine vinegar

1½ teaspoons Dijon mustard

1 garlic clove, minced

Salt and freshly ground pepper to taste

¼ cup olive oil

2 tablespoons vegetable oil

2 tablespoons chopped fresh parsley

1. Whisk the egg yolk, lemon juice, vinegar, mustard, garlic, salt, and pepper.

2. Gently mix in the oils until the mixture forms a creamy consistency.

3. Just before serving, place the greens in one or two large salad bowls. Divide the dressing evenly between the bowls. Toss well to combine. Garnish with parsley.

TOMATOES WITH FRESH BASIL AND OLIVE OIL

SERVES 3–4

Simple and delicious—use only fresh, ripe tomatoes for this recipe.

1 pound yellow, orange, or red plum, grape, or cherry tomatoes (whatever is in season or readily available)

¼ cup fruity or extra-virgin olive oil

10–15 fresh basil leaves, whole or roughly torn

Salt and freshly ground pepper to taste

½ pound buffalo mozzarella, sliced in rounds (optional)

1. Place the tomatoes in a colander and rinse well under cold running water. Drain and pat thoroughly dry with paper towels.

2. Toss the tomatoes with the olive oil, basil leaves, and salt and pepper to taste in a medium-size bowl. If using, add the mozzarella and toss again.

3. Let stand at room temperature until serving time, tossing occasionally. This makes a nice appetizer or side dish.

This recipe can also be prepared with regular-size fresh, ripe tomatoes that you've sliced. Simply brush the slices with a little olive oil and sprinkle with salt, pepper, and the basil leaves. Add some pitted, dry-cured black olives for garnish.

FENNEL AND TOMATO SALAD

SERVES 8–10

If you're lucky, you have access to some fresh, ripe tomatoes from your garden or a neighbor's garden. The anise bite of fennel and the zest of orange give this tomato salad a continental flavor.

1 bunch red leaf lettuce

6 medium tomatoes, quartered

1 bunch fennel, thinly sliced

½ cup arugula, cut in small strips

12 Sicilian dry-cured black olives, pitted (or use jarred)

6 tablespoons olive oil

2 tablespoons lemon juice

2 garlic cloves, finely chopped

1 teaspoon grated orange peel

Salt and freshly ground pepper to taste

1. Arrange lettuce leaves on a decorative platter. Reserve.

2. In a medium-size bowl, add quartered tomatoes, fennel, arugula, and olives.

3. In a screw-top jar, add olive oil, lemon juice, garlic, orange peel, salt, and pepper and shake to combine.

4. Pour dressing over tomato mixture and toss lightly.

5. Place tomato mixture over lettuce on platter.

6. Serve at room temperature or refrigerate, covered with plastic wrap, for no more than 2 days.

TOMATO AND CUCUMBER SALAD

SERVES 6

Artistically arrange the tomatoes, Sicilian dry-cured black olives, crisp green vegetables, and herbs on a decorative flat platter to present a nice centerpiece salad.

4–5 romaine lettuce leaves, washed in cold water and well dried

4 firm ripe tomatoes cut in ¼-inch slices

2 large cucumbers, peeled and cut in ¼-inch slices

1 red onion, peeled and cut in ¼-inch slices

12 Sicilian dry-cured black olives, pitted

¼ cup olive oil

Juice of ½ lemon

1 tablespoon chopped fresh parsley

1 tablespoon chopped fresh mint, or 1 teaspoon crushed dried mint

1 garlic clove, crushed

Salt and freshly ground black pepper to taste

1. Line a large platter with lettuce leaves.

2. Overlap tomato slices in a circle around edge of platter.

3. Overlap cucumber slices in another circle inside tomatoes.

4. Overlap onion slices along center.

5. Garnish between rows with olives.

6. Combine olive oil, lemon juice, parsley, mint, garlic, salt, and pepper in a small bowl or jar. Stir or shake to mix well.

7. Pour dressing over salad and refrigerate to chill before serving.

MEZZALUNA SALAD

SERVES 4

Who doesn't love a good salad? This one is prepared in individual bowls, which makes for a nice, undisturbed presentation. The ingredients can be altered to suit your individual taste. Use only crisp, fresh vegetables.

6 marinated artichoke hearts, drained and thinly sliced

½ small fennel bulb, chopped medium-fine

1 stalk celery, chopped medium-fine

5 tablespoons olive oil

1 bunch arugula, washed, dried thoroughly, and torn into bite-size pieces

1 small head radicchio, washed, dried thoroughly, and torn into bite-size pieces

¼ pound whole-piece Parmesan cheese, shaved thin

2 tablespoons balsamic vinegar

Salt and freshly ground pepper to taste

1. In a medium-size bowl, mix the artichoke hearts, fennel, and celery with 1 tablespoon olive oil.

2. Put 1 tablespoon or so of this mixture in the bottom of 4 individual salad bowls.

3. Divide the shredded arugula and radicchio among the bowls.

4. Top each salad with shaved Parmesan cheese.

5. Pour the remaining olive oil over the individual salads, about 1 tablespoon for each bowl.

6. Pour the balsamic vinegar over each individual salad, about ½ tablespoon for each bowl. Season with salt and freshly ground pepper to taste.

INSALATA DI CICORIA FINA

DANDELION SALAD

SERVES 4–6

We can never get enough of greens. Growing up, this was a big favorite. We used our grandfather's homemade wine for the vinegar. So wonderful . . . we would drink the bottom of the bowl when the salad was gone.

1 pound dandelion greens

1 garlic clove, crushed but left whole

¼ cup olive oil

2 tablespoons red wine vinegar

12 ripe olives, pitted

Salt and pepper to taste

1. Wash the dandelion greens well, rinse, and dry thoroughly.

2. Discard undesirable leaves and cut the greens into 2-inch pieces.

3. Chill the dandelion greens in the refrigerator for about 10 minutes.

4. Rub a wooden salad bowl with the crushed garlic.

5. Place the dandelion greens in the bowl and pour the olive oil and vinegar over leaves.

6. Add the olives and salt and pepper to taste. Mix and toss well. Serve before salad reaches room temperature.

BIG POCKETS

My parents could not afford to buy school uniforms, so I took sewing classes and, with the help of the seamstress, made my own. They always had big pockets. Even though I was embarrassed, I had my own design! I also took a job in the school library to help pay part of the tuition. The library had puppet shows every Saturday, a great way for us to express our inner selves and escape our everyday tribulations.

CANNELLINI BEANS INSALATA

SERVES 6–8

I love this salad so much that I always keep some on hand for unexpected guests. It makes a wonderfully healthy lunch or an excellent appetizer. Beans were always plentiful as I was growing up, and my mother created plenty of different ways to use them. In the ingredients list, I have given you several options for enhancing the recipe. What I like to do is toss in anything appropriate that I find in my refrigerator.

2 cups cannellini beans, or any beans, fresh or canned

2 tablespoons freshly squeezed lemon juice

¼ cup olive oil

Salt and freshly ground pepper to taste

¼ cup chopped fresh parsley

2 garlic cloves, chopped

½ cup Sicilian dry-cured black olives, pitted and halved (optional)

¼ cup crumbled goat cheese (optional)

¼ cup chopped sun-dried tomatoes (optional)

¼ cup sliced red pepper (optional)

Red onion slices for garnish

1. Place beans on a decorative platter. Sprinkle with lemon juice, olive oil, salt and fresh pepper to taste, parsley, chopped garlic, and remaining ingredients, if using.

2. Garnish with onion slices.

3. Serve warm or refrigerate at least 1 hour to allow flavors to blend.

Variation: For a wonderful quick pasta e fagiole, add a ladle or two of the bean mixture to the reserved broth (see sidebar). Add fresh chopped tomatoes or tomato sauce to give the broth a rosy color, adjust seasonings, and add some cooked pasta. Don't forget the grated cheese.

If you are using fresh beans for this salad, it is not necessary to soak the beans overnight. Just rinse them thoroughly, remove any stones or foreign objects, and put in a pot with enough water to cover. Don't add any salt to the water, for the salt will hinder the cooking process. When the water comes to a boil, simmer beans for 15 minutes. Then add a drizzle of olive oil and one crushed garlic clove. Simmer for 1 to 1½ hours or until tender. Remove beans from broth (reserve broth), add beans to a serving platter, and continue with above recipe.

LENTIL SALAD

SERVES 6

Serve this salad as a side dish with any fish or meat, or as a light lunch with cold cooked ziti or another firm pasta.

3 cups lentils, picked over, washed, and drained

⅓ cup red wine vinegar

½ cup olive oil

¼ cup finely chopped red onion

½ cup finely chopped scallions, white part only

2 tablespoons chopped fresh mint

2 tablespoons chopped fresh parsley

Salt and freshly ground black pepper to taste

1. Bring a large saucepan of water to a boil. Drop in the lentils and return the water to a boil, stirring often. Lower the heat and let the lentils simmer steadily for 20–25 minutes or until they are tender.

2. Drain the lentils in a colander, shake to remove excess moisture, and pile into a bowl.

3. While still hot, add the vinegar and olive oil and stir gently but thoroughly. Let lentils sit until they cool completely.

4. Add the onion, scallions, mint, parsley, salt, and pepper; stir again.

5. Cover with plastic wrap and leave at room temperature for 1 hour for the flavors to mellow, stirring occasionally.

6. Taste for seasoning and serve at room temperature.

INSALATA DI FAGIOLI

BEAN SALAD, ITALIAN STYLE

SERVES 2

A short version of my bean salad, this appetizer will introduce you to the combined flavors of fresh cheese, peppers, and olives.

1 (20-ounce) can red kidney beans or black beans, rinsed and drained well

2 tablespoons freshly squeezed lemon juice

Olive oil (as much as desired)

Salt and freshly ground pepper to taste

¼ cup chopped fresh parsley

2 garlic cloves, chopped

½ cup goat cheese (optional)

Sicilian dry-cured black olives, pitted and cut in half (optional)

1 red bell pepper, chopped into bits (optional)

1. Place the beans in a serving dish large enough to accommodate the beans neatly.

2. Toss the beans gently with lemon juice, olive oil, salt and pepper, fresh parsley, and chopped garlic. Top with crumbled goat cheese.

3. If desired, garnish with black olives, and red pepper for crunch and color. Serve at room temperature.

If you have any leftover bean salad, just throw it in a blender and grind away. Add a drop or two more of olive oil, and you will have the best bean dip ever. Serve with crackers or crusty bread.

GNOCCHI INSALATA

SERVES 6–8

Gnocchi doesn't have to be eaten warm to be enjoyed! This chilled version is a nice change from the ordinary. It makes a wonderful lunch or does well as an appetizer or as part of an antipasto plate.

1 pound gnocchi, cooked and chilled (see page 109)

1 cup green peas, fresh or frozen

½ cup pitted black olives

1 green bell pepper, seeded and chopped in bits

½ cup finely chopped red onion

½ cup chopped fresh basil leaves

Pinch of chopped dry mint or fresh mint

1. Place the chilled gnocchi on a decorative serving platter.

2. Drop the peas into salted boiling water and cook until tender, about 3–5 minutes.

3. Drain peas and allow to chill.

4. Combine the gnocchi and peas with the black olives, green pepper, onion, basil, and mint; stir gently until well blended.

5. Toss with dressing (recipe below). Refrigerate salad and serve cold.

DRESSING

3 tablespoons olive oil

2 tablespoons red wine vinegar

2 tablespoons tomato paste or fresh or canned tomato sauce

Salt and freshly ground pepper to taste

Place all the ingredients in a glass jar and shake until well blended.

INSALATA MISTA

MIXED VEGETABLE SALAD

SERVES 4

I like to use a delicate head of chicory for this salad. The thick dressing gives the salad a smooth, tasty flavor and clings nicely to the lettuce.

1 large head chicory, washed and
   well drained

1 garlic clove, halved

1 medium cucumber, peeled and
   thinly sliced

4 medium tender tomatoes, cut in wedges

1 medium carrot, peeled, washed,
   and diced

¼ cup thick mayonnaise

2 tablespoons olive oil

1 tablespoon lemon juice

1 tablespoon red wine vinegar

Salt and freshly ground pepper to taste

1. Discard the outer leaves of the chicory, then gently pull off the remaining tender leaves.

2. Rub a wooden salad bowl with the garlic halves.

3. Add the cucumber, tomatoes, and carrot to the bowl.

4. In a small bowl, whisk together the mayonnaise, olive oil, lemon juice, and vinegar. When well mixed, pour over the salad, add salt and pepper to taste, and toss thoroughly. Adjust seasonings if needed.

CECI INSALATA

CHICKPEA SALAD

SERVES 4–6

Take time to relax and enjoy this nice and easy, nourishing bean salad.

2 (16-ounce) cans chickpeas, well drained

½ cup chopped green pepper

½ cup chopped red pepper

¼ cup finely chopped onion

½ cup olive oil

¼ cup freshly squeezed lemon juice

1 garlic clove, minced

Salt and pepper to taste

1. In a medium-size decorative bowl, combine the drained chickpeas, green and red peppers, and onion.

2. In a small bowl, whisk the olive oil, lemon juice, garlic, and salt and pepper to taste. Add to chickpeas and toss lightly to blend.

3. Marinate 1 hour at room temperature, or cover and refrigerate until needed.

4. Serve at room temperature.

APRON POCKET

When my grandparents visited, my grandmother would plop herself on the rocking chair and rock and rock. After a few minutes, she would slowly reach into her apron pocket, building up the suspense as she stared at us mischievously. Then she'd quickly throw out a handful of pennies and watch us scour for them on the floor—we loved seeing who could get more than the other!

MIXED GREEN SALAD WITH ANCHOVY SAUCE

SERVES 4–6

Try brushing this sauce on toasted slices of a baguette. Serve as an appetizer.

1¼ pounds Boston lettuce

½ pound Belgian endive

2 teaspoons Dijon-style mustard

1 teaspoon anchovy paste

1 small garlic clove, minced

2 tablespoons red wine vinegar

Salt and freshly ground pepper to taste

1⅓ cups olive oil

1. Wash and thoroughly dry lettuce; cut into fairly large, bite-size pieces. There should be about 8 cups. Put in a large salad bowl.

2. Trim endive and cut into very thin slices. Add to bowl.

3. In a small mixing bowl, whisk together mustard, anchovy paste (or you can use 2 canned anchovy fillets, drained and smashed), garlic, vinegar, salt, and pepper. Gradually whisk in olive oil.

4. Pour anchovy sauce over salad greens and toss gently to blend. Serve immediately.

ROASTED PEPPERS SALAD

SERVES 4

This tried-and-true recipe is one of my old-time favorites, handed down from three generations. It's sure to be a big hit at family reunions, get-togethers, or parties. I like a combination of red and yellow peppers, but one or the other alone will do fine. A good brand of canned peppers will suffice if you are unable to obtain fresh ones. Anchovies are salty, so use them with discretion.

4 whole red bell peppers (or 2 yellow, 2 red)

½ cup pure olive oil

½ cup chopped fresh parsley

4 garlic cloves, chopped

1 (2-ounce) can flat anchovy fillets, chopped

½ teaspoon dried red pepper flakes (optional)

Sicilian dry-cured black olives, pitted and halved (optional)

Salt and freshly ground pepper to taste

1. Heat broiler, then place whole peppers on a broiler pan on lowest rack from heat. Turn them often until the skin is charred and blistered, about 10–15 minutes. (Use tongs to turn, so peppers won't bruise.) Do not allow peppers to burn through flesh or they will not be suitable for serving.

2. Remove peppers and put in a heavy paper bag, closing tightly so steam won't escape. Place bag in a bowl, and let cool.

3. Using your fingertips, scrape the seeds from the cooled peppers, and peel away the charred skin.

4. Carefully tear the peppers in long strips, place them on a decorative platter, and cover them with olive oil.

5. Scatter the remaining ingredients evenly over the peppers, cover with plastic wrap, and refrigerate at least 1 hour to blend flavors.

Pepper salad will keep in the refrigerator for at least 3 days.

CAESAR SALAD

SERVES 4–6

Enjoy this delicious, make-ahead, perfect summer salad. So rich and tasty and simple to make.

1 head romaine lettuce, washed and dried

1 garlic clove, crushed

⅓ cup olive oil

¾ cup croutons, made from stale
French bread

Salt and freshly ground pepper to taste

1 fresh egg

Juice of ½ lemon

2 anchovy fillets, diced

2 tablespoons freshly grated
Parmesan cheese

1. Tear lettuce into a bowl, cover with plastic wrap, and refrigerate.

2. In a small bowl, add crushed garlic to olive oil. Let stand overnight.

3. Discard pieces of garlic. Brown croutons on all sides in the garlic-flavored oil in a medium-size heavy skillet. Drain croutons on paper towels and reserve.

4. Add salt and freshly ground pepper to the oil. Set aside.

5. Cook egg in simmering water for 1 minute. Remove from water and break into a cup.

6. Have remaining ingredients ready. When ready to serve, pour garlic oil over chilled lettuce. Pour on egg and lemon juice and toss salad until creamy looking. Add anchovies and adjust seasonings. At the last moment, sprinkle with grated cheese and browned croutons.

INSALATA DI FUNGHI E PARMIGIANO

MUSHROOMS AND PARMESAN CHEESE SALAD

SERVES 4–6

This makes a nice, light afternoon snack. Store the mushrooms in a paper bag until needed, to prevent them from browning too quickly.

½ **pound baby spinach**

½ **pound medium mushrooms, wiped clean with a paper towel to remove any grit (do not wash)**

2 ounces whole-piece Parmesan cheese, sliced into thin slivers

1–2 garlic cloves, finely chopped (optional)

⅓ **cup olive oil**

2 tablespoons freshly squeezed lemon juice

Salt and freshly ground pepper to taste

1. Place the spinach in a wide, decorative salad dish large enough to accommodate all the ingredients.

2. Thinly slice the mushrooms and scatter them over and around the spinach.

3. Add the slivered cheese and chopped garlic, if using.

4. Sprinkle with olive oil, lemon juice, and salt and pepper to taste. Toss lightly without disturbing. Serve at room temperature.

SPINACH AND MUSHROOM SALAD

SERVES 4–6

Salads can be very boring, so I thought I would share this favorite of mine. Very tasty and low in calories, it makes a wonderful lunch. For best results, use fresh, coarsely grated Parmesan cheese.

1 package spinach, washed, picked over, and spun dry

1 pound mushrooms, thinly sliced

2 celery stalks, very thinly sliced (optional)

3 garlic cloves, chopped

⅓ cup olive oil

3 tablespoons freshly squeezed lemon juice

Salt and freshly ground black pepper to taste

¼ pound whole-piece Parmesan cheese

1. Tear spinach into bite-size pieces and put in a large salad bowl.

2. Add mushrooms, celery, and garlic.

3. Sprinkle olive oil and lemon juice over salad; toss lightly.

4. Add salt and pepper and toss well.

5. Generously grate fresh Parmesan over vegetables. Serve at room temperature.

TALL AND STRAIGHT

My father had one leg! He worked in a shoe factory! We had holes in our shoes! You can't make these sorts of things up. At night we would look for newspapers, and each morning we would fold them to fit into our shoes to fill the holes. I had to adjust my steps as I walked to school to reduce the flapping inside my shoes. My heels would wear down because of my crooked gait. In order to walk tall and straight, I would pretend I had a couple of books on my head that would fall if I just tilted even a little.

SPINACH SALAD WITH PANCETTA DRESSING

SERVES 2–3

Here's a winning combination. The pancetta dressing can also be served over steamed fresh green beans or any cooked green vegetable.

10 ounces fresh spinach, washed, stemmed, and dried

8 slices Italian pancetta or bacon

2 garlic cloves, sliced

¼ cup red wine vinegar

¼ cup currants or raisins (optional)

1 teaspoon Dijon-style mustard

Salt and freshly ground pepper to taste

2 tablespoons olive or vegetable oil

1 bunch radishes, thinly sliced (large ones are best)

1. Place spinach in a salad bowl and refrigerate.

2. In a heavy skillet, sauté pancetta or bacon until crisp and brown. Place on paper towels to drain, then crumble and set aside.

3. Pour off all but 3 tablespoons of fat from pan. Turn heat to medium-high and sauté garlic for 1 minute.

4. Pour the vinegar into the pan and add currants or raisins (if using), mustard, and salt and pepper to taste. Stir to blend. Add oil and combine well.

5. Pour the hot mixture over the spinach and toss immediately to coat the leaves. Work fast or the spinach will wilt.

6. Sprinkle the crisp pancetta or bacon and radishes over the salad and serve at once.

HOT SPINACH AND BACON SALAD

SERVES 6–8

I especially like to use large spinach leaves for this recipe. The spinach will stay nice and firm and retain its bite. If the ingredients appear to be too plentiful, you can use less of the bacon, eggs, sugar, or even the spinach, but you will need to adapt the recipe accordingly. Try to have all the ingredients ready before cooking.

1 (4-pound) bag spinach

¾ pound fresh medium-large mushrooms, thinly sliced

20 slices bacon, cut in 1-inch pieces

½ cup olive oil

½ cup red wine vinegar

4 teaspoons herb mixture (rosemary, tarragon, oregano)

4 teaspoons Worcestershire sauce

4 teaspoons Dijon mustard

¼ cup refined sugar

Salt and freshly ground pepper to taste

8–10 hard-boiled eggs, minced

Croutons (optional)

1. Wash the spinach thoroughly in cold water, drain well, and dry with paper towels. Tear into bite-size pieces and place in a large salad bowl. Sprinkle mushroom slices over spinach.

2. Using a large skillet, sauté bacon until crisp. Drain off drippings and remove to paper towels. Crumble bacon back into skillet. Reserve.

3. Add olive oil, vinegar, herb mixture, Worcestershire sauce, mustard, and sugar to skillet. Mix well and heat through. Add salt and pepper to taste.

4. When hot but not boiling, pour the mixture over the spinach and mushrooms. Cover with plastic wrap and let steam for 15 seconds or until slightly wet.

5. Sprinkle with minced hard-boiled eggs and croutons (if using), and serve.

PANZANELLA

SERVES 4

For this salad you may add any leftovers from your refrigerator. Be sure to adjust the vinegar, oil, and seasonings to taste. Panzanella can be served chilled or at room temperature.

8 slices crusty Italian or French bread, 3 days old

½ bunch fresh basil, stems removed

1 pound soft, ripe tomatoes, chopped

1 ripe cucumber, peeled and thinly sliced

Salt and freshly ground pepper to taste

¼ cup olive oil

3 tablespoons red wine vinegar

½ red onion, thinly sliced

½ cup chopped fresh parsley

1. Cut bread into bite-size pieces and put in a large bowl. Sprinkle bread with a little cold water to slightly dampen.

2. Pick over, wash, and dry the basil leaves; cut them into thin strips.

3. Add tomatoes and their juice, sliced cucumber, and basil to bread in bowl and toss well. Add salt and pepper to taste.

4. Drizzle olive oil evenly over salad until glistening but not soaked; add vinegar and toss well. Adjust seasonings.

5. Decorate with sliced onion and chopped parsley. Allow salad to develop its flavors for at least 1 hour before serving it. For a more dramatic effect, bread salad may be put on a bed of lettuce leaves on a platter.

MELANZANA CON OLIO E ACETO

PICKLED EGGPLANT

YIELD: 1 QUART

This eggplant is good as an appetizer with crackers or as an accompaniment to antipasto. It is especially delicious when sandwiched between crusty French bread slices.

Salt

1½ pounds eggplant, sliced very thin

3 garlic cloves, cut in large pieces

2 basil leaves, chopped fine, or ½ teaspoon dried basil

½ teaspoon dried oregano

1–2 hot green peppers (optional)

1½ cups red wine vinegar

Olive oil

1. Sprinkle salt very lightly on the sliced eggplant. Let stand about 30 minutes.

2. Put the eggplant slices into a pile and press until most of the liquid drains out. Squeeze well and wipe dry.

3. Arrange the slices in a 1-quart screw-cap jar that has been sterilized, adding the garlic, basil, oregano, peppers, and vinegar to every other layer until all ingredients are used.

4. Press down firmly and pour enough olive oil to cover the eggplant mixture.

5. Store in refrigerator at least 48 hours. Serve cold or at room temperature.

MOM'S POTATO AND EGG FRITTATA

SERVES 6

A frittata is an Italian peasant version of the French omelette. It was used to turn eggs into a full meal. Use this recipe for a quick lunch or serve in crusty rolls as sandwiches. We can't get enough of this, especially when sprinkled with extra cheese and black pepper or even a shot or two of Tabasco.

8 large eggs

3 tablespoons milk

¼ cup freshly grated Parmesan cheese

2 tablespoons chopped fresh parsley

Salt and freshly ground pepper to taste

¼ cup plus 4 tablespoons olive oil

2 medium potatoes, peeled and thinly sliced

1 medium onion, thinly sliced

1. In a large mixing bowl, beat the eggs with a whisk or fork until foamy. Add the milk, grated cheese, parsley, salt, and pepper. Set aside.

2. Heat ¼ cup olive oil in a large, heavy, flat-bottomed skillet over high heat. Sprinkle a dash of salt on the bottom of the pan, lower the heat, and add the sliced potatoes (the salt will prevent potatoes from sticking). Fry about 5 minutes or until crisp, tossing to brown slightly. Do not burn.

3. Add the sliced onions and cook until tender, tossing gently with a spatula.

4. Put the potato and onion mixture into the bowl with the beaten egg mixture. Stir to blend.

5. Return the skillet to the heat. Drizzle in 4 tablespoons olive oil to coat the pan sides, using a rotating motion. Pour the egg mixture into the pan, reduce the heat to medium-low, and stir briskly with a fork, pulling the cooked egg from the sides to the center of the pan. Continue stirring until the mixture starts to set. Cook slowly until the edges start to brown.

6. For a softer texture, remove the frittata from the heat, cover, and let rest for 5 minutes. If you prefer to brown both sides of the frittata to have a firmer texture, place a large plate on top of the skillet and slide the frittata out. Then, flip it upside down back into the skillet so that the uncooked side is down. Cook for 5 minutes more, remove from the heat, and let rest 5 minutes.

7. Cut into wedges and serve.

FRITTATA ARRABIATA

HOT AND SPICY OMELETTE

SERVES 4

This recipe is a fancy version of a plain omelette. Serve it to friends or just when you feel like going all out. Enjoy!

6 eggs

2 tablespoons warm water

¼ cup freshly grated Parmesan cheese

2 tablespoons chopped fresh parsley

Salt and freshly ground pepper to taste

⅓ cup olive oil

1 medium onion, thinly sliced

¼ pound mushrooms, sliced

3 large hot vinegar peppers, sliced (purchase at supermarket or make them yourself; see page 286)

2 tablespoons shredded mozzarella cheese

6 pitted black olives, halved

2 ounces canned roasted peppers, cut in pieces, or chopped fresh red peppers

Pinch of fresh basil or mint

1. In a large mixing bowl, whisk the eggs until foamy. Add the water, grated cheese, parsley, salt, and pepper.

2. Heat the oil in a large skillet over medium heat. Add the onion, mushrooms, and vinegar peppers to the pan and sauté. Add salt and pepper to taste.

3. When the vegetables are tender, raise the heat to high. Slowly drizzle the egg mixture over the vegetables in the pan, gently pushing the edges of the batter to the middle of the pan where it is the hottest. This will enable the omelette to set properly.

4. When the omelette is three-fourths firm, sprinkle with the mozzarella cheese, olives, roasted peppers, and a pinch of basil or mint. Cook a few more minutes.

5. Turn off the heat, cover the pan, and let the omelette set 5–7 minutes or until it is moist and firm. Cut into wedges and serve immediately.

RAW SALMON FILLETS IN PINZIMONIO

SERVES 6

Pinzimonio is served in native Italy and now found in many fine restaurants. It will not taste right unless you use high-quality extra-virgin olive oil and coarse salt. A goodly amount of freshly ground black pepper is also necessary for a tasty sauce.

2 pounds fresh, cleaned salmon fillets

2 teaspoons sea salt to taste

3 hardboiled eggs, yolks only

1 2-ounce can anchovy fillets, drained and mashed

1 teaspoon garlic, finely chopped

2 tablespoons tarragon

1 tablespoon oregano

Coarse salt and freshly ground black pepper to taste

½ cup extra-virgin olive oil

2 lemons, freshly squeezed

1. Rinse and pat dry salmon fillets. Sprinkle with sea salt and refrigerate 1 to 2 hours.

2. In a small bowl, mix together the finely minced hardboiled egg yolks, mashed anchovies, garlic, parsley, tarragon, oregano, coarse salt, and freshly ground black pepper.

3. Whisk in the olive oil and lemon juice and whip until mixture resembles a heavy cream, or very thin texture as desired. Reserve.

4. Slice salmon into 18 thin slices, place on a decorative serving platter, and spoon pinzimonio over fish. Refrigerate for 45 minutes and serve.

PROSCIUTTO AND MELON

SERVES 8

This recipe makes an excellent, light, and tasty appetizer. If you like a decorative look, serve it on a bed of lettuce with a few black olives on the side. The color combination is very attractive!

1 large cantaloupe or honeydew melon

½ pound imported prosciutto, thinly sliced

1 lime, cut in 8 wedges

1. Cut the melon into 8 wedges. Remove the seeds from each wedge, but leave the skin on.

2. Make crosswise cuts ½ inch apart into each wedge, cutting down close to the skin. Lay the wedges on individual plates or a serving platter.

3. Drape a piece of prosciutto across the top of each melon wedge. Top with a lime wedge.

4. To eat, squeeze the lime onto the prosciutto. Cut into the prosciutto where the melon has been cut, then lift up a piece of melon and prosciutto on your fork.

MOZZARELLA EN CARROZZA

MOZZARELLA IN A "CARRIAGE"

SERVES 7

This is an Italian version of a grilled cheese sandwich. You may use any favorite large loaf of Italian bread, but if you are lucky enough to have an Italian bakery nearby, get a bastone. It is a crusty bread shaped into a large loaf that is slit on top, and is ideal for this recipe.

1 long loaf Italian bread

¾ pound mozzarella or Fontina cheese, sliced ¼ inch thick

1 (2-ounce) can anchovy fillets, washed and drained

2 medium eggs

3 tablespoons milk

1½ cups olive oil, or more if needed

Lemon wedges for garnish

Fresh parsley sprigs for garnish

1. Cut the bread into 14 ½-inch slices. Make 7 sandwiches by adding a slice of cheese and 1 anchovy fillet to each.

2. Whisk the eggs with the milk. Dip each sandwich in the mixture and set aside.

3. Heat the olive oil in a large, heavy skillet over medium heat. Fry the sandwiches on both sides until golden brown. Drain on paper towels, and slice in half.

4. Garnish with the lemon wedges and fresh parsley. Serve immediately.

FRIED MOZZARELLA STICKS

SERVES 6

These delicious appetizers can be served as a finger food, with marinara sauce, or alongside fried eggs.

All-purpose flour for dredging

3 eggs, beaten

Finely ground bread crumbs

Salt to taste

1 pound mozzarella cheese, cut into 3-inch-square chunks

1 cup olive oil

1. Put flour in a shallow dish, eggs in a small bowl, and bread crumbs on waxed paper. Add salt to the eggs.

2. Roll cheese chunks in flour, then dip into eggs and roll in bread crumbs.

3. Once again, dip into eggs and roll in bread crumbs. Reserve.

4. In a heavy skillet, heat olive oil over medium-high heat, and fry cheese chunks until golden brown.

5. Drain on paper towels and serve immediately.

ORIGINAL ARANGINI BALLS

MAKES 8 RICE BALLS

In years past, when a train stopped at a small station in Sicily, the attendant wheeling the tavolo caldo (a trolley containing hot food to be eaten on the train) would make his way to the platform, crying out, "Arangeeeeeeeni!" He would then hand travelers a piece of brown paper containing a warm mound of pale, orange-colored rice. The rice was eaten right off the paper, and then the paper was used to wipe the hands and mouth. This recipe for arangini balls comes close to the original one.

1 pound rice

1 egg, beaten

Olive oil

¾ pound lean ground beef

¼ cup grated Parmesan cheese

2 tablespoons chopped parsley

2 hard-boiled eggs, minced

½ cup cooked baby peas

Salt and freshly ground pepper to taste

Finely ground bread crumbs

Paprika

1. Cook rice in boiling salted water. Drain and mix with half the beaten egg.

2. Heat 1 tablespoon olive oil in a heavy pan and brown beef.

3. Place drained beef in a medium-size bowl and add cheese, parsley, minced eggs, cooked peas, and salt and pepper to taste.

4. Wet hands and take a handful of cooked rice. Place a generous amount of beef in the center, closing the rice up to make a ball. Repeat until all the rice and filling are used.

5. Lightly dip the balls in the remaining beaten egg. Coat with fine bread crumbs mixed with paprika for color.

6. Deep-fry in a heavy pot in enough olive oil to cover balls. Cook until light golden brown, then transfer to paper towels to drain.

CARPACCIO WITH ARUGULA

SERVES 4

Carpaccio is a fine dish of raw beef marinated in lemon juice and olive oil. It is traditionally served with flakes of fresh Parmesan cheese. Use very fresh meat of the highest quality. The lean beef is sliced and pounded paper-thin, sometimes done a couple of hours ahead and kept in between sheets of plastic wrap. It's best to pound it before serving. To make slicing easier, put the meat in the freezer until it is very cold but not frozen.

1 garlic clove, peeled and cut in half

Juice of 1½ lemons

¼ cup extra-virgin olive oil

Salt and freshly ground black pepper to taste

2 bunches arugula

4 very thin slices top round steak

1 cup thinly shaved Parmesan cheese

1. Rub a small bowl all over with the cut side of the garlic.

2. Add lemon juice to the bowl, then whisk in the olive oil. Season with salt and pepper to taste. Allow the sauce to stand for at least 15 minutes before using.

3. Carefully wash the arugula and tear off any thick stalks; spin or pat dry. Arrange the arugula around the edge of a serving platter, or divide on 4 individual plates.

4. Place the beef in the center of the platter and pour on the sauce, spreading it evenly over the meat. Arrange the shaved Parmesan on top of the meat slices. Serve immediately.

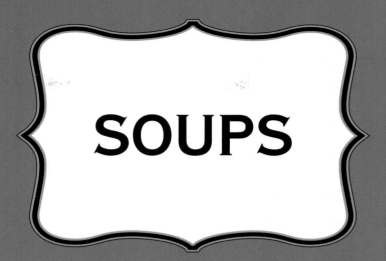

SOUPS

OLD-FASHIONED CHICKEN BROTH

SERVES 10 (GENEROUSLY)

My mother passed on this wonderful recipe to us, and I am sharing it with you.

1 3½-pound fowl, quartered

4 medium carrots, scraped and sliced thick

3 celery stalks with leaves, chopped thick

4 small potatoes, peeled

3 fresh tomatoes, chopped, or 1 cup canned
   tomatoes (more if deeper color is desired)

2 large onions, quartered

4 fresh parsley sprigs

2 tablespoons salt

1 tablespoon freshly ground black pepper

About 10 tablespoons freshly grated
   Parmesan or Romano cheese

1. Wash the fowl thoroughly and remove and discard excess fat. Place the fowl in a large stockpot and add the vegetables and seasonings. Add cold water to 1 inch above the height of the ingredients.

2. Bring the pot to a gentle boil, then reduce heat to a simmer. Partially cover pot and cook slowly for about 2 hours. The fowl should be covered with water or it will be tough. Add more hot water as needed.

3. When chicken is cooked through, remove it from the broth and set it aside in a warm place. Keep the broth simmering for another 30 minutes. Shred the chicken into fairly thin pieces.

4. Adjust seasonings and put the broth and chicken in soup bowls. Sprinkle about a tablespoon of grated cheese on each serving.

5. If you wish, you can cool the broth, then refrigerate it and the chicken overnight. Before serving, remove and discard any congealed fat from the top of the broth. Reheat with the chicken pieces and serve.

Variation: Just before serving, add 2 cups of cooked rice to the strained broth and heat until the rice is hot. Or cook ½ pound tiny pasta such as acini di pepe in 2 quarts boiling water, drain, add to the strained broth, and serve immediately. Note: Do not let pasta sit in the soup because it will absorb much of the broth, leaving less liquid than desired.

FARINA DUMPLINGS

SERVES 6–8

These dumplings are traditional additions to meatless soups, often used when the pasta and trimmings of a soup were eaten up after the first serving. You can save this recipe for day two of a big pot of soup, or make them right from the start for a hearty addition to a lighter soup.

Farina is a light flour that can be purchased at any market. This type of flour was a staple in the Italian homes in my neighborhood, and many a good recipe was created because of its availability. The dumplings in this recipe are boiled in water first, then added to the broth.

1 stick (½ cup) butter

3 eggs

Salt to taste

½ pound (about 1¼ cups) farina

Grated fresh Parmesan cheese

1. Whip butter in a medium-size bowl until light and fluffy.

2. Add eggs, salt to taste, and farina. Stir slightly (batter should be lumpy). If batter seems too thin, add a little more farina. Let stand 15 minutes.

3. Drop small lumps of batter from a teaspoon into a medium-size pot of boiling water. Cover and simmer 10 minutes.

4. Remove from heat and let stand an additional 10 minutes.

5. Remove dumplings from water and drain in a colander.

6. Drop dumplings into boiling hot soup and stir to coat with broth. Serve in deep bowls and top with grated cheese.

CHICKEN SOUP WITH ESCAROLE AND POLPETTINI

SERVES 10–15

Once you accomplish making a homemade soup, it will become a simple and enjoyable task. The secret to this is the secret to all Italian cooking—having the basic ingredients on hand. That will always encourage you to plunge into almost any recipe without fear.

1 plump fowl, about 4–5 pounds

2 celery stalks with leaves, halved

2 fresh parsley sprigs

2 carrots, scraped

1 large ripe tomato, chopped

Salt and freshly ground pepper to taste

1½ pounds escarole, well washed and
    cut crosswise into thin shreds

1 pound ground beef

2 tablespoons freshly grated Romano cheese

1 teaspoon chopped fresh parsley

½ pound tiny pasta such as pastina, orzo,
    or acini di pepe

1. Clean and wash fowl well. Discard excess fat. Place fowl in a soup pot and add cold water to cover. Bring it slowly to a boil and skim the surface often.

2. When the water stays fairly clean, add the celery, parsley, carrots, tomato, and salt and pepper to taste.

3. Cover the pot tightly and cook slowly over low heat until the fowl is tender, about 2½ hours. Strain the broth and discard the vegetables. (The chicken may be used for chicken salad sandwiches another day, or the white meat may be boned and added to the broth.) Refrigerate the broth until the fat has congealed on top. Remove and discard the fat.

4. Reheat the broth over medium heat. Meanwhile, put the escarole in a large skillet with ½ cup water. Simmer for 3 minutes, strain, squeeze out excess water, and add to the broth.

5. For the polpettini ("tiny meatballs"), combine the ground beef, cheese, parsley, and salt and pepper to taste. Shape into balls no larger than a filbert (dip hands in water so that you can make the balls smooth and round), and drop into the hot, semi-boiling soup.

6. Cook the soup for 30 minutes on low heat to combine the flavors thoroughly and cook the meat.

7. Cook the pasta in 2 quarts of boiling salted water. Drain (do not rinse) and add to the soup just before serving.

This soup can be refrigerated for several days. It also freezes well.

STRACCIATELLA SOUP

"LITTLE RAGS" SOUP

SERVES 4

This is a quick soup that looks elegant on the table but takes very little work in the kitchen. It will keep in the refrigerator for at least 3 days, and it freezes well. Use your own homemade broth or canned broth.

2 eggs

⅛ teaspoon salt

2 tablespoons Parmesan cheese, plus more if desired

1 quart homemade chicken broth (page 40), or canned

¼ pound cooked acini di pepe or orzo pasta

Chopped fresh parsley for garnish

1. Combine the eggs, salt, 2 tablespoons Parmesan cheese, and 3 tablespoons cool broth in a mixing bowl. Beat with a wire whisk for about 3 minutes.

2. Bring the remaining broth to the boiling point. Add the egg mixture slowly, stirring constantly with a fork. Let the soup simmer for at least 5 minutes.

3. Add cooked pasta to the soup and simmer 5 minutes more.

4. Pour the soup into individual bowls and sprinkle with parsley and more grated cheese, if desired.

BUBBLE GUM

I remember standing in long lines to buy bubble gum, which only arrived every three weeks. There was a limit of one piece to a customer. My friends and I would cherish that piece, each night placing it into our own private glass of water to keep it hard. In this way, the gum would last us until the next shipment arrived.

ZUPPA DI PESCE
WITH BRANDY AND CREAM

SERVES 6

When I make fish soup, I always buy the cheaper, but very fresh, fish from our local fish market. You should use a boneless chowder fish such as cod, scrod, or flounder for this recipe.

3 tablespoons olive oil

2 medium onions, chopped

2 garlic cloves, crushed

½ teaspoon thyme

1 teaspoon turmeric (or saffron, if available)

1½ pounds fish fillets, rinsed in cold water and cut in bite-size pieces

Salt and freshly ground pepper to taste

1 teaspoon Tabasco (optional)

¼ cup tomato paste

1 cup white wine

5 cups water

¼ cup brandy

2 cups cream, warmed

1. Pour the oil into a large, heavy skillet and heat slightly. Sauté the onions, garlic, thyme, and turmeric until transparent.

2. Add the fish, salt and pepper to taste, and optional Tabasco and cook for 5 minutes, tossing gently.

3. Using a wooden spoon, stir in the tomato paste, wine, and water. Bring to a soft boil, then reduce heat and simmer for 5 more minutes.

4. Remove from heat and slowly add brandy and warmed cream, stirring gently.

5. Return to heat and simmer for 3–5 more minutes.

6. Serve immediately in soup bowls with side dishes of salad and crusty bread.

ZUPPA DI VENERDI SANTO

GOOD FRIDAY'S SOUP

SERVES 2–4

Good Friday is so special and busy that sometimes we need a small, quick meal. What could be better than a nice fish broth of lobster and shrimp?

1 1½-pound lobster

2 (2-ounce) cans anchovy fillets,
  drained and minced

1 garlic clove, minced

2 teaspoons chopped parsley

5 tablespoons olive oil

5–6 cups bottled clam broth

1 full teaspoon tomato paste

½ pound large shrimp, peeled

Salt and freshly ground pepper to taste

Tabasco (optional)

4 slices crusty Italian bread, toasted
  or fried in olive oil (optional)

1. Boil the lobster in a large pot of cold water to cover. Remove after 8 minutes of cooking. Put the lobster in a bowl, remove the shell, pull out the meat, and cut into bite-size pieces, allowing the juices to fall in the bowl. Reserve.

2. Mash together the anchovies, garlic, and parsley, then transfer to a medium-size soup pot with the olive oil. Cook over medium heat until garlic is translucent and anchovies are melted.

3. Combine strained lobster juices with clam juice in a small bowl. Briskly stir the tomato paste into ½ cup of the reserved juices. Add to the soup pot with the remaining broths.

4. Bring to an easy boil, lower the heat, and simmer, covered, for 15 minutes to blend flavors.

5. Add the lobster and shrimp to the broth, bring to a soft boil, and cook uncovered for 2–3 minutes or until shrimp turn pink.

6. Add salt and pepper and Tabasco (if using) to taste.

7. Serve immediately in warm soup bowls into which you have placed the toasted or fried bread.

NONNA'S BEEF SOUP

SERVES 6

This recipe is so versatile. Not only is the soup nourishing, but you can also put the beef on a platter and slice it as you would a roast (or sprinkle it with hot or sweet vinegar peppers for a delicious beef insalata).

1–2 beef soup marrow bones, with marrow, cracked

1 pound beef chuck or eye of round

3 fresh tomatoes, chopped, or 1 (8-ounce) can tomatoes, squeezed to break into small pieces

2 carrots, scraped

1 large onion, quartered

1 potato, peeled

3 celery stalks with leaves, halved

3 parsley sprigs

Salt and freshly ground pepper to taste

½ pound pastina or acini di pepe, cooked and drained just before soup is ready to serve

Freshly grated Parmesan cheese for garnish

1. Place the soup bones in cold water and boil for 3 minutes. Drain and rinse well. You may need to repeat process until water is clear of residue.

2. Place the washed bones, beef, vegetables, and salt and pepper in a large soup pot. Cover with cold water, 2 inches above the ingredients. Slowly bring to a gentle boil, removing any foam that may form on top.

3. Simmer, covered, for 2½–3 hours, stirring from time to time. Add more water if needed to keep the meat submerged so it does not dry out.

4. Remove bones, meat, and vegetables. Shred the beef and reserve. The vegetables may be served as a side dish to this soup.

5. Strain the broth into another large pot and return to the heat. Adjust seasonings as needed. Add the cooked pasta and shredded beef.

6. Pour into individual soup bowls and sprinkle with grated Parmesan cheese. Serve with crusty Italian bread.

This soup freezes well or can be refrigerated for 3 or 4 days.

SOUP BEEF INSALATA

SERVES 4

When my mother made beef soup, she always used lots of meat. After the soup was placed in our bowls, she would take the remaining beef and tear it into shreds, placing it on a decorative platter. Then she would tear vinegar peppers into strips over it so that the juices would cover the meat. This mixture of peppers and beef would be drizzled with pure olive oil and sprinkled with salt and pepper to taste. We would cut crusty Italian bread and devour this wonderful meat salad. This is one of the lost recipes that I would like to share with you.

1 pound cooked beef chuck or eye of round, taken from soup and shredded

4 large hot or sweet vinegar peppers (purchase at supermarket or make them yourself; see page 286)

Olive oil

Salt and freshly ground pepper to taste

1. Place the warm, shredded beef on a serving platter.

2. Tear the vinegar peppers so their juices run over the beef.

3. Drizzle enough olive oil to generously cover the meat and peppers. Add salt and pepper to taste.

4. Toss well and serve warm.

MY HOMEMADE MINESTRONE SOUP

SERVES 6–8

I concocted this recipe at a North End Union luncheon, using the leftovers of the previous day. You might find it a good way to use your leftovers. Ingredients may be omitted or added—use only what you have on hand, just adjust the seasonings. Garlic bread makes an excellent accompaniment.

1 quart cold water

1 (8-ounce) can whole green beans, undrained

1 (8-ounce) can chickpeas, undrained

1 (8-ounce) can red kidney beans, undrained

1 (8-ounce) can medium peas, undrained

1 (16-ounce) can chicken broth, or 2 cups homemade broth

1 medium onion, chopped

1 small zucchini, unpeeled and diced

1 celery stalk with leaves, chopped

2 carrots, peeled and thinly sliced

1 medium cabbage, chopped (remove center core)

1 (8-ounce) can tomato sauce, or 1 cup Simple Marinara Sauce (page 62)

Quick Pesto Sauce (optional; see recipe below)

Salt and freshly ground pepper to taste

½ cup cooked pastina, tubetini, acini di pepe, or rice

Freshly grated Parmesan or Romano cheese

1. Place the first 11 ingredients in a large pot and bring to a slow boil. Lower heat and simmer uncovered for 1½–2 hours, stirring often.

2. Add the tomato sauce and the optional pesto sauce to the soup. Adjust seasonings, adding salt and pepper to taste.

3. Bring soup to a soft boil and add cooked pasta of your choice or rice.

4. Ladle the soup into bowls and sprinkle with grated cheese.

QUICK PESTO SAUCE

¼ cup olive oil

1 garlic clove, chopped

1 tablespoon chopped fresh basil leaves

1 tablespoon chopped fresh parsley

½ cup freshly grated Parmesan or Romano cheese

Blend all the ingredients in a blender until smooth.

MY CABBAGE SOUP

SERVES 6

This soup is quick and easy to prepare. Serve it with delicious, crusty, Italian bastone bread.

1 small head cabbage, regular green or savoy

6 garlic cloves, crushed

Salt and pepper to taste

2 (16-ounce) cans cannellini beans

1 small piece pepperoni, salami, or sopressata

¼ cup olive oil

Pinch of dried red pepper flakes (optional)

1. Cut cabbage into several wedges. Put in a large pot with enough water to cover, 3 of the garlic cloves, and salt and pepper to taste.

2. Bring the pot to a boil and cook until cabbage is tender but not mushy, about 20 minutes.

3. Remove cabbage from water, using a wire mesh scoop.

4. Add beans and pepperoni or other salami to pot. Cook about 20 minutes.

5. In a small skillet, fry remaining garlic cloves in olive oil. Together add them to the pot of beans. Season with salt and pepper to taste and red pepper flakes, if using.

6. Cook slowly for 5–10 minutes. Add cooked cabbage (add more water if needed) and cook an additional 25 minutes. Shut heat off and let sit for 30 minutes to an hour.

7. Serve with butter, white vinegar, and Tabasco on the side, and a loaf of bastone bread.

ITALIAN-STYLE SPLIT PEA SOUP

SERVES 6–8

This is great for lunch or as a first course, especially with a ham dinner. It can be refrigerated for several days or frozen.

1½ cups green split peas, picked over, washed, and drained

1 large onion, chopped

2 celery stalks, chopped

1 large leek, chopped

1 large garlic clove, halved

1 large ripe tomato, chopped

1 large carrot, peeled and chopped

3 quarts cold water

¼ cup olive oil

Salt and freshly ground pepper to taste

1. Place the peas in a 4-quart stockpot with the vegetables and cold water. Drizzle with olive oil.

2. Let the stock come to a boil. Stir well and add salt and pepper to taste. Simmer for about 1½ hours, or until the peas are tender but not mushy.

3. Ladle into large soup bowls and serve with croutons or garlic bread.

A good way to begin preparing a recipe is to have the basic ingredients on hand. The basics for Italian cooking are usually tomatoes (canned and/or fresh), fresh garlic, fresh parsley, freshly grated Italian cheese (Romano or Parmesan), fresh bread crumbs, and good olive oil.

CREAMY HOT POTATO SOUP

SERVES 6–8

This soup can also be served cold. When serving hot, be careful not to curdle the cream. If you haven't tried potato soup, have it soon. It is great when served before dinner and helps make a special presentation. Serve it in nice, decorative bowls.

I favor white pepper so as not to speckle the soup. White pepper is very strong, so add just a small pinch.

3 tablespoons butter

1 medium onion, thinly sliced

4 leeks (white bulb only), washed and finely chopped

3 celery stalks (and some of the tender yellow tops), washed and finely chopped

4 cups canned chicken stock

4 medium potatoes, sliced about ¼ inch thick

Salt and white pepper to taste

1 pint light cream or whole milk

Chives or parsley, finely chopped, for garnish

1. Melt the butter in a fairly deep stock pot. Add the onion, leeks, and celery and cook until transparent and tender. Don't let brown.

2. Add the broth and bring to a boil.

3. Add the potatoes and salt and pepper to taste. Reduce heat to medium-low, cover, and simmer until potatoes are tender. Cool slightly.

4. Place in a blender or food processor and puree until smooth.

5. Before serving, add cream and heat until piping hot. Adjust seasonings and garnish with fresh chives or parsley.

LA MINESTRA MOM'S WAY

Straight from my grandmother, her mother, and her mother's mother, this recipe reflects a true "old style." It takes a while to prepare but is very nourishing and flavorful. It should be started the day before you wish to serve it.

See your butcher for a fresh prosciutto bone. Don't concern yourself with its size, but have the butcher cut it into small pieces.

1 cup white navy or pea beans

1 fresh prosciutto bone with meat attached

½ pound pepperoni, cut in chunks; or 2 pounds spareribs, boiled, drained, and rinsed well; or 2 pigs feet, boiled, drained, and rinsed well

7–8 garlic cloves, crushed

1 large savoy cabbage (outer leaves removed), quartered

½ cup olive oil

Salt and freshly ground pepper to taste

Dried red pepper flakes for garnish

1. Wash the beans well, removing any imperfect ones. Soak overnight.

2. Soak the prosciutto bone for 6–8 hours in a bowl of water in the refrigerator, changing the water often.

3. Boil 6 cups of water. Gradually add the beans to the boiling water. Simmer for 2 minutes and remove from heat. Set aside to soak for 1 hour, then rinse the beans and strain.

4. Boil the prosciutto bone and the meat of your choice for 20 minutes. Rinse and strain. This will remove any fat or residue.

5. Put the clean prosciutto bones, your chosen meat, and the prepared beans in a large heavy pot. Cover with cold water to an inch over the bone and beans. Add 3 of the crushed cloves of garlic. When the water comes to a boil, lower the heat and simmer. When the prosciutto meat starts to pull away from the bone (about 30 minutes), shut off the heat. Separate the meat from the prosciutto bones and put the meat back in the pot.

6. In a separate large pot, cook the cabbage until tender. Do not overcook. Strain, reserving some of the liquid. Put the cabbage in the pot with the beans and prosciutto.

7. Fry the other 4–5 cloves of garlic in the olive oil until brown. Add to the cabbage and beans. If the sauce seems too thick for your taste, add some of the cabbage broth. Simmer the entire mixture for 5 minutes, stirring with a wooden spoon.

Add salt and pepper to taste (be careful with the salt, as prosciutto and pepperoni are highly salted).

8. Remove the pan from the heat and let rest for at least 2 hours so that all the flavors will be well combined. Refrigerate until ready to serve.

9. When you are ready to serve, reheat La Minestra on a low burner, heating only as much soup as needed. Serve in large bowls, topped with red pepper flakes. It is excellent with crusty Italian round bread.

PASTA E FAGIOLE

PASTA AND BEANS

SERVES 4–6

We ate this very popular and easy-to-prepare soup at least twice a week as a filler before the main course. It can be used as a lunch dish or as a first course at dinner.

TO PREPARE BEANS

½ **pound white navy or pea beans**

6 **cups cold water (sometimes I use leftover or canned chicken broth for a richer flavor)**

¼ **cup olive oil**

2 **garlic cloves, crushed**

Salt and freshly ground pepper to taste

1. Wash the beans thoroughly and discard any imperfect ones.

2. Put the water in a large pot. Add the beans, olive oil, garlic, salt, and pepper. Simmer until the beans are tender, about 1½ hours.

MARINARA SAUCE

1 **garlic clove, chopped**

Pinch each of dried red pepper flakes, basil, and mint

3 **tablespoons olive oil**

1 **(8-ounce) can whole plum tomatoes with juices, squeezed into pieces**

Salt and freshly ground pepper to taste

1. In a small heavy skillet, slowly sauté the garlic and seasonings in the olive oil on low heat until golden brown.

2. Add the tomatoes and a pinch more of each of the seasonings. Add salt and pepper to taste. Simmer, uncovered, for 10 minutes on low heat.

TO FINISH SOUP

1 **teaspoon salt**

2 **quarts water**

½ **pound ditali, small shells, or elbow macaroni**

Freshly grated Parmesan cheese

1. Put the salt in the water and heat to boiling in a large saucepan.

2. Gradually add the pasta. Boil rapidly, uncovered, about 12 minutes or until al dente. Reserving 1 cup of liquid, drain the pasta in a colander, and rinse it under cold water to prevent sticking. Reserve.

3. When the beans are tender, add the drained pasta and the marinara sauce to the pot. If more broth is desired, add the 1 cup of reserved liquid from the pasta. Simmer 10–15 minutes.

4. Ladle into large soup dishes and sprinkle with grated Parmesan cheese. Serve immediately or the pasta will swell and absorb all the broth.

PASTA E PISELLI

PASTA AND PEAS

SERVES 6–8

This soup was a familiar one while I was growing up. I didn't appreciate it then, but I love it now. It makes a tasty and nourishing lunch, especially with garlic bread.

¼ **cup olive oil**

1 small onion, chopped

1 large garlic clove, chopped

2 teaspoons tomato paste

1 (14-ounce) can peeled Italian plum tomatoes

Pinch each of dried basil, mint, and red pepper flakes

1 (8-ounce) can medium sweet peas, undrained

Salt and freshly ground black pepper to taste

1 pound small shells, ditali, or elbow macaroni

Freshly grated Parmesan or Romano cheese for garnish

1. Heat the olive oil in a heavy saucepan and sauté the onion and garlic. When transparent, add the tomato paste. Mix well.

2. Add the canned tomatoes and juices, squeezing the tomatoes to break them up. Sauté for a minute or two, then add basil, mint, and red pepper flakes. Stir gently for about 3 minutes over medium-low heat.

3. Add the undrained can of peas. Simmer the sauce while you cook the pasta, adding more seasonings if desired and salt and pepper to taste.

4. Meanwhile, bring 2 quarts of salted water to a boil. Add the pasta. Boil rapidly, uncovered, about 10 minutes or until tender. Drain in a colander, reserving 2 cups of the water. Do not rinse.

5. Transfer the pasta back to the pot, and add the tomato sauce and peas mixture. Stir gently and add the pasta water until the sauce has a nice broth texture.

6. Serve immediately with plenty of grated cheese.

LENTIL SOUP

SERVES 4–6

Even if you do not like lentils, you will not be able to resist this soup. My daughter used to turn up her nose at lentil soup when she was young. Now, as a married woman, she keeps containers of it in the freezer to serve to her friends gathered around the fireplace on a cold winter night. And she doesn't hesitate to accept the rave reviews!

½ **pound lentils, picked over, washed, and drained**

1½ **quarts cold water**

2 **or 3 celery stalks with leaves, finely chopped**

2 **small carrots, chopped**

1 **tablespoon chopped fresh parsley**

1 **onion, chopped**

1 **garlic clove, chopped**

1 **tablespoon olive oil**

3 **ripe tomatoes, peeled and chopped, or 1½ cups canned tomatoes with juices, squeezed**

Salt and freshly ground pepper to taste

½ **pound ditali, small shells, or elbow macaroni**

Freshly grated Parmesan cheese

1. Place the lentils and water in a large pot. When the water comes to a soft boil, add the remaining ingredients except the pasta and grated cheese.

2. Simmer, covered, for 30 minutes or more, until the lentils and vegetables are tender.

3. Meanwhile, cook the pasta in 2 quarts of salted water until al dente. Drain the pasta, reserving 1 cup of liquid.

4. Add the pasta to the soup. Taste for seasonings and simmer 5 minutes. If the soup seems too thick, add some or all of the reserved pasta water.

5. Ladle into large soup bowls, sprinkle with grated cheese, and serve immediately for lunch or dinner along with a garden salad or antipasto.

This soup freezes well or can be refrigerated for several days.

MEDITERRANEAN THREE-BEAN SOUP

SERVES 4

The use of string beans in this soup gives it a distinct taste. It is important that you use fresh beans to appreciate the combination of the different bean flavors.

⅓ **cup olive oil**

2 leeks, coarsely chopped

2 celery stalks, coarsely chopped

2 garlic cloves, minced

4 cups chicken broth, fresh or canned

Salt and freshly ground pepper to taste

1½ cups cooked or canned kidney beans

1½ cups cooked or canned garbanzo beans

**1 pound string beans, trimmed and cut in
  1-inch pieces**

Grated Parmesan or Romano cheese

1. Heat the oil over moderate heat in a large soup pot.

2. Add the leeks, celery, and garlic and sauté 3–4 minutes. Add the remaining ingredients except the grated cheese.

3. Bring the soup to a boil, then lower heat. Simmer for 20 minutes.

4. Pour soup into bowls and serve with grated cheese.

ZUPPA DI CECI CON ACCIUGHE

CHICKPEA SOUP WITH ANCHOVIES

SERVES 6

Beans, beans, beans! What would we ever do without them? They are such a great staple and so adaptable to any recipe. Whether you prepare them fresh or from cans (in which case the texture might be softer), their flavor never changes. Use any small pasta for this recipe, or just enjoy the soup and beans alone.

Olive oil (enough to cover bottom of pan)

Pinch of dried basil

1 garlic clove, finely chopped

Dried red pepper flakes (optional)

1 ounce anchovy fillets, chopped

2 tablespoons tomato paste

½ cup warm water

2 (16-ounce) cans chickpeas, undrained

1 pint water

Salt and freshly ground pepper to taste

½ pound small shells or elbow pasta, cooked

Grated Parmesan cheese

1. Using a medium-size stockpot, heat olive oil and sauté basil, garlic, red pepper flakes, and anchovies on low heat until anchovies are dissolved.

2. Dilute tomato paste in ½ cup warm water.

3. Add tomato paste mixture to anchovy mixture. Mix well, using a wooden spoon, and simmer for 5 minutes.

4. Add undrained chickpeas and 1 pint water. Bring to a boil and add salt and pepper to taste.

5. Simmer about 10 minutes, then add cooked pasta.

6. Stir well and serve immediately in bowls. Sprinkle well with grated Parmesan cheese.

Anchovies are salty, so be careful when seasoning with salt.

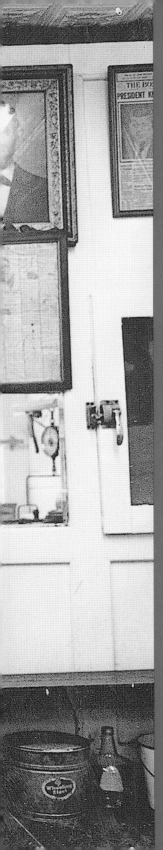

SAUCES
AND
GRAVIES

SIMPLE MARINARA SAUCE

YIELD: 4 CUPS

The difference between plain meatless tomato sauce and marinara is texture and color. Tomato sauce is prepared with tomato paste, giving it a darker, richer body and flavor. Marinara sauce is light, almost pinkish, and can be cooked in 10 or 20 minutes for a delicate effect. It also can be frozen. Use it over cooked thin spaghetti or linguine.

½ cup virgin olive oil

2 garlic cloves, chopped

Pinch each of dried red pepper flakes, basil, and mint

1 (28-ounce) can crushed or whole plum tomatoes, with juice, or 12 peeled fresh tomatoes

Salt and freshly ground pepper to taste

1. In a large, heavy skillet over low heat, very slowly heat the olive oil, garlic, red pepper flakes, basil, and mint. Let cook for about 5 minutes or until the garlic is golden brown.

2. Raise the heat to medium-high. When the oil is really hot, add the tomatoes. (If you are using the plum or fresh tomatoes, crush them in your hands or put them in a blender for 1 second before adding them to the pan. This will speed up the cooking process and give a smoother consistency to the sauce.) Let the sauce come to a soft boil, then lower the heat.

3. Add salt and pepper to taste, and adjust the seasonings. Let the sauce simmer, uncovered, for about 5 minutes, stirring occasionally with a wooden spoon.

Variations: This is a wonderful sauce to use as a base for other recipes. Add a can of clams, or sliced mushrooms, or sliced black olives. Be inventive! I gradually add the juices from the canned clams or mushrooms to the sauce as well, until I produce the texture my family enjoys. Other additions might include a can of crabmeat or a pound of cut-up baby squid or lobster meat.

SUNDAY GRAVY

SERVES 10–12 GENEROUSLY

This tomato sauce with meat is called gravy because the meat drippings become the base for the sauce. It is meant to feed the whole family abundantly. You may cook up to 3 pounds of pasta and have enough sauce and meat to make everyone happy. It refrigerates and freezes well. You may use any or all of the meats listed.

1 pound sweet Italian sausage

2 pounds meatballs (page 159)

4–5 lean pork chops

1 pound lean spareribs

1-pound piece of beef or pork

½ cup olive oil

1 medium onion, chopped

1 garlic clove, chopped

Salt and pepper to taste

A few pinches each of dried basil, red pepper flakes, and mint

1 (6-ounce) can tomato paste

1 (28-ounce) can peeled and crushed tomatoes

1 (28-ounce) can water

Salt and freshly ground pepper to taste

1. Fry the meats of your choice in ¼ cup olive oil in a large, heavy saucepan. Add more oil if the pan seems too dry to brown meats without burning.

2. When meats are browned, transfer them to a platter. Add the remaining ¼ cup olive oil to the residual juices in the pan. When the oil is hot, sauté the onion, garlic, and seasonings until transparent.

3. Stir in the tomato paste and blend well. Add the tomatoes and stir until blended with the tomato paste and oil. Stir in an extra pinch of the seasonings. Add water, using the 28-ounce can from the tomatoes. (Keep adding water until the sauce attains the thickness you desire. I use a full can.)

4. Let the sauce come to a full boil and add salt and pepper to taste and adjust seasonings. Return the meat to the pan. Simmer over medium heat, uncovered, for at least 1 hour or until all of the meat is fully cooked. Stir gently every 15 minutes or so, using a large wooden spoon.

5. Place the cooked meat on a decorative serving platter. Pour some hot sauce over pasta in another bowl, reserving additional sauce for individual servings at the table.

The addition of pork will make an oily—though delicious—gravy. When you are using a significant amount of pork, skim the excess oils off the top of the sauce. Pork also tends to produce a thin sauce, so go easy when adding additional water, or add an extra can of paste at the beginning of the preparations. This will help maintain the body of the sauce.

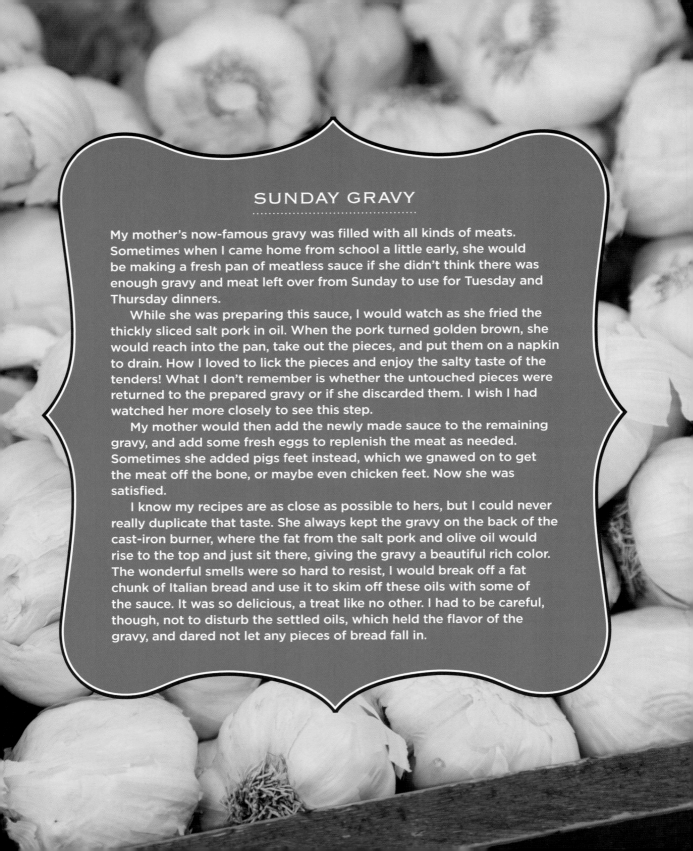

SUNDAY GRAVY

My mother's now-famous gravy was filled with all kinds of meats. Sometimes when I came home from school a little early, she would be making a fresh pan of meatless sauce if she didn't think there was enough gravy and meat left over from Sunday to use for Tuesday and Thursday dinners.

While she was preparing this sauce, I would watch as she fried the thickly sliced salt pork in oil. When the pork turned golden brown, she would reach into the pan, take out the pieces, and put them on a napkin to drain. How I loved to lick the pieces and enjoy the salty taste of the tenders! What I don't remember is whether the untouched pieces were returned to the prepared gravy or if she discarded them. I wish I had watched her more closely to see this step.

My mother would then add the newly made sauce to the remaining gravy, and add some fresh eggs to replenish the meat as needed. Sometimes she added pigs feet instead, which we gnawed on to get the meat off the bone, or maybe even chicken feet. Now she was satisfied.

I know my recipes are as close as possible to hers, but I could never really duplicate that taste. She always kept the gravy on the back of the cast-iron burner, where the fat from the salt pork and olive oil would rise to the top and just sit there, giving the gravy a beautiful rich color. The wonderful smells were so hard to resist, I would break off a fat chunk of Italian bread and use it to skim off these oils with some of the sauce. It was so delicious, a treat like no other. I had to be careful, though, not to disturb the settled oils, which held the flavor of the gravy, and dared not let any pieces of bread fall in.

FRESH EGGS IN MARINARA SAUCE

SERVES 4

How we loved this mint-flavored (fresh from my grandfather's farm) tomato sauce! My grandfather carefully added several dropped eggs to the sauce and cooked them until they were firmly set. The eggs are a wonderful substitute for meat, and they can be added to any leftover sauce to stretch it for another meal. This recipe is also called Eggs in Purgatory because the eggs are hotly spiced. Serve it for a delicious breakfast or brunch with crunchy garlic bread.

12 fresh tomatoes, blanched and peeled
  (see page 68)

1 small onion, chopped

1 small carrot, chopped

1 stalk celery, chopped

¼ cup olive oil

Dried red pepper flakes (optional)

Salt and freshly ground pepper to taste

2 garlic cloves, chopped

1 tablespoon fresh mint, or a pinch of
  dried mint flakes

6 fresh eggs

¾ pound linguine or other thin pasta

1. Put the tomatoes in a blender and process briefly just to coarsely mash them.

2. Using a large deep skillet, sauté the onion, carrot, and celery in olive oil until translucent.

3. Add the tomatoes, red pepper flakes, and salt and pepper to taste. Mix well and simmer for at least 5 minutes, stirring with a wooden spoon.

4. Add the garlic and mint to the sauce and stir until well blended. Adjust seasonings and simmer for at least 10 minutes, stirring well.

5. Raise heat to medium-high and bring sauce to a soft boil. Crack eggs, one at a time, onto a small plate and slide each raw egg, uncrowded, into the tomato sauce. Continue until all 6 eggs are used.

6. Lower heat, cover skillet, and cook for 5 minutes. Uncover and, with a wide wooden spoon, gently coax the eggs away from each other without breaking them.

7. Ladle sauce over the tops of the eggs to better cook them. Cover and simmer for about 15 minutes or until the eggs are firm and set. At this point you should be able to transfer them to a plate without breaking the yolks.

8. Cook pasta separately in salted boiling water according to package directions.

9. Drain pasta and put on a serving platter. Add sauce. Place eggs on top of the pasta or serve on the side.

QUICK MEAT SAUCE

YIELD: APPROXIMATELY 6 CUPS

The total cooking time for this sauce is approximately a half hour; it can be cooked ahead and reserved. The sauce refrigerates well for several days and freezes excellently.

¼ cup olive oil

1 pound ground meat (½ pound beef, ½ pound pork)

1 small onion, chopped

1 garlic clove, chopped

A couple pinches of dried basil, red pepper flakes, and mint

Salt and freshly ground pepper to taste

1 (28-ounce) can peeled and crushed tomatoes

1. Heat the olive oil in a large skillet. When it is rippling hot, add the ground meat and start to brown it, stirring with a wooden spoon. When partly browned, add the onion, garlic, and seasonings. Continue browning until the meat is a little crisp on the bottom of the pan.

2. Add the tomatoes and mix until the sauce starts bubbling. At this point lower the heat and add additional salt and pepper to taste, stirring well. If the mixture is too thick, add some warm water to smooth it a bit.

3. Sprinkle in an additional pinch of basil, red pepper flakes, and mint. Let the sauce simmer, uncovered, on low heat for about 20 minutes, stir it often.

4. Serve over a pound of cooked pasta, or use as a topping for eggplant, lasagne, manicotti, ravioli, or stuffed peppers.

TO FREEZE OR REFRIGERATE SAUCES AND SOUPS

Place meal-size portions of soups and sauces in freezer storage bags and secure tightly. The bags will take up less space than containers, and the sauce or soup can be reheated in the microwave right in the bag.

BOLOGNESE SAUCE

SERVES 6–8

There are many old versions of this authentic sauce. Although only fresh tomatoes were used at the time of its creation, in later years canned tomatoes made it easier for the working person to re-create this sauce. The ground tomatoes used here give the sauce good body and texture. This sauce is wonderful with homemade pastas.

¼ **cup olive oil**

1 **pound ground meat (preferably ½ pound each of beef and pork)**

3 **garlic cloves, chopped**

1 **small onion, chopped**

1 **tablespoon each of dried basil, mint, and red pepper flakes**

1 **(6-ounce) can tomato paste**

1 **cup dry white wine**

1 **(28-ounce) can peeled tomatoes, with no puree added**

Salt and freshly ground pepper to taste

½ **cup heavy cream or half-and-half**

1. Heat olive oil in a large, heavy, stainless steel skillet. Add ground meat and cook on high heat until partly browned but not burned, stirring often with a wooden spoon.

2. Add garlic, onion, and seasonings. Cook until meat is totally browned and a little crisp on the bottom.

3. Lower heat and add tomato paste, stirring constantly until paste is well blended.

4. Add wine, mix well, and cook on medium-high heat at least 2–3 minutes, stirring often.

5. Add tomatoes and keep stirring until sauce is bubbly. Lower heat, adjust seasonings to taste, and simmer sauce for about 10–15 minutes, stirring often.

6. Add cream or half-and-half. Stir and simmer a few minutes or until sauce is creamy.

7. Serve over manicotti, lasagne, ravioli, or homemade fettuccine.

COOKED SAUCE WITH FRESH TOMATOES

YIELD: APPROXIMATELY 6 CUPS

The difference in this sauce is its sweet, fresh taste. The recipe makes enough sauce to coat at least 1 to 1½ pounds of any store-bought or homemade pasta. If you wish to add some fish or meat to the sauce, you may do so immediately after the sauce is prepared and just keep cooking until the fish or meat is cooked.

12 ripe tomatoes, blanched and peeled

½ cup olive or vegetable oil

1 carrot, scraped and chopped

1 small celery stalk with leaves, chopped

1 medium onion, chopped

1 garlic clove, chopped

Pinch each of dried basil, mint, and red pepper flakes

Salt and freshly ground black pepper to taste

1. Put peeled tomatoes in a pot with no water. Let them boil until they are cooked, about 10 minutes, then mash or blend them in a blender until they have the consistency of a cooked sauce.

2. Heat the oil in a large, heavy saucepan. Add the carrot, celery, onion, garlic, basil, mint, and red pepper flakes. Sauté until the vegetables are tender, but not burned.

3. Pour in the tomatoes and mix well. Let the sauce come to a soft boil. At this point you can determine if you wish to add some water. You also can add salt and pepper and additional basil, red pepper, or mint.

4. Stir for a couple of minutes, lower the heat, and let simmer for 15 minutes or more, stirring with a wooden spoon. I like the oils to accumulate on top of the sauce at this point because I feel they seal in all the flavors, so I stir very gently, trying to scrape the bottom of the pan without disturbing the accumulation of oils on top.

TO BLANCH FRESH RIPE TOMATOES

Cut a cross along the bottom of each tomato. Drop in boiling water and cook for 1 minute or until skin loosens or splits (touch with a knife to ensure splitting). Remove from boiling water and dip in cold water, then peel off skin. Blanched tomatoes can be frozen for future use in soups or stews.

AGLIO E OLIO

GARLIC AND OIL SAUCE

YIELD: 1 CUP

This is the original and widely used peasant sauce we enjoyed while growing up. It is delicious on spaghetti (about ½ pound is the right amount). If you like garlic, you would also like this sauce with shrimp, as shrimp scampi, or as a sauce with clams.

1 cup extra-virgin olive oil

5 garlic cloves, slivered

Salt and freshly ground black pepper to taste

¼ teaspoon dried red pepper flakes (optional)

1 tablespoon chopped fresh parsley

Freshly grated Parmesan cheese

1. In a medium-size heavy skillet, heat the oil until warm. Add the garlic and simmer slowly for about 5 minutes or until the garlic is golden. Do not burn. You may remove the garlic at this point or leave it in if you enjoy a strong garlic flavor.

2. Add the salt, black and red pepper, and parsley. Let simmer for about 5 minutes to blend flavors. If using with pasta, add some of the hot pasta water to the sauce in the skillet and let boil lightly for about 2 minutes. The pasta water adds a nice thickness and helps eliminate some of the oily taste.

3. Add sauce to hot strained pasta and serve immediately with lots of freshly ground black pepper and grated cheese.

A squeeze of lemon juice in the sauce adds a nice, zippy flavor.

PESTO SAUCE

SERVES 4

This sauce is served uncooked, at room temperature, over cooked pasta. It makes an elegant dish when used with tortellini, fettuccine, or other favorites. It is also excellent when added to minestrone or pasta primavera. When all the ingredients are on hand, the sauce takes about 5 minutes to prepare. It also can be refrigerated or frozen indefinitely for future use; just warm it up at room temperature.

2 cups olive oil

2 cups fresh parsley leaves

4 garlic cloves

½ cup pignoli (pine nuts)

1 tablespoon freshly ground black pepper

1 teaspoon salt

1 cup freshly grated Pecorino or
   Romano cheese

½ cup lemon juice

2 firmly packed cups whole fresh basil
   leaves, stems removed

1. Put all the ingredients except the basil into a blender and grind thoroughly.

2. Add the basil and grind until a creamy texture is achieved. No cooking is needed. This amount of sauce is enough for 1 pound of pasta of your choice.

PUTTANESCA SAUCE

SERVES 6–8

This is such a zesty and robust sauce that it was named after the gypsies. I have omitted the salt because of the anchovies, but you be the judge. If you're not the daring type, you can omit some of the seasonings also. The first six ingredients, however, are important to the flavor of the sauce and should not be left out.

2 tablespoons olive oil

1 large onion, halved and slivered

6 garlic cloves, coarsely chopped

1 heaping teaspoon tomato paste

2 (28-ounce) cans Italian plum tomatoes

2 (2-ounce) cans anchovies in oil

¾ cup pitted and coarsely chopped Sicilian dry-cured black olives

¼ cup drained capers

1 teaspoon each dried basil, oregano, and red pepper flakes

Freshly ground black pepper to taste

1 pound pasta of your choice

Freshly grated Parmesan (optional)

1. Heat olive oil in a heavy saucepan. Add onion and garlic and cook on low heat until transparent. Add tomato paste and blend well.

2. Crush tomatoes slightly and add to the pan along with their juices. Cook for 5 minutes on medium heat.

3. Coarsely chop the anchovies and add to the saucepan, along with their oil, stirring gently with a wooden spoon.

4. Stir in the olives, capers, basil, oregano, red pepper flakes, and black pepper to taste. Blend gently and simmer over medium heat for about 20 minutes, stirring occasionally.

5. While sauce simmers, bring 6 quarts of water to a boil. Add pasta of your choice, such as fettuccine, rigatoni, or linguine. Cook according to package directions or until al dente.

6. Drain pasta and place on decorative platter. Top with the hot sauce and serve immediately. Pass the Parmesan!

To chop canned olives easily and neatly, drain and, using a small knife, cut the olives up and down in the can. This also works well with pineapple.

MY ANGELO'S RED PEPPER SAUCE

YIELD: ENOUGH FOR AT LEAST 4 SERVINGS OF FISH

Because we had an abundance of peppers, thanks to a neighbor with a huge garden, my husband, Angelo, concocted this recipe to accompany our pescia fritta. We think it is so wonderful that it is now a must with our family's fried-fish dinners.

4 raw long finger peppers (hot or sweet)

3 ounces raspberry vinegar

½ cup milk

1 tablespoon soy sauce (optional)

¼ cup lemon juice

1 teaspoon chopped fresh parsley

1 garlic clove

2 tablespoons butter or margarine

Flour

1 teaspoon chopped parsley for garnish

1. Cut stems off peppers, slice, and put in a food processor.

2. Add all other ingredients except butter, flour, and parsley. Slowly beat on low pulse until mixture is nicely smooth, about 1 minute.

3. Heat butter in a medium-size skillet and add pepper mixture. Simmer uncovered for 2–3 minutes.

4. Stirring well with a wooden spoon, add flour, a little at a time, until mixture has thickened slightly.

5. To serve, spread sauce on 4 warmed plates and top with a crispy piece of fish. Sprinkle with chopped parsley.

ALTERNATIVE SAUCES FOR FRESH PASTA

SPINACH SAUCE

YIELD: 2½ CUPS

¼ cup butter or margarine

1 (10-ounce) package frozen chopped spinach

1 teaspoon salt

1 cup ricotta cheese

¼ cup grated Parmesan cheese

¼ cup milk

⅛ teaspoon ground nutmeg

1. Melt butter in a 2-quart saucepan over medium heat. Add spinach and salt and cook for 10 minutes.

2. Reduce heat to low and add remaining ingredients. Mix sauce well and cook until just heated through; do not boil.

WALNUT SAUCE

YIELD: 1⅓ CUPS

¼ cup butter or margarine

1 cup coarsely chopped walnuts

½ cup milk

2 tablespoons minced fresh parsley

1 teaspoon salt

1. Melt butter in a 9-inch skillet over medium heat. Add walnuts and lightly brown for about 5 minutes, stirring occasionally.

2. Add remaining ingredients and cook until heated through.

CREAMY BROCCOLI SAUCE

YIELD: 3½ TO 4 CUPS

1½ pounds broccoli, cut into florets

¼ cup olive oil

4 garlic cloves, chopped

Salt and freshly ground pepper to taste

¼ teaspoon dried red pepper flakes

1 cup heavy cream (or half-and-half)

¾ cup grated Romano or Parmesan cheese

1. Cook broccoli florets in water, uncovered, until tender. Drain well and set aside.

2. Heat olive oil in a medium-size saucepan. Add garlic, salt, pepper, and red pepper flakes. Sauté on low heat until garlic is lightly browned, about 5–7 minutes.

3. Add cream and cook 20 minutes to thicken.

4. Add cooked broccoli and cheese to sauce mixture; stir to blend.

Removing the green piths from the center of a garlic clove helps prevent unpleasant acids in the body.

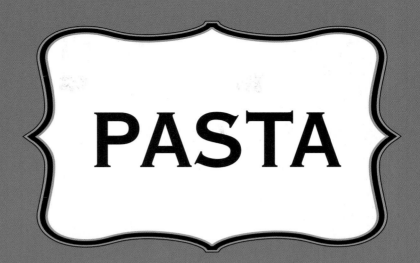

PASTA

SOME TIPS FOR COOKING AND SERVING PASTA

Since all pasta is cooked the same way, it is not necessary to repeat the cooking directions for each dish. However, here are a few general pointers so that your pasta will not be cold and gummy before the sauce is done:

- Store-bought pasta will take about 10 to 15 minutes to cook; homemade or fresh pasta from the delicacy shop only takes about 3 or 4 minutes. These cooking times are measured from the time the cooking water returns to a full boil after the pasta is added.

- There should be plenty of water in the cooking pot to allow the pasta to float around easily and uncrowded. Always have the cooking water rapidly boiling when you first put the pasta into it, and softly boiling as the pasta is cooking. Don't start cooking the pasta until your sauce is ready or the ingredients for the sauce are fully ready.

- After the pasta has been cooked and sauced, it should be served immediately. Don't let it stand at room temperature; don't even try to keep it warm or hot in the oven while you eat your appetizer. The pasta should be served as soon as it is prepared. The only exception would be primavera, which keeps well and therefore can be made in advance.

- A true Italian serves the pasta as the first or main course, with the meat and salad coming after it.

RAVIOLI

Because this recipe can be somewhat tedious, I suggest you invite a friend over to prepare it with you. That way you can share both the work and the rewards. If you make the ravioli one day and freeze them, and the sauce another day and freeze it, you'll be putting together your meal without a lot of last-minute fuss. To make the ravioli, you will need a lightly floured, flat, unpainted surface; I use my kitchen counter or an old table without any veneer. A heavy rolling pin on ball bearings will make the dough much easier to roll out. Don't get discouraged! It will take you a few times to get comfortable with making ravioli.

BASIC RAVIOLI DOUGH

6 cups unsifted unbleached flour (King Arthur preferred)

1 teaspoon salt

3 eggs

Boiling hot water (about ¾ cup)

1. Pour the flour on your preparation surface and form a well in the center. Add the salt to the well. Add the eggs to the well, breaking them gently with your fingers. Mix the flour and eggs together until they form a cornmeal texture.

2. Make another well and gradually add hot water, constantly shifting the flour on top of the water (so you won't burn your hands), until you are able to handle the mixture. The dough should be soft and pliable. If you find it too moist, add more flour to the work surface and knead the dough directly on top of it. If the dough is too dry, keep wetting your hands with warm water as you work the dough until it handles well.

3. The dough should be kneaded for about 8 minutes or until it becomes smooth enough to roll. A thorough kneading mixes the ingredients and develops elasticity in the dough. Knead dough by folding the opposite side toward you. Using the heel of your hand, gently push the dough down and away from you. With your fingertips, squeeze it and push it back to you. Fold the dough over envelope-style, and repeat the process over and over. When the dough has been kneaded enough, its surface will feel satiny and will look smooth. For a beginner, this might take 10–12 minutes, while an experienced person may need 5–8 minutes. Throughout this process, use as little additional flour as possible.

4. Place the kneaded dough in a bowl, pat it with some water, and cover with a clean cotton cloth or an inverted bowl to prevent drying. Let it rest for 30 minutes before attempting to roll it out. Remember, the dough should be very smooth in order to work well. While the dough is resting, you can make the filling.

Many people feel that they should add at least a half-dozen eggs to this recipe, because that's what Grandma used to do. That is fine, but it should be remembered that the resting period for a dough with this amount of eggs must be longer—at least an hour. Working people without much time should keep this in mind. A dough with many eggs that is not sufficiently rested will simply "bounce back" in the rolling process.

RAVIOLI FILLING

2 pounds ricotta cheese

3 medium eggs plus 2 additional egg yolks

½ cup freshly grated Parmesan or Romano cheese

1 garlic clove, pressed

½ cup chopped fresh parsley

Salt and freshly ground pepper to taste

Mix the ingredients thoroughly in a large, wide bowl. Reserve.

TO FINISH PREPARATION

1 recipe Quick Meat Sauce (see page 66), heated

Approximately 1 pound freshly grated Parmesan or Romano cheese

1. Divide the dough in half, keeping the other half covered with an inverted bowl. Roll out the dough on a lightly floured surface until it is about ⅛ inch thick. Repeat with the second half.

2. Drop teaspoonfuls of filling about 2 inches apart on one sheet of dough until the filling is used. Cover with the other sheet.

3. With your fingertips, gently press around each mound of filling to form a little filled round. Cut apart into 2-inch squares with a pastry cutter or a special ravioli cutter (available at a specialty shop in all sizes and shapes). Make sure the edges are well sealed. Sprinkle the finished ravioli with a little flour and let rest.

4. Meanwhile, bring approximately 8 quarts of salted water to a boil in a large pot.

5. Using a spatula, gently put the ravioli into the rapidly boiling water. The ravioli will keep rising to the top of the water during cooking, crowding each other. Lower the heat to medium and gently press the ravioli back down into the water, using a large, flat, slotted soup skimmer. This step is important because it allows the ravioli to cook evenly. Continue this process for at least 10 minutes.

6. Taste to see if dough is tender enough to serve. (I always wait for the pasta to cool before sampling; somehow it changes its texture after it is out of the water.)

7. Strain gently and thoroughly, one third at a time, and place ravioli on a large serving platter. Alternate 3 layers of ravioli, sauce, and grated cheese. Continue until all the ravioli is on the platter, ending with sauce and grated cheese.

Ravioli can be made earlier in the day it will be served; just sprinkle with flour and cover with a dry cloth. Ravioli can also be frozen in the following manner: Place a single layer on a cookie sheet and put in the freezer about 20 minutes. When they are frozen, transfer them to a plastic freezer bag. Continue this process until all the ravioli are frozen. They will keep indefinitely in this way. When ready to use, gently drop into boiling water as you would any fresh product.

MANICOTTI

SERVES 8–10

If you have ever eaten manicotti made with the store-bought pasta, you should be sure to try this recipe. There's no comparison. Homemade manicotti is much lighter and fluffier.

Basic Ravioli Dough (page 77)

2 pounds ricotta cheese

2 pounds spinach, boiled, drained, squeezed dry, and chopped

4 large egg yolks

2½–3 cups freshly grated Parmesan cheese

1 cup shredded mozzarella cheese (optional)

1 large garlic clove, pressed

¼ cup chopped fresh parsley (reserve 2 tablespoons for topping)

Salt and freshly ground pepper to taste

½ recipe Quick Meat Sauce (page 66)

1. Follow the ravioli dough recipe until the rolling-out stage. Then, divide the dough in half and roll it on a lightly floured surface until it is paper thin. Cut into 5- by 6-inch rectangles. Continue until all the dough is used up.

2. Cook the pasta rectangles in 8 quarts of boiling salted water in a large pot. Add a drizzle of oil to prevent the pasta from sticking together. Cook about 12–15 minutes or until tender, stirring often with a wooden spoon. Rinse well under cold water, but be careful to prevent the pasta from tearing. Drain well and reserve while you make the filling. Run the pasta rectangles under cold water occasionally and loosen them with your hands until you are ready to use them.

3. Mix together the ricotta, spinach, egg yolks, 1 cup grated cheese, ½ cup shredded mozzarella (if using), garlic, parsley, and salt and pepper to taste.

4. Spread 2 tablespoons of the mixture on each piece of cut pasta. Roll envelope-style, carefully tucking all ends together halfway through the roll to prevent the filling from oozing out.

5. Place the filled manicotti side by side in a baking pan with the tucked ends on the bottom of the pan. Cover the manicotti with a layer of sauce and remaining grated cheese and ½ cup shredded mozzarella (if using). Sprinkle with the 2 tablespoons of reserved parsley.

6. Bake in a preheated 400°F oven, covered with foil, on the middle rack, 15–20 minutes. Remove from oven and let rest 20–30 minutes, then serve with additional sauce.

Manicotti may be prepared in advance and refrigerated uncooked. When ready, bake as usual. Stuffed peppers and a salad complement this elegant meal nicely.

CRESPELLE

SERVES 6–8

This recipe is a batter dough, which you can use as a manicotti shell or a cannelloni, putting in any filling of your choice. You can also use the crepes for a light dessert, filled with chopped, sugared strawberries or blueberries.

4 eggs, beaten well

1 cup all-purpose flour

Pinch of salt

1 cup water

Olive oil

Filling such as ricotta, meat, or a combination of the two

Tomato sauce

Grated Parmesan cheese

Shredded mozzarella cheese

Chopped fresh basil (optional)

1. Place beaten eggs in a large mixing bowl.

2. Sift flour with a pinch of salt.

3. Add flour to the eggs gradually, while beating with an electric mixer on slow speed, until mixture is smooth.

4. Add water and 2 tablespoons olive oil to bowl; beat on slow speed until mixture is lump-free. (If small lumps remain, stir with a wire whisk or put batter through a strainer.) Cover bowl with a damp cloth and let rest 30 minutes.

5. Heat a 9-inch nonstick skillet over medium-high heat. Brush pan lightly with olive oil.

6. Remove pan from heat, stir the batter in the bowl, and pour 2 tablespoons into a single spot at the edge of the skillet, tilting so batter just coats bottom.

7. Cook crepe until bottom is set, about 5 seconds, loosening the edges and underside with a spatula.

8. Turn the crepe over and cook until second side is set but not browned, about 5 seconds. (Lower heat as needed, to keep pan from burning crepes.) Continue until all batter is used up, stirring batter occasionally.

9. Transfer finished crepes to a warm platter, stack, and cover with a clean towel until needed.

10. Fill crepes with 2 tablespoons of your favorite filling, such as ricotta, meat, or a combination of the two. Roll each manicotti and place in an ovenproof dish, seam-side down.

11. Lightly spoon enough tomato sauce over the manicotti to keep the edges from drying out. Generously sprinkle with grated Parmesan and shredded mozzarella.

12. Cover pan with foil and bake in a pre-heated 400°F oven for 20 minutes.

13. Serve warm with extra heated sauce on the side. Garnish with chopped fresh basil.

Crepes can be prepared in advance by placing each crepe between 2 sheets of waxed paper and allowing to cool completely. Put in plastic bags and refrigerate for up to 3 days. You can also freeze these for at least 1 month. Bring to room temperature before using.

LASAGNE IMBOTTITO

BAKED LASAGNE

SERVES 6–8

Lasagne is referred to as full (imbottito) because it is layered to fill the baking pan completely.

LASAGNE TOMATO SAUCE

¼ cup olive oil

1 small onion, chopped

1 garlic clove, chopped

1 (6-ounce) can tomato paste

1 (14-ounce) can peeled and crushed tomatoes

1 (14-ounce) can hot water

Pinch each of dried red pepper flakes, basil, and mint

Salt and freshly ground pepper to taste

1. Heat the olive oil. Add the onion and garlic and sauté for about 3 minutes. Do not allow them to burn.

2. Add the tomato paste and stir until dissolved. Add the tomatoes and mix well. Add the hot water, stir well, and let the mixture come to a soft boil.

3. Add the seasonings, stir until they are blended, and let the sauce simmer while you prepare the lasagne. Or, if you wish, the sauce may be made as much as a day or two in advance and refrigerated before you finish the lasagne.

TO FINISH PREPARATION

2 tablespoons salt

1 tablespoon olive oil

1 pound lasagna noodles

2 pounds ricotta cheese

3 eggs

1 garlic clove, pressed (optional)

1¾ cups freshly grated Parmesan or Romano cheese, plus more for topping

¼ cup chopped fresh parsley

Salt and freshly ground pepper to taste

¾ pound mozzarella cheese, shredded, plus more for topping

1. Put the salt and olive oil in 8 quarts of rapidly boiling water. Add the noodles and cook about 15 minutes or until tender. Stir constantly with a wooden spoon to prevent sticking. Do not overcook. Drain and rinse under cold water and reserve.

2. Meanwhile, combine the ricotta cheese, eggs, garlic, ¾ cup of the grated cheese, parsley, salt, and pepper in a large bowl. Mix well.

3. Bring the tomato sauce, ricotta filling, and cooked noodles to a clean work surface. Set out a 9 x 13-inch baking dish.

4. Pour ½ cup of the tomato sauce into the bottom of the baking pan. Over this, place a layer of lasagna noodles (you may slightly overlap). Top with 1 cup tomato sauce. Spread ⅓ of the ricotta mixture here and there, reaching the edges of the pan. Sprinkle ⅓ of the Parmesan and mozzarella on the top. Start again with the noodles and repeat the layering process

2 more times until all the ingredients have been used, finishing with the tomato sauce and topping it with the grated Parmesan cheese.

5. Bake in a preheated 350°F oven for 40 minutes. Let rest for about 1 hour. Cut into 2-inch squares and serve with the remaining sauce, heated, and more grated cheese.

Lasagne can be prepared early in the day on which it will be served and then baked prior to serving.

BAKED STUFFED ZITI

SERVES 6–8

This dish can be varied according to the sauce you use in it. If you use my Simple Marinara Sauce (page 62), you will have a very light dish, which will be almost pink in color. If you want a more filling dish, one that is practically a complete meal, use the Quick Meat Sauce (page 66) or the Sunday Gravy (page 63). It will then have a dark color.

1 pound ziti or any large macaroni

1 recipe for sauce or gravy (see introduction above)

1 pound ricotta cheese

½ pound mozzarella cheese, shredded, plus more for topping

¼ cup freshly grated Parmesan cheese, plus more for topping

2 large eggs

Salt and freshly ground pepper to taste

2 tablespoons chopped fresh parsley

1. Cook pasta according to directions, stirring often. Drain well and turn into a large bowl. Toss with a ladleful of sauce to keep it from sticking together.

2. Combine the ricotta, mozzarella, Parmesan, eggs, salt, and pepper. Using a whisk, mix until well blended.

3. Add mixture to the cooked, hot pasta and toss lightly with a wooden spoon. Turn into a medium-size baking pan with a little sauce added to the bottom to prevent the pasta from scorching.

4. Spread a layer of sauce over the pasta. Top with mozzarella and Parmesan. Sprinkle with the chopped parsley.

5. Cover with foil and bake in a preheated 350°F oven on the middle rack for 25 minutes. Allow it to rest for 20 minutes before serving. Serve with the remaining hot sauce.

This dish should normally be prepared just prior to eating it, but it can be kept in the refrigerator after cooking for up to 3 days. To reheat, put 1 heaping tablespoon of water and ¼ cup of sauce in the bottom of a heavy skillet. Put baked ziti into the skillet, cover, and steam on low heat until thoroughly heated.

BAKED STUFFED SHELLS

SERVES 6–12

There are many recipes for ricotta-stuffed pasta, but not too many are explained explicitly. You will first need to start your shells cooking, while you make a quick tomato sauce and prepare the ricotta stuffing. Use a baking pan that will accommodate shells snugly.

24 jumbo-size boxed pasta shells

1 small onion, chopped

3 tablespoons olive oil

1 (28-ounce) can peeled and crushed tomatoes

Pinch each of crushed dried mint and red pepper flakes

Salt and freshly ground pepper to taste

3 pounds firm ricotta, drained

4 whole eggs plus 2 yolks

2 cups shredded mozzarella cheese (about ½ pound)

½ cup freshly grated Parmesan or Romano cheese

1 tablespoon chopped fresh parsley

1. Cook shells in boiling salted water according to package directions. They should be cooked only until they are firm enough to handle, but not too hard. Drain and let cool.

2. Meanwhile, in a medium-size skillet, sauté onion in olive oil until translucent. Add tomatoes and stir until well blended. Add mint, red pepper flakes, and salt and pepper to taste; stir gently and set aside.

3. In a large mixing bowl, combine ricotta, eggs and yolks, salt and pepper to taste, 1 cup shredded mozzarella, ¼ cup grated cheese, and parsley.

4. Spread some tomato sauce on the bottom of a baking pan.

5. Spoon ricotta filling into cooked shells and arrange in baking pan so that shells are close together.

6. Cover with more sauce to cover shells and sprinkle with remaining cheeses.

7. Cover with foil and bake in a preheated 350°F oven for 20–30 minutes until heated through and the cheeses have melted.

This dish may be prepared a day or two ahead and left in the refrigerator. Extra sauce may be added before cooking.

FRITTATA DI SPAGHETTI

SPAGHETTI PIE

SERVES 4

This is a good recipe for using up any leftover pasta to concoct a new dish! Excellent for lunch or a late-night snack. To make it you'll need a heavy 12-inch skillet, preferably cast iron.

¾ **pound spaghetti, cooked and cooled**

3 **tablespoons melted butter**

2 **eggs, beaten**

1 **cup grated Parmesan cheese**

Salt and freshly ground pepper to taste

Chopped fresh parsley

2–3 **tablespoons olive oil**

1. Toss the spaghetti with the butter, beaten eggs, Parmesan cheese, salt and pepper to taste, and chopped parsley. Mix thoroughly.

2. Put the olive oil in a heavy 12-inch skillet, preferably cast iron. When the oil is hot, pour in the spaghetti mixture and shape it into a round pie.

3. Using medium heat, gently work the pasta so that it browns evenly, by gently turning it around in the same direction to avoid sticking.

4. When one side is brown, slide the omelette onto a large plate, then return it to the skillet to allow the other side to brown. Add another tablespoon of oil if needed.

5. Leave the pasta omelette to cool slightly before serving; this will give it a better flavor. Cut into wedges and serve with crusty Italian bread.

FETTUCCINE

SERVES 8–10

Fettuccine is good with Quick Meat Sauce (page 66) or Pesto Sauce (page 70) or a mixture of butter, grated cheese, and chopped fresh parsley. The pasta can be made ahead and covered with lots of flour and a clean cloth before it is cooked. Uncooked fettuccine also freezes well; arrange the pasta in a single layer on a cookie sheet and put in the freezer. When frozen, transfer pasta to a plastic bag.

6 cups unbleached flour (King Arthur preferred)

1 teaspoon salt

3 eggs

About ½ cup boiling water

1. Pour 5 cups flour on a smooth work surface. Make a well in the center and sprinkle with salt. Drop the eggs in the well, break the yolks with your fingers, and stir a bit. Then, mix the flour and eggs together until they form a cornmeal texture. Gradually mix in boiling water, using as much as necessary to form a smooth, pliable dough. (Be careful not to burn your hands. Always throw the flour on the water before touching it with your hands. This will cool it off a bit.)

2. Knead the dough for about 10 minutes until it is shiny and smooth. Form it into a loaf shape, pat the top with some water, and cover with an inverted bowl for 30 minutes.

3. Divide the dough in half, keeping the remainder covered. Roll the dough into a large round shape, about ⅛ inch thick. Liberally sprinkle flour from the remaining cup of flour all over the dough to prepare for the next step.

4. Starting at the top, gently fold over about 2 inches of dough. Continue to fold over dough so that the final width will be about 3 inches. The dough must be floured enough so that the layers do not stick together.

5. Beginning at one end of the roll, cut the dough into strips ¼ inch wide or a width you desire. (Be sure to use a sharp knife or the edges will be jagged.) Sprinkle more flour on the cut pieces and gently toss them with your fingers until the noodles loosen and open to form long strands.

6. When you are ready to cook, boil the fettuccine in 6 quarts of water seasoned with 1 tablespoon salt. Boil gently, uncovered, stirring often, for about 5–7 minutes or until tender.

7. Drain into a colander and transfer to a large serving bowl. Cover with your chosen sauce and serve immediately.

LA SPADELATTA

SERVES 4

For no apparent reason, this is a dish no one has heard of for years. I am told that Tuscany never abandoned it entirely and it is undergoing a revival today. Spadelatta is spaghetti with a tomato-cream sauce. You can add the finishing touch in a serving bowl at the table.

¾ **pound spaghetti**

1 pint light cream

1 heaping tablespoon tomato paste (or more if needed)

Salt and pepper to taste

Dried red pepper flakes to taste (optional)

½ **cup freshly grated Parmesan cheese**

1. In a large pot, bring salted water to a rolling boil.

2. Add the spaghetti and let the water return to a boil. Lower heat to a rolling boil and stir well.

3. While the spaghetti cooks, warm the cream in a large skillet over low heat (don't allow the cream to boil).

4. When the cream is hot, add the tomato paste, salt and pepper to taste, and, if using, red pepper flakes.

5. Stir with a wooden spoon until dissolved (the quantity of the paste is up to you, but this should not look like a tomato sauce—the cream mixture should be a pale pink).

6. When you have cooked the spaghetti al dente, drain.

7. Immediately pour it into the cream mixture, add the parmesan cheese and toss vigorously.

8. Place the pasta in a warmed bowl and serve immediately.

PERCIATELLI ALLA NAPOLETANA

SERVES 4–6

This is another delicious way to cook pasta. If fresh tomatoes are used, scald in boiling water for a few minutes until skin can easily be peeled off, then peel and cut in small pieces. Fresh ground meat can be substituted for the sausage meat. The peas can be shelled and refrigerated in advance.

¼ cup olive oil

½ pound ground Italian sausage

1 (16-ounce) can whole peeled tomatoes, squeezed, or 2 pounds fresh tomatoes

½ pound fresh peas

Salt and pepper to taste

1 pound perciatelli or bucatini (hollow-thick macaroni)

½ pound diced or shredded mozzarella cheese

Grated Parmesan cheese

1. Heat the olive oil in a large, heavy skillet and brown the meat.

2. Quickly add the squeezed canned tomatoes, fresh peas, and salt and pepper to taste. Cook briskly over high heat for about 5 minutes.

3. Lower the heat and let simmer, covered, for about 20 minutes or until peas are tender and sauce has thickened, stirring often with a wooden spoon.

4. Cook perciatelli in boiling salted water, following the package directions or until al dente.

5. Drain pasta and turn into a warm serving bowl. Immediately add the sauce and diced mozzarella, tossing gently. Serve with grated Parmesan cheese on the side.

HomeMade

Pasta

Ravioli

Gnocchi

Lasagna Sheets

PERCIATELLI WITH TUNA AND CANNED TOMATOES

SERVES 2

For a nice color, pitted black olives and freshly chopped parsley can be added, if desired. Anchovies can be salty, so go easy on the spices. A romaine salad goes well. Grated cheese is not usually used with any pasta and fish dishes, but many do like it.

½ **pound perciatelli pasta or linguine**

2 **tablespoons olive oil**

4 **rolled anchovy fillets with capers (canned)**

3 **garlic cloves, minced**

1 **(14-ounce) can crushed tomatoes**

¼ **cup dry white wine**

1 **(5-ounce) can whole chunk white Albacore tuna in water, drained well**

Salt and pepper to taste

Pinch of red pepper flakes (optional)

1. Cook the pasta in a pot of boiling salted water until al dente.

2. Meanwhile, heat the olive oil in a large, heavy skillet over medium heat. Add the anchovies with capers and the garlic and sauté for 2 minutes.

3. Mix in the tomatoes and the white wine. Raise heat to medium-high and cook until sauce thickens slightly, about 5 minutes.

4. Add the tuna and mix to break up large chunks.

5. Drain the pasta and place in a serving bowl. Pour the sauce over the pasta and mix gently.

6. Season with salt and pepper to taste and a pinch of red pepper flakes. Serve immediately.

ORANGE OR ROSY PASTA

SERVES 2–4

This colorful pasta is good with Simple Marinara Sauce (page 62) or Pesto Sauce (page 70) or made Alfredo-style. It also can be used for lasagne or manicotti. Experiment and make your own creation.

2 cups unbleached flour (King Arthur preferred)

2 large eggs

3 tablespoons strained carrots or beets for babies, or tomato paste

Boiling water

1. Mound flour on a work surface or in a large bowl and make a deep well in the center. Break the eggs into the well.

2. Beat the eggs lightly with a fork, then stir in the carrots, beets, or tomato paste. Using a circular motion, mix the flour from the sides of the well into the eggs. If the dough is too crumbly to stick together, slowly add a few drops of boiling water.

3. Pat the dough into a ball and knead on a lightly floured surface for 10 minutes or until the dough is shiny, smooth, and elastic. Cover and let rest for 20 minutes.

4. On a lightly floured surface, roll out ¼ of the dough at a time to about ⅛-inch thickness. Keep the unrolled portions covered with a large inverted bowl.

5. Cut and cook as described for Fettuccine (see page 89).

SPINACH PASTA

Spinach noodles are good with melted butter, plenty of grated cheese, and black pepper. Or be creative and use them with your favorite pasta sauce.

½ **(10-ounce) package frozen leaf spinach**

¼ **cup water**

Pinch of salt

2 cups unbleached flour (King Arthur preferred)

2 large eggs

1. Cook the spinach in the salted water in a covered saucepan on medium heat for 5 minutes.

2. Meanwhile, mound the flour on a work surface or in a large bowl. Make a deep well in the center and break the eggs into the well.

3. Beat the eggs lightly with a fork. Using a circular motion, draw the flour from the sides of the well into the eggs. Gradually mix all the flour with the eggs.

4. Add the hot, undrained spinach (the juices will provide the water needed to make the dough). Being careful not to burn your hands, blend the spinach into the flour-egg mixture. If the dough is too crumbly to stick together, slowly add a few drops of boiling water.

5. Pat the dough into a smooth ball and knead on a lightly floured surface for 10 minutes or until the dough is shiny, smooth, and elastic. Cover and let rest for 20 minutes.

6. On a lightly floured surface, roll out ¼ of the dough at a time to about ⅛-inch thickness. Keep the unrolled portions covered with a large inverted bowl.

7. Cut and cook as described for Fettuccine (see page 89).

SAL'S LINGUINI ALLA VONGOLE EN BIANCO

SAL'S LINGUINI WITH WHITE CLAM SAUCE

SERVES 2

This white clam sauce can be made ahead and reheated. It refrigerates and freezes well. If you desire a more bountiful dish, add about ½ cup chopped mushrooms, canned or fresh, to the clams and continue cooking as directed. They work very well together.

6 tablespoons butter

1 garlic clove, chopped

1 shallot clove, chopped

3 scallions, sliced

4 shakes Tabasco

½ large ripe tomato, quartered

Squeeze of lemon

½ pound canned whole clams, or 12 fresh shucked clams (reserve juices)

2 pinches chopped fresh parsley, plus more for garnish

⅓ cup dry white wine

½ pound thin linguine

Freshly grated Romano cheese for garnish

1. Start heating a pot of salted water for the pasta, following package directions.

2. Heat 4 tablespoons butter in a small saucepan. Add the garlic, shallot, and scallions and sauté until transparent. Add the Tabasco, quartered tomato, and squeeze of lemon. Cook slowly for about 5 minutes. Add the reserved clam broth.

3. Raise the heat and let the mixture come to a boil. Add the clams, chopped parsley, and white wine. Boil gently for a few minutes so that the clams are barely poached.

4. Put the pasta in the salted boiling water and cook for 7 minutes or until al dente. Strain well by shaking the colander. Transfer to a deep serving dish, toss with the remaining 2 tablespoons butter, and then pour the clam sauce on top. (Tossing the pasta with butter will prevent it from absorbing too much sauce.)

5. Sprinkle with chopped parsley and grated cheese and serve immediately.

LINGUINE WITH RED CLAM SAUCE

SERVES 4–6

In this recipe we are cooking the clams together with the tomatoes and spices, making a sauce that is lighter and more on the pink side than it would be if we started with a marinara sauce.

3 (10-ounce) cans of clams

¼ cup olive oil

2 garlic cloves, minced

1 (28-ounce) can plum tomatoes, undrained

Salt and freshly ground pepper to taste

1 teaspoon each oregano and red pepper flakes

1 pound thin linguine

Butter (optional)

Grated Parmesan (optional)

1. Bring a large pot of salted water to a boil for cooking the linguine.

2. Drain clams, reserving liquid.

3. Heat oil in a heavy, medium-size skillet (preferably cast iron). Add garlic and sauté until tender.

4. Place tomatoes in a bowl and, with a fork, squeeze the pulp into the juice. Add tomatoes and juice to the skillet and simmer over medium-high heat for 10 minutes.

5. Add salt and pepper, oregano, and red pepper flakes. Stir often with a wooden spoon.

6. Add clams and enough of the reserved clam liquid to make a pink sauce. Adjust seasonings and cook for 5 minutes longer. Remove from heat and reserve.

7. Cook linguine in boiling water for 7 minutes or until al dente. Drain and put in a warm bowl. Toss with a pat of butter (optional).

8. Cover linguine with some of the clam sauce and toss gently, adding salt and pepper if needed. Serve immediately and pass remaining sauce and grated cheese around the table.

PASTA WITH BROCCOLI SAUCE

SERVES 6

This pasta dish can be eaten hot or cold, as a side dish or a main course. The total preparation time is approximately 45 minutes.

1 bunch of broccoli (about 1½ pounds)

½ cup olive oil

4 garlic cloves, chopped

Salt and freshly ground pepper to taste

¼ teaspoon dried red pepper flakes

3 cups warm water

½ pound pasta (ziti, gnocchi, or small shells)

⅓ cup freshly grated Romano or Parmesan cheese, plus more for garnish

1. Cut off and discard about ½ inch of the end of the broccoli stem. Cut the broccoli into florets. Trim the tough leaves, peel the stems, and cut them into 1½-inch lengths. Set all the pieces aside.

2. Heat the olive oil in a heavy skillet or medium saucepan. Add the garlic, salt, pepper, and red pepper. Sauté slowly on low heat until the garlic is lightly browned.

3. Remove the pan from the burner and gently pour in the warm water to start the sauce. Let the water-and-oil sauce boil briskly for a minute, then add the cut broccoli. Cook on medium heat to a soft boiling stage. Add more salt, pepper, and red pepper to taste.

4. Cook the pasta according to package directions, reserving some of the water before draining. (This can be added to sauce if more broth is desired.)

5. Put the drained pasta in a large skillet and pour the cooked broccoli sauce on top. Sprinkle with grated cheese, cover, and simmer for 5 minutes or until the cheese is melted. Or, to make it peasant-style (Ma's way), add the cooked pasta to the pan of broccoli, toss a couple of times until well mixed, then serve. Sprinkle each serving with more Parmesan or Romano cheese.

FARFALLE WITH FRESH TOMATOES AND RICOTTA

SERVES 4

This pasta dish will be warm, but the ricotta and tomatoes will give it a cool taste. It's good as a light lunch or for dinner with a nice tossed salad. Be sure to use only fresh ricotta cheese (drain if too watery). Try to buy ricotta in a specialty store that features fresh cheeses. Some supermarkets have a section reserved for this and other kinds of cheese—if you shop in one, be sure everything is fresh. Farfalle has a bow-tie shape.

2 large semi-ripe, firm tomatoes, finely chopped

Salt and freshly ground pepper to taste

4 large fresh basil leaves, torn in small pieces

1 (16-ounce) container firm ricotta cheese, drained

1 tablespoon chopped fresh parsley

2 tablespoons grated Parmesan cheese

1 pound farfalle pasta

1. In a large bowl, combine the chopped tomatoes and their juices, salt and pepper to taste, and 2 torn leaves of basil.

2. In a medium bowl, mix the ricotta, chopped parsley, and grated Parmesan. Reserve.

3. Cook farfalle pasta according to package directions or until al dente. Drain well and toss with the tomato mixture. Adjust seasonings.

4. Place the pasta on a semi-flat serving platter or in a decorative bowl large enough to accommodate all the ingredients.

5. Top with the ricotta mixture and gently toss. Try not to disturb the texture of the ricotta.

6. Top with the remaining basil leaves and serve immediately.

FETTUCCINE AND BROCCOLI WITH LIGHT ALFREDO SAUCE

SERVES 4–6

Use 2% milk and low-sodium chicken broth, allowing the sauce to be light and smooth, and help produce a silky texture. The addition of Parmesan cheese will give it a soft binding. Color-wise I like to use ground white pepper, but if using be careful when adding for it has a strong taste. This recipe is too easy to be so good.

¾ pound fettuccine

4 cups (about 10 ounces) broccoli florets, washed and dried

¼ cup unsalted butter (optional)

2 cups 2% low-fat milk or half-and-half

1 cup low-sodium chicken broth, canned or fresh

3 tablespoons corn starch or flour

Salt and freshly ground pepper to taste

½ cup freshly grated Parmesan cheese

1. Bring 3 quarts salted water to a rapid boil; gradually add fettuccine, being sure water continues to boil. Cook uncovered until tender but firm, stirring occasionally.

2. While pasta is cooking, add broccoli to a saucepan with enough water to cover. Bring water to a boil. Reduce to medium heat, cover, and cook for 3 minutes or until broccoli is tender-crisp. Drain well and reserve. Thoroughly drain the cooked fettuccine. Place in a large, warmed serving bowl. Toss with unsalted butter, if using, and reserve.

3. In a 2½ quart pot, on medium heat, briskly whisk together 1 cup milk, chicken broth, corn starch or flour, and salt and pepper to taste. Whisk until smoothly thickened. Do not allow to burn. Add remaining cup of milk and whisk briskly to form a creamy, slightly thick sauce.

4. Add the broccoli florets, tossing until well-coated. Stir in the grated cheese.

5. Toss hot broccoli sauce mixture in bowl with cooked fettuccine. Serve immediately.

FETTUCCINE ALLA CARBONARA

SERVES 2

You may use pancetta, an Italian ham, in place of the prosciutto for an even more authentically Italian flavor. For best results, have all ingredients at room temperature.

½ **pound fettuccine**

¼ **cup melted butter**

¼ **cup heavy cream**

2 **egg yolks**

3 **slices prosciutto, chopped**

⅔ **cup grated Parmesan cheese**

Salt and freshly ground pepper to taste

¼ **cup walnuts, finely chopped (optional)**

1. Using a large pot, bring 4 quarts of salted water to a boil and add fettuccine.

2. While pasta cooks, warm melted butter and heavy cream in a small saucepan. Remove from heat; allow to cool slightly.

3. When butter and cream have cooled somewhat (if mixture is too warm, the eggs will curdle), use a whisk to stir in the egg yolks.

4. Using a large, heavy skillet over medium heat, cook prosciutto until its fat is rendered and the meat is crisp.

5. Add cooked, well-drained fettuccine to the skillet with prosciutto. Pour butter and cream mixture over pasta and add ⅓ cup grated Parmesan cheese. Toss thoroughly over low heat until the sauce coats every strand. Season to taste with salt and freshly ground pepper.

6. Remove to serving platter and garnish with remaining cheese, chopped walnuts, and more black pepper to taste.

PASTA CON ACCIUGHE

PASTA WITH ANCHOVIES

SERVES 4–6

A favorite tradition in our neighborhood, especially at Lent or on Christmas Eve, this pasta with anchovies is light, tasty, and easy to make. Eliminate the added water, and the sauce alone makes a delicious spread that can be used on any toasted bread.

2 tablespoons salt

½ cup olive oil

2 garlic cloves, minced

2 (1¾-ounce) cans flat anchovies, undrained

1 teaspoon capers

¼ teaspoon dried red pepper flakes (optional)

Sicilian dry-cured black olives, pitted and chopped

1 pound thin spaghetti or thin linguine

1 teaspoon chopped fresh parsley

Freshly grated Parmesan cheese

1. Boil 6 quarts of water in a large pot and add salt.

2. In a medium-size heavy skillet, heat olive oil on medium heat.

3. Add garlic, anchovies with their oil, capers, and red pepper flakes. Sauté 4–5 minutes, crushing with wooden spoon, until the anchovies dissolve and a sauce is formed. Remove from heat, but keep warm. Taste and add olives according to taste preference.

4. Add spaghetti to boiling water and cook about 10–15 minutes or until al dente.

5. Take 1 cup of the pasta water and add to warm anchovy sauce.

6. Drain the cooked pasta and place on a serving plate.

7. Heat the anchovy sauce until bubbling and immediately pour over pasta. Gently lift pasta, allowing the sauce to spread evenly.

8. Sprinkle with chopped fresh parsley and grated Parmesan cheese. Serve at once.

PASTA AL FREDDO

SERVES 4

This cold pasta salad is a wonderful summer dish, especially good to have on hand when you need a quick bite to eat. It stores well in the refrigerator for several days.

1 pound rigatoni or ziti pasta

½ cup olive oil

¼ cup red or white wine vinegar

4 garlic cloves, finely chopped

1 tablespoon chopped fresh parsley

1 cup chopped fresh basil leaves

½ teaspoon salt

Freshly ground black pepper to taste

10 ripe tomatoes or 2 cups canned peeled
    plum tomatoes (juice reserved)

6 Sicilian dry-cured black olives, pitted
    and chopped (optional)

Freshly grated Parmesan cheese

1. Bring 6 quarts of salted water to a boil and add pasta. Bring pasta back to a soft boil and cook, stirring often, about 7 minutes or until al dente.

2. Strain, rinse under cold water, and drain well, shaking the colander lightly. Transfer the pasta to a large serving platter. Reserve.

3. Combine the oil and vinegar in a large bowl and whisk until well blended. Add the garlic, parsley, basil, salt, and pepper and stir well.

4. Peel the fresh tomatoes, if desired, and slice them in small pieces. If you are using canned tomatoes, squeeze them slightly to remove as many seeds as possible and then dice.

5. Spoon the tomato mixture on top of the pasta. Gently lift the pasta without disturbing the tomatoes to allow some of the juices to pour into the pasta. Add the olives.

6. Cover with plastic wrap and marinate in the refrigerator for a couple of hours. (Add the reserved tomato juice if this sauce looks too dry.)

7. Serve with Parmesan cheese.

LINGUINI AI TRE FORMAGGI

LINGUINE WITH THREE CHEESES

SERVES 4–6

Here is a good appetizer or side dish to serve with the meat of your choice. It will take a half hour to prepare and cook.

2 tablespoons olive oil

1 garlic clove

¼ cup chopped fresh Italian parsley

1 pound linguine

½ cup crumbled Gorgonzola cheese

¼ cup freshly grated Parmesan cheese

¼ cup freshly grated Romano or pecorino cheese

Salt and freshly ground black pepper

1. Fill a large pot with 6 quarts of salted water and start heating it for the pasta.

2. Heat the olive oil in a large skillet and push the garlic through a garlic press into the oil. Add half of the parsley and sauté for a few minutes. Set the skillet aside until the pasta is cooked.

3. Add linguine to the rapidly boiling water. Cook the pasta until it is al dente. Reserve some pasta water, then drain the pasta, transfer it to the skillet, and toss with the garlic and oil mixture.

4. In a large bowl, add the cheeses. Immediately place pasta in the bowl, tossing quickly. Add hot pasta water if consistency is too thick. Add salt and pepper to taste, if needed, and the remaining parsley. Serve immediately.

MOM'S PASTA AND RICOTTA ALLA ROMANA

SERVES 2

Jacqueline Kennedy used to visit a certain now-defunct restaurant in our neighborhood just to order this peasant dish. The sauce may be made ahead, but the pasta should be cooked imme-diately before serving.

**½ pound fresh plum tomatoes, or
1 cup canned plum tomatoes**

½ pound fine linguine or spaghettini

2 tablespoons olive oil

1 garlic clove

3 tablespoons minced fresh basil

¼ cup chopped fresh Italian parsley

Salt and freshly ground black pepper to taste

1 cup ricotta cheese

3 tablespoons freshly grated Parmesan cheese

1. Fill a large pot with 3 quarts of salted water and start heating it for the pasta.

2. Remove the hard portion of the fresh tomatoes near the stem. Chop the toma-toes until you have 1 cup. Reserve the juice in another cup. If you are using canned tomatoes, squeeze them to elimi-nate the seeds, and reserve the juice.

3. When the water is rapidly boiling, add the pasta. Cook until tender or al dente, about 6–10 minutes.

4. While the pasta is cooking, heat the olive oil in a saucepan. Push the garlic through a garlic press into the oil, or mince it and add it to the oil. Sauté for 1 minute on medium-low heat.

5. Add the chopped tomatoes, basil, parsley, salt, and pepper. Cook until the mixture is reduced to a sauce consistency. Add the reserved tomato juices if the sauce looks drier than you like.

6. Drain the cooked pasta thoroughly (reserve some cooking water). Return the pasta to the pot. Stir the ricotta into the hot pasta, tossing with a wooden spoon. Pour in the hot tomato sauce and toss again. Sprinkle with Parmesan cheese and serve at once. This produces a thick, cheesy dish. (If you prefer a moister con-sistency, use some of the reserved water from the pasta and add as desired.)

QUICK PRIMAVERA

SERVES 8

This primavera can be kept in the refrigerator for several days to be used for lunch, an appetizer, or a main course. It can be served cold or at room temperature.

1 pound zucchini

1 pound ripe plum tomatoes

4 large mushrooms

3 tablespoons vegetable oil

6 shallots

6 parsley sprigs, chopped

2 tablespoons minced fresh basil, or
    1 tablespoon dried basil

1 small garlic clove, crushed

½ cup chopped cooked broccoli

Pinch each of dried oregano, mint, and red
    pepper flakes

Salt and freshly ground black pepper
    to taste

1 pound ziti, rotini, or tortellini

¼ cup grated fresh Parmesan, pecorino,
    or Romano cheese

1. Fill a large pot with 6 quarts of salted water and start heating it for the pasta.

2. Wash and trim the zucchini, tomatoes, and mushrooms, but do not peel.

3. Pour the oil into a large skillet, but do not put the pan over the heat yet.

4. Dice the unpeeled zucchini and tomatoes into the oil and then dice and add the shallots. Slice the mushrooms into the mixture. Add the chopped parsley, basil, garlic, cooked broccoli, oregano, mint, and red pepper flakes. Turn the heat to medium-high and cook, stirring often with a wooden spoon. After 5 minutes, add salt and pepper. Turn off the heat and reserve. By now, the water should be boiling for the pasta.

5. Cook the pasta according to the package directions, or for less time for a firmer pasta. Gently strain the pasta when it is cooked and shake it briskly to remove excess water.

6. Transfer the pasta to a large serving platter. Pour the sauce over it, a small amount at a time, and toss with two forks to mix before adding more. Add half the grated cheese and toss again. Taste, and add more salt and pepper if needed.

7. Serve immediately, with the remaining cheese in a separate bowl to be used according to individual taste. Or refrigerate, covered, up to several days if desired.

POTATO GNOCCHI

SERVES 6–8

Gnocchi, also known as dumplings, are a great delicacy. They can be served with any tomato sauce (see the sauce chapter) or substituted for the pasta in the Pasta with Broccoli Sauce recipe (page 98). Top with plenty of freshly grated Parmesan cheese, black pepper, and dried red pepper flakes and watch your family's delight! A salad and light wine will complete the meal. Gnocchi also can be served as a side dish or appetizer.

1 pound potatoes

2 cups unbleached flour (King Arthur preferred)

1. Wash, pare, and cube the potatoes. Cover them completely with boiling salted water, cover the pot, and cook about 20 minutes or until tender when pierced with a fork. Drain the potatoes, but do not rinse them with cold water; they should remain boiling hot. Reserve some hot water for further use.

2. Put the cooked potatoes on a flat work surface and mash. Immediately measure the flour on top of the potatoes and mix well to make a soft elastic dough.

3. Knead the dough until it is pliable, adding some of the reserved hot water if needed. To knead the dough, fold the opposite side over toward you. Using the heel of your hand, gently push the dough away from you. Give it a quarter turn, always turning in the same direction. Repeat the process rhythmically until the dough is smooth and elastic (5–8 minutes), using as little additional flour as possible.

4. To make the gnocchi, break off small pieces of dough. Using the palm of your hand, roll the pieces to pencil thickness. Cut them into pieces about ¾ inch long. Curl each piece by pressing lightly with your index finger and pulling your finger along the piece of dough toward you. Gnocchi may also be shaped by pressing each piece lightly with a floured fork to form an indentation.

5. Bring 3 quarts of salted water to a boil. Add gnocchi gradually, a few pieces at a time. Boil rapidly, uncovered, for about 8–10 minutes or until tender. Drain. Top with sauce of your choice and serve.

TO FREEZE GNOCCHI, FETTUCCINE, OR RAVIOLI

Place freshly made pasta on a tray and put in the freezer. When frozen, transfer to plastic bags and store in the freezer until needed.

RICOTTA GNOCCHI A LA LOUISE

SERVES 4–6

These fluffy balls were prepared for us by my friend Louise Saluti at one of our Sons of Italy lodge meetings. Deservedly so, she was surrounded by the members as they oohed and aahed between mouthfuls of these delicious morsels.

1 pound ricotta cheese

1 egg, slightly beaten

1 teaspoon salt

2½ cups unbleached flour (King Arthur preferred)

1. In a large bowl, mix the ricotta, egg, and salt.

2. Add the flour and work mixture with your hands until a soft dough is formed.

3. Turn onto a floured board and knead lightly until the dough is firm and smooth. The dough should be soft, but not sticky. If sticky, keep flouring hands until it feels comfortable to handle.

4. Break off small pieces of dough. Using the palm of your hand, roll the pieces to a double pencil thickness, about 10 inches long.

5. Cut into 1-inch pieces. Press each piece lightly with a floured fork to form an indentation.

6. Set pieces aside and sprinkle with additional flour to keep them from sticking to each other or to their surface.

7. Continue until all the dough has been used up, then drop the gnocchi into 4 quarts of salted boiling water. When the gnocchi floats to the top, drain immediately and transfer to a bowl.

8. Serve immediately with Simple Marinara Sauce (page 62) or Creamy Broccoli Sauce (page 73), tossed with freshly grated Parmesan cheese.

My friend Louise bakes the gnocchi and sauce in a foil-covered pan in a preheated 375°F oven for 15 to 20 minutes.

PASTA CON PISELLI E FORMAGGIO

PASTA WITH PEAS AND CHEESE SAUCE

SERVES 4–6

The Romans made much of this especially delicate preparation that unites homemade pasta, green peas, cream, and cheese. This dish is a delightful appetizer for a simple roast, or it can be the main course for supper or lunch.

1 pound fresh egg noodles (like tagliarini)

3 cups fresh shelled peas or frozen petite peas, thawed

2 tablespoons butter

⅛ teaspoon nutmeg

2 cups whipping cream

1 egg, beaten

1 cup freshly grated Parmesan cheese, plus additional for topping

1. Bring 4 quarts of salted water to a rapid boil over high heat. Drop noodles into the water. When water returns to a boil, cook noodles for 2 minutes, then add the peas and cook 5 minutes longer if using fresh peas, or 2 minutes longer if using frozen peas. Drain noodles and peas.

2. Using a wide, heavy skillet over medium heat, melt the butter. Add nutmeg and 1½ cups cream and stir, using a wooden spoon.

3. When the cream is warm, add pasta and peas and bring to a boil.

4. Remove the pan from the heat and stir in the beaten egg.

5. Add 1 cup grated cheese and stir mixture until well blended. Add more cream if sauce seems too thick.

6. Sprinkle with more grated cheese and an extra dash of nutmeg. Serve immediately.

LA PASTINA

SERVES 3

Good old pastina! Whenever we were sick, mom made it for us. My grandchildren remember her making this for them as well.

3½ cups water

2½ cups baby pastina

1–2 eggs, well beaten

Butter to taste

Salt and pepper to taste

Milk, as desired

1. In a small pan, bring the water to a boil (follow measurements from box).

2. Add the pastina.

3. When the pastina is tender, slowly swirl in the beaten egg(s).

4. Add butter and salt and pepper to taste.

5. When done, add more butter and a little milk. Serve hot in bowls.

CORNER KITCHEN

Our apartment was three flights up, with only four rooms to house six people. An old oil stove was the only source of heat, and in a corner of the kitchen sat a copper hot water boiler, which my mother constantly scrubbed with Bon Ami until it shined. This quickly emptied, however, so the water was usually cold. Mother always kept a kettle on the back of the cast-iron stove for additional hot water. The bathroom (which contained neither bath, shower, nor heat) was outside our apartment, in the hallway. We bathed in a bathhouse where, for a penny, we were given a towel and access to an open shower where we could all bathe.

PAGLIA E FIENO

SERVES 4–6

If I had to choose among the many old-world dishes, this would be a strong favorite. It is so quick and easy and very popular in our local Italian restaurants.

1 pound fresh or store-bought wide egg noodles

4 tablespoons butter

1 cup light cream

¼ pound pancetta, cut in small cubes

1 cup frozen peas, thawed

1½ cups grated Parmesan cheese

½ teaspoon freshly grated black pepper

1. Cook noodles in 6 quarts of salted boiling water until al dente. Drain, toss with 2 tablespoons butter, and reserve.

2. In a small saucepan, warm light cream (do not boil). Reserve.

3. Using a large, heavy skillet, sauté the remaining 2 tablespoons butter and the pancetta until the meat is fairly crisp.

4. Drain off fat. Add the warmed cream, peas, 1 cup grated cheese, and pepper. Stir thoroughly on medium heat, using a wooden spoon, until cream is fairly bubbly and sauce thickens slightly.

5. Add reserved noodles to skillet and, over medium-high heat, toss mixture until pasta is well coated with sauce.

6. Add remaining ½ cup grated cheese and serve immediately.

ZITI WITH WHITE CREAM SAUCE

SERVES 4

We always counted on pasta to get us through the day. There was always plenty of it, and lots of different, inexpensive ways to prepare it. Here we have a simple departure from the red sauce recipe. Simply, it is flour, butter, and cheese—the same ingredients that appear in many of our foods of yesteryear.

1 pound ziti (with no lines)

4 tablespoons butter

2 tablespoons flour

1 cup milk

Salt and freshly ground pepper to taste

Freshly grated Romano or Parmesan cheese

1. Cook ziti in salted boiling water according to package directions until tender. Drain and put on a serving platter. Toss with 2 tablespoons butter and keep warm.

2. Melt remaining butter over very low heat. Stir in flour until well blended, then add milk slowly, turning constantly with a wooden spoon.

3. When mixture is well blended, bring to a soft boil and cook for 10 minutes or until sauce has thickened, stirring often. Add salt and pepper to taste and stir well.

4. Pour sauce over warm, cooked ziti. Sprinkle with grated cheese and serve immediately.

If a thinner sauce is desired, add more milk to flour mixture.

PASTA CON UOVO E FORMAGGIO

PASTA WITH EGGS AND CHEESE

SERVES 2–4

Sometimes when I came home from school, and my mother had all her chores completed, she would make this wonderful snack for me. I would always top it with plenty of black pepper and lots of Parmesan cheese. In those days there was no such product as grated cheese. We always had a big chunk of this cheese sitting in the fridge and the cheese grater hanging nearby. We ground our own pepper from a wonderful pepper mill. My father would sit at the kitchen table when he came home from work and just crank away until we had enough for the evening meal.

We can recapture those days by using only fresh ingredients, such as pure olive oil and fresh eggs. In this dish, rice may be substituted for the pasta. It will taste just as wonderful.

½ **pound small pasta shells, or ½ pound cooked rice**

2–3 **tablespoons pure olive oil**

2 **eggs, slightly beaten**

Freshly grated Romano or Parmesan cheese

Freshly ground black pepper to taste

1. Cook shells in boiling salted water according to package directions until al dente. Drain some of the water until you have only enough to cover the pasta, with a little extra to spare.

2. Return the pasta to medium heat and slowly drizzle in the olive oil, enough only to barely cover the top of the pasta.

3. Using a fork, work the beaten eggs into the mixture, stirring well. Add 3 tablespoons of grated cheese and black pepper to taste.

4. Serve immediately in deep dishes or bowls. Cover with additional cheese and pepper to taste. If desired, drizzle more olive oil over pasta and cheese.

LEMON FETTUCCINE

SERVES 6

This pasta dish can also be served as an accompaniment to any meat or salad dish. My husband, Angelo, added some baby scallops to the lemon cream sauce and let it simmer until thickened.

2 lemons

1 cup heavy cream, warmed

Salt and freshly ground black pepper to taste

¾ pound fresh fettuccine (or substitute store-bought)

1. Bring 6 quarts of salted water to boil in a large pot.

2. Meanwhile, using a vegetable peeler, scrape rind from the lemons in long thin strips; set aside.

3. Squeeze and strain the juices from the lemons and pour into a skillet wide enough to accommodate the pasta when it is cooked.

4. Add warmed cream and salt and pepper to taste. Bring to a soft boil for 1 minute and reduce heat to simmer. Stir with a wooden spoon until a smooth sauce is formed.

5. Cook fettuccine in the boiling water until slightly cooked, about 3–5 minutes. Drain, add to the skillet, and toss with the hot cream sauce.

6. Divide into portions and top each one with the julienned lemon rind and freshly ground pepper. Serve immediately.

LOG CABIN

In the winter especially, I took out lots of books from the local library. I would warm my feet on the opened oven door and read and read. Abe Lincoln was my favorite topic—I could never read enough about him. Maybe because he lived in a log cabin, I could picture him warming his feet by the fire.

PIZZA, CALZONE, POLENTA, AND BREAD

PIZZA

SERVES 2–6

Pizza is certainly the most perfect food. When I was a young girl, my mother would give me my allowance of thirty-five cents every Friday, and I would visit the pizza parlor to order a pizza to go. A whole pizza (they really made them much smaller then) for myself! I always loved my mother, but never as much as when I bit into my Friday treat. To this day I feel like a little girl whenever I sit down to my own pizza pie.

BASIC PIZZA DOUGH

¾ cup lukewarm water

1 package dry yeast

⅛ teaspoon sugar

3 cups unbleached flour (King Arthur brand gives a quality lift)

1 teaspoon salt

¼ cup olive oil

Vegetable oil

1. Place the lukewarm water in a small bowl and sprinkle the yeast and sugar over it. Let stand in a warm, draft-free place for 10–15 minutes, until a foam forms on top.

2. In a large bowl, combine 1 cup of the flour and the salt.

3. Add the olive oil to the yeast mixture. Pour the mixture into the bowl of flour.

4. Gradually add the second cup of flour, stirring with a wooden spoon. When the dough begins to pull away from the sides of the bowl, turn it out onto a floured board.

5. Gradually knead the rest of the flour into the dough until the dough is smooth, elastic, and no longer sticky, about 10 minutes. The amount of flour needed will vary, depending on how moist the dough is and on the weather; a damp or humid day will cause excess moisture.

6. Coat a medium bowl with vegetable oil and place the ball of dough in it, rolling to coat it on all sides. Cover it tightly with plastic wrap and set in a warm place until it has doubled in bulk, about 45–60 minutes. To test if the dough has doubled, gently press two fingers into it; if they leave impressions, the dough is ready. While the dough is rising, prepare the sauce.

BASIC PIZZA SAUCE

The sauce can be made ahead and then reheated when it is needed. This recipe makes about 1½ cups of sauce.

¼ cup olive oil

1 garlic clove, crushed

1 tablespoon tomato paste

1 (8-ounce) can peeled and crushed tomatoes

Pinch each of dried oregano, red pepper flakes, basil, and mint

Salt and freshly ground black pepper to taste

1. Heat the oil in a saucepan and add the garlic. Simmer on low heat until the garlic is golden brown, but not burned.

2. Add the tomato paste and stir to mix well. Add the tomatoes with their juice, herbs, salt, and pepper. Bring to a soft boil, stirring often, and let simmer 10 to 20 minutes.

TO FINISH PIZZA

Olive oil

3 Italian sausages, fried until lightly browned and sliced (optional)

¼ pound pepperoni, sliced (optional)

1 medium green bell pepper, seeded and sliced in thin rings (optional)

¼ pound mushrooms, thinly sliced (optional)

½–1 (2-ounce) can anchovy fillets, drained (optional)

1 medium Bermuda onion, thinly sliced (optional)

½ pound shredded mozzarella cheese

½ cup freshly grated Parmesan or Romano cheese

1. Preheat the oven to 450°F. (To produce a heavenly, crispy pizza, the first thing to remember is that a very hot oven is very important! This will brown the crust and cook the sauce quickly so it will not seep through the dough.)

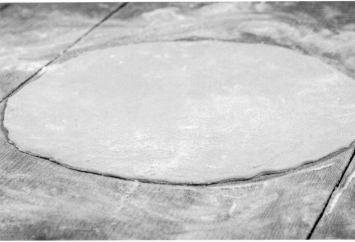

2. Lightly flour a clean flat surface, enough so that the dough does not stick. Flatten the dough with your hands until it forms a circle. Start punching it all around with the back of a clenched fist to shape it into a large 14- to 15-inch circle, sprinkling it with flour as needed. Make a rim all around the circle, using your fingertips.

3. Rub 1 tablespoon of olive oil onto the surface of a large pizza pan. Arrange the circle of dough on the pan.

4. Add the pizza sauce to the center of the dough and spread it almost to the edges. Scatter over the entire dough the sausages, pepperoni, peppers, mushrooms, anchovies, and onion slices, as desired. Top with the mozzarella and Parmesan or Romano cheeses.

5. Drizzle olive oil evenly over the entire pizza. Put the pizza on the top rack of the 450°F oven and cook for 20 minutes. This will seal the crust and tomatoes immediately and heat the oil on the bottom of the pan to cook the dough. When the dough is golden, move the pizza to the middle rack, lower the oven temperature to 375°F, and cook 10–15 minutes.

CALZONE

SERVES 4–6

This is a delicious warm lunch, or it can be served cold on a summer day. When I serve it warm, I sometimes top it with a dab of marinara sauce for a scrumptious taste. All that is needed to complete the meal is a tossed salad.

1 1-pound chunk of prosciutto or boiled ham, cubed

2 pounds ricotta cheese, drained if very wet

1 cup freshly grated Parmesan or Romano cheese

3 eggs

Salt and freshly ground pepper to taste

Basic Pizza Dough (page 120), or 1 pound store-bought pizza dough

Olive oil

½ pound mozzarella, cubed

1 cup homemade or canned tomato sauce

1. Using a large bowl, mix prosciutto or ham, ricotta, grated cheese, eggs, salt, and pepper (the cheese will produce a salty taste, so test carefully). Set this filling aside.

2. Stretch the dough to make a 12- to 14-inch round. Leave the dough slightly thick so that the filling will not ooze out.

3. Put the dough on a lightly oiled pizza pan, avoiding the edges. Gently spoon the filling onto half the pizza round. Fold the other half of dough over to form a large turnover. Use your fingertips to press the edges tightly together until all the dough is sealed.

4. Moisten the top and sides of the calzone with olive oil, using a pastry brush or the palm of your hand to spread it evenly. Cut a few slits in the middle of the calzone. Place some cubes of mozzarella and a ladleful or two of tomato sauce in each of these slits. Use all the cheese and sauce.

5. Bake the calzone in a preheated 350°F oven for 40–45 minutes or until golden brown. It is best to use the medium rack of the oven.

6. Let the calzone rest for at least 20 minutes to allow the cheese mixture to set. Cut in slices and serve as an appetizer or as a lunch dish, topped with additional tomato sauce if desired.

CALZONE WITH SPINACH-RICOTTA FILLING

SERVES 4–6

Calzone is great with a variety of ingredients. Many of my friends layer it with salami, baked ham, and provolone cheese—sort of an Italian sub. It is good with any vegetables, such as broccoli, mushrooms, or spinach. Once you become accustomed to preparing this wonderful food, you will become more creative with it.

1 cup firmly packed spinach leaves, washed and dried

1 cup ricotta cheese

½ cup freshly grated Parmesan cheese

1 egg yolk

1 garlic clove, pressed

Salt and freshly ground black pepper to taste

Basic Pizza Dough (page 120), or 1 pound store-bought pizza dough

Olive oil

½ pound mozzarella, cubed

1. Finely mince the spinach leaves and blend with the ricotta cheese, Parmesan cheese, egg yolk, garlic, salt, and pepper.

2. Before adding the filling, remember to put the dough on the pan you will be using. Then prepare and fill the dough as directed in the previous calzone recipe. Brush the top and sides of the calzone with olive oil. Cut a few slits in the middle, and place the mozzarella cubes in each these slits.

3. Bake the calzone in a preheated 350°F oven on the middle rack for 40–45 minutes or until golden brown.

4. Let the calzone rest for at least 20 minutes before serving to allow the cheese mixture to set.

FOCACCIA

SERVES 4

There are so many ingredients that you can use to top the flat, usually round bread called focaccia. In this recipe I give you my favorites, but you can experiment with any leftovers or seasonings of your choice. Focaccia is a wonderful snack or appetizer and makes a tasty and satisfying lunch.

1 pound pizza dough

1 small onion, thinly sliced

2 tablespoons olive oil

Salt and freshly ground pepper to taste

1 cup shredded mozzarella

1 can anchovies, drained and chopped

1 garlic clove, chopped

1 tablespoon crushed rosemary

Oregano (optional)

1 teaspoon red pepper flakes

Sicilian dry-cured black olives, pitted and chopped (as desired)

Grated cheese (any kind will do)

1. Stretch dough into a rectangular shape onto a pizza tray.

2. Sauté onion in olive oil until tender. Season with salt and pepper to taste.

3. Spread onion mixture over dough and sprinkle with mozzarella, anchovies, garlic, rosemary, oregano, red pepper flakes, olives, and lots of grated cheese.

4. Bake in a 450°F oven for about 20 minutes or until almost browned.

5. Cut in squares and serve hot or cold.

When using store-bought pizza dough, put it on a lightly floured wooden board and punch it down several times, turning. This will activate the gluten and help you to stretch the dough easily.

POLENTA

SERVES 6–8

A staple of northern Italy and most Italian homes in the North End of Boston, polenta is a sort of mush made from cornmeal. It can be cooked to the consistency of cream of wheat and eaten with milk and honey or butter and cheese. Leftovers can be cut into slices that are fried, broiled, baked, or toasted and served with a variety of sauces and fillings. Like pasta or rice, polenta accents and absorbs any flavor it is matched with.

Polenta can be used in appetizers, side dishes, or main courses. For example, try this hors d'oeuvre: On skewers, alternate cubes of leftover polenta and Fontina cheese that have been dipped in beaten egg and rolled in seasoned bread crumbs; deep-fry and serve hot. Or, for a hearty inexpensive meal on a cold winter night, serve polenta the old-fashioned Italian way: Spread it on a large board in the middle of the table and top it with cacciatore sauce and freshly grated Parmesan cheese. Seat your family or guests around the table, pour the wine, and have each person pick a corner and start eating.

1¾ cups yellow cornmeal

2 cups cold water

1 teaspoon salt

5 cups water

3 tablespoons olive oil

Melted butter or Fontina cheese

1. In a bowl, combine the cornmeal, 2 cups of cold water, and salt. Mix and set aside.

2. In a large, heavy pot, bring the 5 cups of water to a boil. Add the olive oil and stir in the cornmeal mixture. Always stir clockwise. With a wire whisk, beat the cornmeal until it thickens, about 5 minutes. This will keep the polenta smooth and free of lumps. Cook it over medium heat, stirring constantly with a wooden spoon, for 30 minutes. Use a wooden spoon with the longest handle you can find and wear long sleeves, for polenta will bubble and can splatter. If the batter gets too thick, add a ladleful of water and continue stirring.

3. When the polenta is the consistency of cream of wheat, cover the pot and leave it on the heat for 3 minutes more without stirring. Shake the pot a little; this will allow some steam to get under the polenta so it will detach itself from the bottom of the pot easily.

4. Turn the polenta onto a smooth surface or into a lightly oiled round bowl. The polenta should be allowed to set and become firm enough to cut, but it should still be warm when it is served.

5. Cover the polenta with melted butter or Fontina cheese. To cut it, use a wooden spatula if you have one, or a piece of string or dental floss. It is customary to avoid anything metal because the taste of metal will destroy the taste of the polenta.

6. Serve with additional salt and pepper to pass around, dried red pepper flakes, and grated Romano or pecorino cheese.

DIGGING FOR GOLD

My grandparents had a clever way of turning a humble and inexpensive meal into a treasure hunt. When Nonna served polenta to her twelve children, she would pour it onto a wooden board. My grandfather would then hide a penny or two in the polenta. Then Nonna would make several deep indentations in the polenta and pour the sauce in the holes. Each child was given a section of the board from which they could eat. The anticipation of finding the coins was so exciting, it was almost like digging for gold. Little did they all know that the real gold was the memories that were being created.

SAUSAGE GRAVY FOR POLENTA

SERVES 4–6

Italian sausage makes a scrumptious sauce over polenta, which is bland, or ziti or spaghetti.

1½ pounds Italian sausages, cut in chunks

½ cup water

Olive oil

3 garlic cloves, chopped

1 small onion, chopped

2½ cups plum tomatoes

1 (28-ounce) can peeled and crushed
    tomatoes

Salt and freshly ground pepper to taste

Pinch each of red pepper flakes,
    sweet basil, and mint

1. In a wide, medium-size saucepan, sauté sausages with water, simmering on medium heat until water evaporates.

2. Add enough olive oil to cover the bottom of the pan, and allow sausages to brown. Remove with a slotted spoon and reserve.

3. Add the chopped garlic and onion to the pan and brown slightly.

4. Squeeze the plum tomatoes into the pan and stir well. Add the can of tomatoes and stir until mixture comes to a soft boil.

5. Add salt, pepper, red pepper flakes, sweet basil, and mint to taste. Stir and add reserved sausages. Simmer gently for 20 minutes, stirring frequently with a wooden spoon.

6. Adjust seasonings and serve as sauce for slightly warm and firm polenta or homemade pasta.

FRIED POLENTA

SERVES 2–4

During my childhood we ate polenta so often that there was always some left over in the refrigerator. My grandfather, who was the cook of cooks, often fried the leftover polenta. He faithfully stood by the stove and diligently pressed and arranged the polenta over the bottom of a cast-iron skillet until it was cooked to his liking. This he would use in place of bread. It was served with greens, such as sautéed spinach, escarole, or broccoli rabe. To us, leftover polenta was better than the fresh version of the day before. Tastier than bread, it was filling also. Remember to use only wooden objects when touching the polenta.

4–6 cups cooked polenta, at room temperature

Olive oil

String (for cutting)

1. Place the cooked polenta on a wooden board that is covered with a sheet of waxed paper. With a wooden spoon, press down on the polenta until it is in a pie shape, but still thick.

2. Heat enough olive oil to cover the bottom of a medium-size cast-iron skillet. Cook oil until smoking, using medium-high heat.

3. Remove the skillet from the heat and place near the board with the polenta. Use the waxed paper to lift the polenta from the board and invert it carefully into the sizzling skillet. Peel off the waxed paper.

4. Return the skillet to the heat and fry the polenta, constantly pressing down with a wooden spoon until of even thickness all around and touching the pan on all sides. Cook on medium heat without turning until polenta is crusty and golden brown at the bottom.

5. Invert polenta pie onto a large platter.

6. Heat more olive oil to cover the bottom of the skillet. Return the polenta to the skillet and brown on reverse side.

7. Transfer the completed pie to the same platter, cut into wedges using the string, and serve with vegetables of your choice.

ZEPPOLE CON BACCALÀ

YIELD: 2 ½ DOZEN LARGE OR 4–5 DOZEN SMALL ZEPPOLE

You may know this traditional favorite as carnivale fritters or pizza fritta. Called zeppole in Italian, this treat can be made in many ways. My recipe uses baccalà (salted cod), but zeppole can also be filled with anchovies or any vegetable, such as cooked cauliflower or broccoli.

I hope you enjoy this version, which comes straight from my grandmother and is cooked in the same fashion as the old-time zeppole. Watch the directions for an important step that the Italians believe is necessary for a successful dough. (Hint: If you know why Christians believe in Easter, you will recognize its connection to dough.)

2 pounds boneless dried salt cod (baccalà)

1 square fresh yeast or 1 packet dry

2¼ cups warm water

1½ teaspoons salt, or to taste

2 tablespoons olive oil

8 cups unbleached flour (King Arthur preferred)

1 tablespoon freshly ground black pepper, or to taste

Vegetable oil with olive oil added

1. Soak the salt cod in enough cold water to cover for 24 hours. Change the water at least 6 times to remove the salt. Keep refrigerated. When you are ready to cook, drain and rinse well in cold water. Boil about 15 minutes (or until tender), drain, and refresh under cold water until cooled. Tear cooked baccalà into bite-size chunks; reserve.

2. In a large bowl, dissolve yeast in ¼ cup of the warm water, using fingertips. Let stand 5–10 minutes or until it is bubbly and creamy. (If yeast does not activate, starter must be repeated. Check the expiration date on your package of yeast to be sure it is still good.)

3. Add salt and 2 tablespoons olive oil, then pour starter into a very large stainless bowl. Slowly whisk in flour and remaining warm water until dough is thicker than pancake batter, using more water if needed. Dough should be heavy and sticky.

4. Wet hands and knead dough until smooth and shiny. Do this by loosening dough from edge of bowl and gently folding dough over and over, from top to bottom, always staying in one direction, until well mixed.

5. Stir in black pepper and cooked fish chunks and, with wooden spoon or even wet hands, mix until fish is well coated with the dough, again folding in one direction. Rub dough lightly with olive oil on all sides.

6. Bless the dough (make a cross sign with hands) and cover tightly with plastic wrap, then place a heavy towel on top to keep warm. Let rise in a warm place about 1½–2 hours or until doubled in size. When dough has doubled, stir with a wooden spoon and reserve.

7. Fill a large, heavy frying pan with 2 inches of vegetable and olive oil. Heat oil over medium heat.

8. Bring the bowl with the dough to the stove and add ½ cup of dough to the hot oil for small zeppole or 1 cup of dough for large zeppole. Dip the spoon you are using in oil, then in dough, to enable dough to slide off into the oil without sticking; continue this step each time.

9. Fry zeppole, uncrowded, until deep golden-brown and crisp on both sides. Bear down slightly with your spoon on the dough to cook well. Add more oil as needed, removing any burnt particles in pan.

10. Remove cooked zeppole, using a slotted spoon, and drain on paper towels. Sprinkle with salt and serve warm or at room temperature with lemon wedges.

Unused dough may be covered and refrigerated until needed. Stir dough well before using.

LA PIZZAGIENA

ITALIAN EASTER PIE

SERVES 15–20

Many thanks to my aunt, Lucy Baldassare, who generously shared her mother's glorious recipe with our family. I now pass this recipe on to you, with my aunt's blessing, so that you may share this wonderful Easter tradition with your family. The dough is so manageable, you could cry. The secret is to allow it to rest, covered, for at least half an hour. This recipe makes a large amount, so you may want to share a piece or two with a friend. You will need a heavy rectangular baking pan, 13 inches long by 9 inches wide by 3 inches deep.

CRUST

5 cups unbleached flour (King Arthur preferred), unsifted

2 tablespoons freshly ground black pepper

½ cup vegetable shortening

4 eggs, slightly beaten

¾ cup warm water

Egg wash (2 eggs beaten with 3 tablespoons milk)

1. Using a large bowl, add measured flour and black pepper, mixing slightly with a fork.

2. Add shortening and, working fast, press together, using your fingertips to blend evenly.

3. Make a well in the flour and add the beaten eggs and warm water (use ¼ cup water at a time until you have a soft and pliable but firm dough).

4. Press dough firmly together, adding more water if needed.

5. Turn onto a slightly floured surface and knead thoroughly, at least 5-7 minutes.

6. Cover with a bowl and let rest 30 minutes or more.

7. Cut ⅔ of the dough and roll it out, turning often, to fit the bottom and up the sides of the ungreased baking pan.

8. Roll out the remaining dough for the top crust and set aside (make a few slits).

This recipe keeps 5 days or more in the refrigerator. It requires no yeast (therefore no waiting for the dough to rise), yet the finished product is of no comparison to other styles of preparation. You will surely pass this one on to your children.

2 pounds ricotta cheese

1 large pepperoni (about 1 pound)

1 double Abbruzese salami (about ⅓ pound)

1 large sopressata (about ¾ to 1 pound)

¼ pound Genoa salami

½ pound mozzarella cheese, cubed

12 medium eggs

½ cup freshly grated Romano cheese

1 tablespoon freshly ground black pepper

2 pounds fresh cheese (such as formaggio or fresco)

1 pound prosciutto, thinly sliced

1. Using a very large bowl or deep soup pot, combine all ingredients except fresh cheese and prosciutto.

2. When mixture is thoroughly blended, use your fingertips to break the fresh cheese into large pieces and toss gently with the cold-cut meats mixture. Try not to crush this delicate cheese when tossing. Reserve.

3. Line bottom crust with half of the prosciutto slices.

4. Gently pour ricotta mixture into the prosciutto-lined baking pan or pans, and cover top with remaining prosciutto slices. Cover entire mixture with reserved dough.

5. Take the edges of the top and bottom dough, press together, and roll inward. Continue around the edges of the pan to form a decorative edge similar to a pie.

Crimp edges, then press gently with the tines of a fork.

6. Take any remaining scraps of dough, roll together, and cut into 2 lattice strips to form a cross; place in the middle of top crust. Brush all over with egg wash and prick the dough in 3 or 4 scattered places on the top to allow steam to escape.

7. Place in a preheated 400°F oven for 30 minutes, then lower heat to 350°F. Continue cooking for 30–40 minutes or until golden brown.

8. Let cool in refrigerator overnight or even for up to 2 days for better flavor and easy slicing. Cut in wedges and serve. If the pie is not firm or cool enough, it will tear when it is sliced.

Have your butcher slice the meats in thick strips. Be sure to remove the skin before chopping the cold-cut meat into small cubes.

BLACK PEPPER TARALLI

These taralli were made by one of our own senior citizens from the North End of Boston. They are crispy and great for dipping in your morning coffee. Taralli are found hanging in our pastry and bread shops on long strings, enabling them to dry out after being cooked in boiling water. You may add more or less black pepper than the recipe calls for.

6 eggs

½ cup vegetable oil

1 packet dry yeast

4 cups unbleached flour (King Arthur preferred)

1 heaping teaspoon freshly ground black pepper

1½ teaspoons fennel seeds

1. In a large mixing bowl, beat eggs thoroughly. Add oil and beat again.

2. Mix yeast with 1 cup flour, then beat this mixture into the first mixture.

3. Add remaining flour gradually, along with black pepper and fennel seeds. Stir well.

4. Place dough on a wooden board or counter. Knead until smooth, about 10 minutes.

5. Break off 24 small pieces of dough and roll each one into a pencil shape. Bend the "pencils" to form a circle, and secure the edges by pinching the ends together.

6. Place in a pot of boiling water a few at a time and cook until they float to the surface. Remove from the water and allow to cool on a wire rack.

7. When cool, bake on ungreased cookie sheets in a preheated 350°F oven for 25–30 minutes or until golden brown and dry.

PANE GRATTO

YIELD: 2 CUPS

These delicious bread crumbs are good on pasta, broccoli rabe, or escarole. The recipe makes enough for 1 pound of spaghetti or 1 pound of cooked vegetables.

¼ cup extra-virgin olive oil or melted butter

2 cups finely ground dry bread crumbs (made from French bread)

Salt and freshly ground pepper to taste

6 medium garlic cloves, minced

2 tablespoons freshly grated Parmesan cheese

1. Preheat oven to 400°F.

2. Heat the olive oil or butter in a small, heavy skillet. When hot, toss the bread crumbs into the pan and cook, stirring constantly, until the oil is used up. Add salt and pepper to taste.

3. Spread on a baking sheet and toast in the oven until golden brown, about 1–2 minutes.

4. Place bread crumbs in a small bowl and toss with the minced garlic and grated cheese. Serve over pasta or vegetables.

A WHOLE PIZZA

My father worked as a dinker in the same factory as his father. He would get up at five in the morning, attach his leg with suspenders, splash his face with cold water, have a cup of coffee, and walk down three narrow flights of stairs to meet up with his father. Together they would take a train to the shoe factory, about an hour or so away. There he made the holes in leather pieces that were used for the lacing. There was no minimum wage then, only piecework—the workers were given the materials and a specific task, and they only got paid according to each piece completed. To do more pieces, my father would hurriedly punch holes at the factory and bring home the pieces and laces for me to thread. At the end of the week, he would give me some money for the work I had done. That was my first lesson in working and saving money. Every Friday I would take some of what I had earned and treat myself to a whole pizza, which in those days cost thirty-five cents.

MEAT, POULTRY, AND GAME

VEAL SCALOPPINE

SERVES 2

This is a favorite in most Italian restaurants. A very quick, simple recipe if all the ingredients are on hand.

6 tablespoons unsalted butter

6 veal scallops (2 ounces each)

Flour to coat veal

Salt and freshly ground pepper to taste

Chopped fresh parsley for garnish

1. Melt the butter in a sauté pan over medium-high heat.

2. Lightly dredge the veal with flour, shaking off the excess.

3. When the butter is hot but not burning, place the veal in the sauté pan. Lightly brown the slices on one side, turn them over, and cook quickly, 1 minute or so, on the other side. You must work fast to produce a tender veal.

4. Transfer the veal slices to a warm platter. Stir the sauce well, scraping up any bits that may be stuck to the pan. Pour it over the veal.

5. Season with salt and pepper and sprinkle with fresh parsley. Serve immediately with buttered pasta or rice.

VEAL MARSALA

SERVES 2

Have all the ingredients nearby and ready. Work quickly! Once you are prepared, this dish can be cooked and served in fewer than 10 minutes.

6 tablespoons unsalted butter

6 veal scallops (2 ounces each)

Flour to coat veal

Salt and freshly ground pepper to taste

2 shallots, chopped

3 or 4 ounces marsala wine

6 fresh mushrooms, thinly sliced

Chopped fresh parsley for garnish

1. Using medium-high heat, melt the butter in a sauté pan.

2. Lightly dredge the veal with flour, shaking off any excess.

3. Place the veal in the sauté pan and lightly brown on one side. Sprinkle with salt and pepper, turn over, and add chopped shallots. Cook 1 minute more.

4. On high heat, add the marsala and boil rapidly to burn off the excess alcohol. Add the mushrooms and cook briefly to blend flavors.

5. Transfer the veal to a warm platter. Pour the sauce over the veal, sprinkle with chopped parsley, and serve immediately.

Boneless chicken breasts can be substituted for the veal scallops.

VITELLO SPEZZATINA

VEAL AND PEPPERS SAUTÉ

SERVES 2–4

For this recipe, it is important not to overcook the vegetables; they should be crisp. The tender meat and crunchy vegetables recapture the grand old custom of keeping food as close as possible to its natural state.

1½ pounds lean veal

Olive oil

3 large garlic cloves, peeled

3 large bell peppers, chopped

2 large white onions, chopped

Salt and freshly ground pepper to taste

Red pepper flakes (optional)

Chopped fresh parsley

1. Have butcher slice the veal ¼ inch thick, as for cutlets. Cut into ¼-inch slices.

2. Cover the bottom of a 12-inch frying pan with olive oil to a depth of ¼ inch. Slice garlic cloves lengthwise into thirds and sauté slowly over low heat until translucent. Do not burn. Remove the garlic.

3. Add the veal. Turn heat up to medium-high and immediately add the peppers and onions; cover.

4. Cook for 1½ minutes. Turn the veal, lower heat, and continue to cook until done (approximately another 3 minutes).

5. Season to taste with salt, pepper, and red pepper flakes if desired. Sprinkle with fresh parsley.

VEAL AND MUSHROOMS OREGANATO

SERVES 4–6

Veal shoulder is an inexpensive cut of meat, and with the bone is a favorite in our Italian kitchens because of its wonderful flavor.

6 veal shoulder steaks

½ cup flour seasoned with oregano and parsley

Olive oil

2 garlic cloves, crushed

1 (15-ounce) can mushrooms, drained, or ¼ pound fresh mushrooms

2 tablespoons dried oregano

Salt and freshly ground pepper to taste

1 (8-ounce) can whole tomatoes

¼ cup dry white wine

1. Dredge the steaks in the seasoned flour. Shake off the excess flour.

2. Heat enough oil in a heavy skillet to cover the bottom. Cook the crushed garlic in the oil gently until golden brown.

3. Add the steaks and cook until brown on both sides.

4. Add the mushrooms to the meat and sauté, uncovered, for 5 minutes. Sprinkle with oregano and salt and pepper to taste.

5. Add the tomatoes, with their juice, and the wine; simmer gently until steaks are tender. Adjust seasonings and serve hot with tomato mixture over meat.

VEAL PICCATA

VEAL WITH PROSCIUTTO

SERVES 4

This recipe makes a special company dinner. When buying veal, always look for pale-colored meat with no fat or gristle.

¼ cup unsalted butter

1 pound veal scallops

2 tablespoons flour

Salt and freshly ground black pepper to taste

⅛ pound prosciutto, sliced very thin and slivered

1 tablespoon unsalted butter

1 teaspoon chopped fresh parsley

2 teaspoons lemon juice

1. Heat the butter in a frying pan.

2. Dredge the meat in flour seasoned with salt and pepper.

3. Place the meat in the frying pan and cook over high heat for 2 minutes on each side. Transfer the meat to a warm platter and keep it warm.

4. Place the prosciutto in the frying pan and cook it 3 minutes, stirring quickly. Remove it from the pan and place it over the veal.

5. Add the butter and parsley to the pan gravy. Scrape the pan well, cook for 2 minutes, and add the lemon juice.

6. Pour the sauce over the meat. Serve immediately with sautéed sliced zucchini or squash.

VEAL CUTLETS PARMIGIANA

SERVES 4

Truly a favorite for all times, this dish has been in my family forever. It is simple to make and is so appealing that there is no doubt you will win praises. Cutlets may be prepared in advance, such as early in the day. You also can cook and refrigerate them for a couple of days. For this recipe you will need at least 2 cups of my Simple Marinara Sauce. Spaghetti is a wonderful accompaniment, along with a fresh salad. (Chicken may be substituted for the veal.)

6 boneless veal cutlets (4 ounces each)

2 eggs

3 tablespoons milk

3 cups dry bread crumbs, or more if needed

¾ cup freshly grated Parmesan cheese

¼ cup chopped fresh parsley

Salt and freshly ground pepper to taste

2 cups olive oil

2 cups Simple Marinara Sauce (page 62)

½ pound mozzarella cheese, shredded

1. Place veal between sheets of waxed paper. With smooth surface side of mallet or rolling pin, pound to ¼ inch thickness.

2. In a medium-size shallow dish, beat eggs with milk. Place bread crumbs in another dish and mix with ¼ cup Parmesan, chopped parsley, and salt and pepper to taste.

3. Coat cutlets with egg, then bread crumbs, pressing down slightly so that crumbs will adhere to both sides. Place on waxed paper to set.

4. Heat olive oil in medium, heavy skillet over medium-high heat. Add cutlets, a few at a time, and fry about 1 minute on each side until golden brown and crisp. Drain on paper towels.

5. Place cutlets on a heavy baking sheet and cover each cutlet with tomato sauce. Sprinkle with ½ cup grated Parmesan and mozzarella. Bake in a preheated 375°F oven for 10–15 minutes or until cheese is melted and tops are golden brown.

VEAL SHOULDER STEAKS VENETIAN STYLE

SERVES 4–6

Our family loved meat that was still attached to the bone. Veal was easily available and was reasonably priced, so there was always plenty to go around. This recipe is typical of the style we remember coming home to.

6 veal shoulder steaks

½ cup flour

Salt and freshly ground pepper to taste

3 tablespoons olive oil

2 garlic cloves, chopped

3 ripe fresh tomatoes, chopped

Pinch of dried red pepper flakes

¼ cup white wine

¼ pound fresh button mushrooms

2 tablespoons chopped fresh parsley

1. Dip veal steaks in flour seasoned with salt and pepper.

2. Heat olive oil in heavy skillet. Add veal and, using medium heat, fry until golden brown on both sides.

3. Add garlic and sauté with meat until golden brown.

4. Add chopped tomatoes, red pepper flakes, and salt and pepper to taste. Stir well until a nice sauce is formed.

5. Add wine, mushrooms, and chopped parsley; mix well.

6. Simmer gently until veal is tender.

VEAL PICCANTE

VEAL WITH ANCHOVIES

SERVES 2

This is a very simple recipe, as are most of the veal recipes in this book. All that is required are the best ingredients and careful attention to each step.

¼ cup unsalted butter

6 veal scallops (2 ounces each)

Flour to dredge veal

6 flat anchovies, drained and chopped

12 capers (in water), drained

½ lemon

Freshly ground black pepper to taste

Chopped fresh parsley

1. Heat the butter in a sauté pan over medium-high heat.

2. Dredge the veal in flour and shake off the excess.

3. Place the veal in the pan and lightly brown on one side. Turn it over, raise the heat to high, and add the anchovies and capers. Let the mixture get red hot.

4. Squeeze the half lemon (juice only) over the veal. Add pepper to taste. Shake pan vigorously, sprinkle the veal with parsley, and serve immediately.

LA PANZETTA

This is an old recipe and one that should be treasured. Serve it on special occasions because it is a "fussy" dish. The combination of the fatty meat, the very rich and custard-like cheese and eggs, and the gravy makes it succulent and delicious. The meat will need to be ordered in advance from your butcher, as it is not easily available. Have him cut a pocket all the way through the meaty end of the flank. For the gravy, you will be following the Sunday Gravy recipe, substituting this meat for the meat in that recipe.

¼ **pound ricotta cheese**

5 **eggs**

1½ **cups freshly grated Romano cheese**

½ **cup chopped fresh parsley**

4 **garlic cloves, chopped**

Salt and freshly ground pepper to taste

1 4½- **to 5-pound veal flank, with pocket cut**

Olive oil

Tomato sauce from Sunday Gravy recipe, doubled (page 63)

1. Blend the ricotta and eggs with the grated cheese, parsley, garlic, salt, and pepper.

2. Pour a little of this mixture into the cavity of the veal. If any of it leaks out because of a slight tear in the meat, pour mixture back into the bowl and sew up that tear with a large needle and thread. Place your stitches very close together. Pour the mixture back into the opening. When the opening is filled, sew it up with the needle and thread. Again, place the stitches very close together to keep the filling from seeping through. You may need to lay the veal flat as you are preparing it. (Don't worry if you lose a little filling.)

3. Heat the olive oil in a roasting pan large enough for the veal to lie flat. Gently lift veal and place in pan. Sprinkle the veal all over with about 1 tablespoon of salt and 1 tablespoon of pepper. Fry the meat until it is very brown and crisp on both sides, turning gently with a large, strong spatula or a large fork (do not pierce the

meat). Remove it from the pan and set it aside in a warm place. This will set the egg and seal the meat openings.

4. Start cooking your tomato sauce in the same pan, using the drippings from the veal. When the sauce comes to a boil, add the veal, lower the heat to medium, and cook for at least 3½ hours. (You can also bake the veal and sauce in a 350°F oven for the same amount of time, if you wish.) Adjust the heat as necessary to keep the sauce from drying out. The meat is cooked through when it gently lifts from the bone without falling apart.

5. Lift the meat onto a large platter and let it rest while you serve a first course of pasta (about 1 to 2 pounds), spooning the gravy from the panzetta over the pasta.

6. Slice the veal between the bones as you would a prime rib. Serve with the gravy.

IF IT'S TUESDAY, THIS MUST BE . . .

Italian families in the North End used to have the same basic menu schedule for each day of the week. On Sunday we had tomato gravy with meat, either meatballs, sausages, pork, or braciole (rolled stuffed beef). Monday was soup day, usually beef or chicken, with a salad. On Tuesday and Thursday we ate the leftover tomato gravy and meat from Sunday (my mother would also drop some eggs into the sauce). Wednesday was variety night. We would have either chicken cacciatore, sausages and potatoes with vinegar peppers, pork chops, minestra (cabbage and beans), or roast chicken and potatoes. Of course, on Friday no meat was allowed, so my mother would make stuffed calamari with spaghetti, fried fish, or sometimes deep-dish pizza—my favorite. On Saturday my mother economized with dishes like tripe with tomato sauce or, you guessed it, franks and beans, but on some occasions we would have steak, which my grandfather would grill over the flame of our gas stove. It smelled wonderful, but my mother didn't appreciate all the grease on her shiny stove! All these meals stand out in my memory with gratitude for the love and care my mother gave her family through this good food.

VEAL PANINO

SERVES 2–4

Veal cutlets must be delicately pounded with a food mallet before they are cooked or they will curl up and toughen. Even better, have a butcher do this. This recipe makes a wonderful presentation. Chicken can be substituted for the veal.

4 veal cutlets, pounded very thin
  (3 ounces each)

2 thin slices prosciutto

2 thin slices Fontina cheese

1 small garlic clove, pressed

Chopped fresh parsley

Olive oil

1 teaspoon freshly grated Parmesan cheese

Egg wash of 2 eggs, ¼ cup milk

2 lemons

1 tablespoon melted butter

1. Pound the cutlets very thin. Sandwich between the cutlets the thin slices of prosciutto, Fontina cheese, bits of pressed garlic, chopped parsley (about 1 teaspoon per sandwich), a few drops of olive oil, and grated cheese (½ teaspoon per sandwich).

2. Using two serving forks or tongs, gently dip the veal sandwich in the egg wash. Then fry the sandwich in ½ cup hot olive oil. If the oil is not hot enough when you add the cutlet, the egg will slither into the oil and leave the cutlets bare and unattractive. If the oil is really sizzling, the egg will puff into a protective shell and seal in the juice of the meat and cheeses.

3. Once the egg has adhered and the meat is cooking nicely, lower the heat and cook for at least 10 minutes on one side and 5 minutes more on the other side.

4. Sprinkle with juice of one lemon and melted butter.

5. Transfer to a warm platter and serve immediately with lemon wedges sprinkled with fresh parsley. Hot buttered noodles work well with this and other veal dishes.

VEAL BRACIOLE SICILIAN STYLE

SERVES 4–6

For this recipe you will need a prepared tomato sauce in which to add the braciole. Serve with pasta and salad for a complete meal.

7 large thinly sliced veal scallops

1 cup fresh bread crumbs

1 egg, slightly beaten

1 tablespoon chopped fresh parsley

2 small garlic cloves, chopped

¼ cup grated Romano or Pecorino cheese

¼ cup pignoli nuts, slightly crushed

Salt and freshly ground pepper to taste

Olive oil

4 cups hot cooked tomato sauce

1. Spread veal slices on counter and pound slightly to flatten.

2. Put bread crumbs in a medium bowl and add beaten egg, parsley, garlic, grated cheese, pignoli nuts, and salt and pepper to taste. Mix together to form a soft paste.

3. Spread this paste evenly over veal slices, leaving edges bare. Roll each veal slice tightly and tie with string or secure with toothpicks.

4. Using a heavy skillet, brown veal braciole in enough olive oil to cover bottom of pan.

5. When meat is nicely browned, add to hot cooked tomato sauce. Use a pan large enough to keep meat from crowding. Cook 20–25 minutes or until tender, but not falling apart.

6. When ready to serve veal, place on a serving platter, remove string or toothpicks, and cut in thin slices. Pour some hot sauce over braciole and serve with pasta.

VEAL STEW WITH TOMATOES AND PEAS

SERVES 4

The aroma of this stew will make your neighbors come knocking. Don't be surprised if they linger until dinnertime. A good loaf of Italian bread will complement this hearty winter meal.

½ cup olive oil

2 garlic cloves, mashed

¾ cup flour

1½ pounds boned shoulder of veal, cut in cubes

Salt and freshly ground pepper to taste

1 cup dry white wine

1 tablespoon chopped fresh parsley

1 (14-ounce) can tomatoes, or 2 large ripe tomatoes, seeded and chopped

1 cup fresh peas; or 1 (10-ounce) package of frozen small peas, thawed; or 1 (12-ounce) can peas

1. Heat the oil in a large stew pan, then add the garlic and brown gently. Discard the garlic.

2. Spread the flour on waxed paper. Dip the pieces of veal in the flour, coating them on all sides. Shake off the excess flour.

3. Add the veal to the pan with salt and pepper. Over medium-high heat, brown the veal thoroughly on all sides. When the meat is well browned, add the wine and parsley. Cook slowly until the wine evaporates.

4. Add the tomatoes, enough warm water to cover the meat, and more seasonings as needed. Stir gently, scraping up any residue on the bottom of the pan.

5. When the tomato sauce begins to boil, cover the pot and set the heat to simmer. Cook slowly until the veal is very tender, about 30–45 minutes. More water may be added during cooking time if necessary to keep stew from drying out.

6. Add the peas, toss well, and adjust seasonings. Cook until peas are done. If using canned peas, add them just before serving.

OSSOBUCO

SERVES 4

Ossobuco means, literally, "bone with a hole" and refers to the fact that the veal shanks are sawed crosswise, exposing the marrow-filled hole through the middle of the bone.

1 stick (½ cup) butter

½ cup chopped onions

½ cup chopped celery

½ cup chopped carrots

1 garlic clove, minced

1 heaping tablespoon chopped fresh parsley

About ½ cup flour

Salt and freshly ground pepper to taste

3 veal shanks, cut in half

½ cup olive oil

½ cup white wine

½ cup chicken broth

1 bay leaf

2 cups canned chopped Italian plum tomatoes (strain juices)

1. Melt the butter in a large Dutch oven over medium heat. When it is hot, but not burning, add the onions, celery, and carrots. Stir often. When the onions are transparent, turn off the heat. Add the garlic and parsley and stir for a few minutes.

2. Put about ½ cup of flour in a paper bag. Add salt and pepper and the veal shanks. Shake the bag vigorously. Shake the excess flour from the shanks.

3. In a separate skillet, brown the shanks in olive oil. Remove them from the skillet and place them on top of the vegetables in the Dutch oven.

4. Use the drippings in the skillet as a base for your sauce. Start by pouring out any excess fat. Add the wine to the remaining drippings and cook rapidly, until the mixture thickens.

5. Add the broth, bay leaf, and tomatoes. Bring the sauce to a boil, then pour it over the veal and vegetables in the Dutch oven.

6. Cover the Dutch oven and bake in a preheated 350°F oven for 1½ hours. Baste often. Add more broth if it starts to dry out. The sauce should gently cover the veal shanks and should be fairly thick.

7. Remove the bay leaf. Serve as is or over noodles. Don't forget to provide a spoon for each person to scoop out that wonderful, tasty marrow.

Ossobuco may be prepared in advance, refrigerated for 2 or 3 days, and reheated before serving.

OSSOBUCO MILANESE STYLE

SERVES 4

This dish has been showing up on a lot of restaurant menus lately, although it frequently requires advance notice. The meat is succulent, and don't forget to eat the marrow in the bones. It is both nutritious and delicious!

2 tablespoons butter

4 veal shin bones, each 4 inches long and with meat

2 tablespoons flour

Salt and freshly ground pepper to taste

½ cup dry white wine

1 cup chicken broth, or more as needed

1 teaspoon chopped fresh parsley

1 garlic clove, chopped

4 strips lemon peel, each 1 inch long

1 anchovy fillet, chopped

1 tablespoon stock

1. Heat 1 tablespoon butter in a deep heavy skillet.

2. Roll the bones in the flour. Place them in the skillet, add salt and pepper, and cook over medium heat until browned. Turn the bones occasionally.

3. Add the wine and continue cooking until the wine evaporates. Add the cup of broth, lower the heat, cover the skillet, and cook for 1 hour. Add more broth, if necessary.

4. Five minutes before serving, add the parsley, garlic, lemon peel, and anchovy. Cook 2 minutes longer, turning the bones over once.

5. Place the bones on a serving dish. Add the stock and 1 tablespoon butter to the pan gravy and mix well until the sauce thickens. Pour the sauce over the bones.

CALVES LIVER ALLA VENETIANA

SERVES 4

We don't often see liver on restaurant menus, probably because its taste does not appeal to many. I think this recipe is appealing and may even tempt non-liver-fans to give it a try.

1 pound calves liver (membrane trimmed), cut in thin strips

Salt and pepper to taste

2 medium onions, peeled and thinly sliced

¼ cup butter, or 2–3 tablespoons olive oil, or equal measurements of both

Red wine or wine vinegar (optional)

1. Season strips of liver with salt and pepper to taste; reserve.

2. Using a heavy skillet, cook onions slowly in butter, or oil, or both until golden yellow; do not burn. Lightly salt, if desired, and push to side of pan.

3. Turn up the heat and cook liver quickly for 2–3 minutes, or long enough to cook both sides of the liver to desired doneness.

4. Serve liver with onions spooned over. Red wine or wine vinegar can be swirled on the bottom of the pan until a nice sauce has developed. Serve the sauce over the liver.

BEEF BRACIOLE IN TOMATO SAUCE

ROLLED STUFFED BEEF

SERVES 4

Nick Varano puts his heart and soul into the Italian dishes that are served at his Boston restaurant, Strega. He watches over each and every meal and insists on perfection. Nick's concept for Strega was influenced by his many travels throughout Italy. He accumulated much knowledge from the different kitchens and people along the way, and that knowledge was not wasted! I love the fact that chef Sal Firicano knows exactly what Nick expects and is always moving his menus closer to the kind of food that is eaten by Italians at home. His combination of ingredients is always surprising and totally delicious.

Nick added this braciole recipe to his menu, conveniently borrowed from Mamma Rosetta's collection, and she naturally gave her approval. You'd better make a couple—this will be a big favorite!

1½ pounds flank, skirt, or top round steak

2 garlic cloves, finely chopped

½ cup chopped fresh parsley

¾ cup freshly grated Parmesan cheese

½ teaspoon salt

1 teaspoon freshly ground black pepper

⅓ cup olive oil

1 (28-ounce) can peeled and crushed tomatoes

Pinch each of dried basil, red pepper flakes, and mint

Salt and freshly ground black pepper to taste

1. Lay the meat out flat on a smooth work surface. Flatten it to a ½-inch thickness, pounding it lightly with the dull edge of a meat cleaver, or use a meat mallet. Keep the meat in one piece.

2. Cover the steak with the garlic, parsley, grated cheese, salt, and pepper. Roll up the steak, jelly-roll fashion, and tie it with cotton string or secure it with several toothpicks.

3. Heat the olive oil in a large, heavy skillet and brown the meat thoroughly on all sides. This should take 10 minutes.

4. Add the tomatoes and seasonings to the browned braciole. Cover the skillet and simmer the meat for about 1 hour or until tender. Do not overcook or it will fall apart.

5. When the meat is ready, place it on a large serving platter, cut the string (or remove the toothpicks), slice, and serve with the sauce poured over it. This may be accompanied by cooked pasta.

Braciole can be made in advance. It can be refrigerated for 3 to 5 days after cooking, and it freezes well if it is covered with the sauce.

MEATBALLS

YIELD: 10–15 MEDIUM MEATBALLS

For a soft, moist meatball, add uncrowded to a light tomato sauce; keep sauce gently boiling to allow meatballs to float to the surface.

1½ pounds ground meat (1 pound beef and ½ pound pork)

2 medium eggs

¾ cup soft bread crumbs, or enough to hold mixture together

¼ cup chopped fresh parsley

½ cup freshly grated Parmesan or Romano cheese

1 large garlic clove, finely chopped

Salt and freshly ground pepper to taste

1. Combine all the ingredients in a large bowl. Toss gently with your hands until the meat has become thoroughly blended with all the seasonings. The mixture should be fairly moist.

2. To form the meatballs, wet your hands in a small bowl of lukewarm water and then pick up about ⅓ cup of the meatball mixture. Roll it in the palm of your hands to form a smooth ball about 2½ inches in diameter.

3. Drop the meatballs directly into your basic tomato sauce recipe. Or, if you prefer a crusty meatball, fry in approximately 3 tablespoons of olive oil on medium heat for about 5 minutes, turning to brown evenly. Then drop them into gently boiling tomato sauce as they are browned. Meatballs take 20 minutes to cook well.

TO FREEZE MEATBALLS

Put uncooked meatballs on large trays and place in the freezer. When completely frozen, remove from trays and put in plastic freezer bags, a few in each bag. Defrost as needed or put bags in boiling water and cook until soft. Add to sauce.

ITALIAN BEEF STEW

SERVES 4–6

Experiment with different kinds of wine in this stew. Burgundy will keep it on the sweet side, while a dry white wine will keep it light.

2 pounds cubed lean beef

Flour to coat beef

¼ cup olive oil

2 ounces salt pork, diced into small pieces

3 large onions, thickly sliced

Salt and freshly ground black pepper to taste

3 garlic cloves, slivered

10 sprigs parsley, leaves only, chopped

½ teaspoon dried red pepper flakes (optional)

½ cup red wine

3 large potatoes, cut in chunks

3 celery stalks, sliced

3 or 4 carrots, peeled and sliced in chunks

2 medium fresh tomatoes, diced, or 1 (14-ounce) can plum tomatoes, squeezed, with their juice

½ pound mushrooms, thickly sliced

½ cup hot water

1. Dredge the meat in flour. Shake off the excess.

2. Heat the olive oil and salt pork in a heavy pot or Dutch oven. Remove the salt pork when it is slightly browned. Add the onions, beef, salt, and pepper. Cook for 10 minutes, stirring often.

3. Add the garlic, chopped parsley, and red pepper flakes. Let the mixture heat thoroughly. Add the wine to the pot. Stir and simmer, covered, for 10 minutes.

4. Add the potatoes, celery, carrots, tomatoes with their juice, and mushrooms. Stir and cook for 10 minutes longer.

5. Add the hot water, cover, and simmer for 40 minutes, stirring at least twice to prevent sticking.

6. Uncover the stew and simmer 10 minutes more or until the meat is tender. Adjust seasonings.

This stew refrigerates well for several days.

STEAK TARTARE

SERVES 4

Do not purchase already ground beef. Use only top of the round, tenderloin, or sirloin well-trimmed of fat and cut into chunks. Place in food processor and blade pulse on and off until meat is chopped into approximately ⅛-inch-thick pieces. Do not overprocess.

1 pound lean beef, chopped (use food processor)

1½ teaspoons salt

2 teaspoons dry mustard

1 garlic clove, minced

1 onion, grated

1 tablespoon Worcestershire sauce

½ cup minced parsley

1 egg yolk

Paprika and capers for garnish

1. Combine the beef, salt, dry mustard, garlic, onion, Worcestershire sauce, parsley, and egg yolk. Toss lightly and gently.

2. Mound on individual cold plates as desired.

3. Sprinkle with paprika and garnish with some small capers, strained. Have a pepper grinder handy.

4. Serve immediately.

TRADITION

Tradition is so important and, thankfully, respected in our American-Italian homes. In Italian kitchens, cooking has always been looked upon as a pleasure, not as a chore, and this attitude is still apparent today. Italians take food seriously, but think cooking and eating should be fun, too. Italian cooking has a beautiful simplicity about it. Beginners can produce these Italian dishes without difficulty, in ordinary kitchens with ordinary utensils, and expensive ingredients are often not essential. My cookbook represents many regional styles of cooking, making it rich and diverse. The recipes are completely authentic and promise to give you a real sense of pleasure.

TRIPPA DI MAMMA

SERVES 6

Maurizio Badolato's famed Limoncello Ristorante is one of the grand old-fashioned family-run restaurants in the North End of Boston. Along with Mamma Concetta, they lovingly design their menus in a truly regional tradition, with dishes prepared as if they were in their home-town of Calabria, Italy. At Limoncello's you will enjoy a taste that will long be remembered. This recipe for tripe is one of their specials, one that never fails to satisfy your taste buds.

3 pounds honeycomb tripe

½ cup olive oil

1 garlic clove, chopped

½ large onion, chopped

1 tablespoon dried red pepper flakes

3 bay leaves

Pinch each of dried basil, mint, and oregano

Dash of Tabasco

3 ounces canned tomato paste

1 (28-ounce) can peeled and crushed tomatoes

Salt and freshly ground pepper to taste

½ cup freshly grated Parmesan cheese, plus more for serving

1 tablespoon chopped fresh parsley

1. Rinse the tripe under cold water and scrub with salt until it is white and clean.

2. Place the tripe in a deep pot filled with about 5 quarts of cold water. Cover and let it come to a soft boil. Continue cooking for about 1 hour or until tender. Drain and rinse under cold water until it is cool enough to handle. Cut it into pieces about 3 inches long and 1 inch wide. Reserve.

3. Heat the oil in a large pot. Sauté the chopped garlic, onion, red pepper flakes, bay leaves, basil, mint, oregano, and Tabasco. Add the tomato paste and stir briskly. Add the can of tomatoes and the salt and pepper to taste. Stir constantly until all the ingredients are blended and gently boiling.

4. Add the tripe and simmer, covered, for about 30 minutes, adding hot water if sauce is too thick. Adjust seasonings as needed.

5. Add the grated cheese and parsley and simmer for an additional 15 minutes. Remove the bay leaves. Shut off the heat and wait about 30 minutes before serving.

6. Serve with plenty of grated cheese and additional salt and pepper.

ITALIAN SOUL FOOD

This dish can be prepared a day or two ahead of serving. It refrigerates well and can be frozen. Tripe is both a peasant dish and a delicacy. It is a Saturday-afternoon favorite at Italian neighborhood restaurants. Honeycomb tripe can be purchased at the local butcher shop and often at the supermarket as well.

SOFFRITTO

SERVES 3–4

What wonderful images this recipe brings to mind. Days of peasant cooking that would delight even a hunter's appetite—enough so that I know he would leave his fireside to follow the exciting aromas from my mother's Italian kitchen in the North End! This dish is deliciously nutritious. Serve with crusty, hot bread and a nice salad.

3 beef hearts (approximately 2 pounds total)

Olive oil

1 large onion, thinly sliced

2 garlic cloves, chopped

1 (6-ounce) can tomato paste

1 teaspoon each salt and freshly ground pepper

1 teaspoon dried red pepper flakes

1 teaspoon dried basil

½ teaspoon dried oregano

½ cup white wine

1. Wash beef hearts, place in a stainless steel pot, and cover with water. Simmer until cooked, about 20 to 30 minutes.

2. Drain, allow to cool, and wipe each heart with a damp cloth. Cut away all the fat and membranes, and dice the meaty part into bite-size pieces. Reserve.

3. In a medium-size heavy skillet, heat enough olive oil to cover the bottom of the pan. Fry hearts with the onion and garlic until the vegetables are tender but not limp.

4. Using a wooden spoon, gently stir in the tomato paste and salt and pepper until mixture is well blended. Add the red pepper flakes, basil, oregano, and additional salt and pepper if needed. Stir until meat is nicely coated.

5. Add the wine and simmer, uncovered, for 30 minutes or until a nice sauce forms, adding more wine if needed.

6. Allow to sit at least 30 minutes before serving to better capture the flavors.

You can fry small fresh hot peppers along with the garlic and onion for a pungent flavor, but omit the red pepper flakes.

LAMB STEW

Nothing can beat a bowl of stew. It is warm and nourishing and full of love.

3 pounds lamb chunks

Flour to coat lamb

½ cup oil

2 garlic cloves, crushed

3 large onions, thickly sliced

1 heaping tablespoon tomato paste

1 (14-ounce) can whole tomatoes, or 2 cups
  Simple Marinara Sauce (see page 62)

Pinch each of dried red pepper flakes, mint,
  oregano, and basil

Salt and freshly ground pepper to taste

1 cup red wine

4 carrots, thickly sliced

3 or 4 celery stalks, sliced

2 large potatoes, thickly sliced

1. Put the meat in a large bowl and sprinkle with flour, turning often until all sides are coated.

2. Put the oil and garlic in a large, heavy pot. Sauté on low heat for about 20 minutes so that the oil absorbs all the flavor of the garlic without burning.

3. Remove the garlic from the oil. Raise the heat to high and fry the lamb and onions until they are well browned, turning often.

4. Lower the heat to medium. Add the tomato paste and stir well. Add the tomatoes or marinara sauce and seasonings, and stir until mixed thoroughly. Sauté for about 5 minutes, turning often. Add salt and pepper to taste.

5. Sprinkle the cup of wine all over and simmer, covered, for 20 minutes. Stir several times during cooking.

6. Add the carrots, celery, potatoes, and more of the seasonings. Stir well and cover. Cook for another 30 minutes or until the meat is tender.

7. Turn off the heat and let the mixture rest (covered) for about 20 minutes. If the stew seems too dry, add more wine.

This stew refrigerates and freezes well.

AGNELLO AL LACRYMA CHRISTI

"CRYING LAMB"

SERVES 6–8

Lamb will always be one of the star attractions in an Italian home at Easter. For a wonderful and easy recipe, try this lamb delight. To prepare it, you will need the freshest meat from your favorite butcher.

5- to 6-pound leg of lamb, wiped with paper towel

6 garlic cloves, slivered

1 teaspoon each crushed rosemary and tarragon

¼ cup olive oil

Salt and freshly ground black pepper to taste

3 pounds Maine potatoes, peeled and thinly sliced

Butter

Paprika (optional)

Dry white wine (optional)

1. Preheat oven to 400°F.

2. Make short, deep slashes in lamb and stuff them liberally with some of the garlic slivers and herbs. Brush the meat with olive oil and sprinkle with salt and pepper.

3. Layer potatoes in a buttered baking pan, topping each layer with dots of butter, and sprinkle with salt and pepper to taste. Spread with remaining garlic slivers and more herbs.

4. Place lamb on a rack in the baking pan to sit directly over the potatoes, allowing lamb drippings, known as the "tears," to fall over the potatoes. Dust with paprika if using. Set pan on middle rack of oven.

5. Roast in the hot oven, uncovered, for 1½ hours for medium-rare, or until the lamb has cooked to desired degree of doneness and potatoes are browned. Cover with aluminum foil if it browns too fast.

6. Remove meat and potatoes from pan and place on a warmed platter.

7. If a sauce is desired, add some white wine to the meat drippings in pan and stir on low heat until well blended. Serve sauce over warm sliced meat.

LAMB WITH WHITE WINE SAUCE

SERVES 6

This delicious dish can be made in advance and refrigerated or frozen.

3 pounds leg of lamb, boned and
　　cut in cubes

½ cup flour

1 garlic clove

1 teaspoon dried rosemary

¼ cup olive oil

Salt and freshly ground pepper to taste

1 cup dry white wine

1 teaspoon tomato paste

¼ cup warm water

1 cup canned peeled plum tomatoes,
　　squeezed to break into small pieces

1 (8-ounce) can peas (optional)

1. Put the lamb cubes and flour in a paper bag. Shake the bag to coat the meat evenly with flour.

2. Chop the garlic and rosemary together into tiny bits. Heat the olive oil in a Dutch oven over high heat. Sauté the garlic and rosemary until golden.

3. Add the lamb to the Dutch oven. Brown it thoroughly by turning it over and over on all sides. Add salt, a few grinds of pepper, and the wine. Stir gently and cook for about 5 minutes. Reduce the heat to medium.

4. Dilute the tomato paste in the warm water. Add it to the Dutch oven and stir gently, then add the tomatoes. Bring all the ingredients to a soft boil, reduce heat, and simmer 1 hour, stirring occasionally. Remove the lamb from the heat.

5. I like to throw a can of peas in the pot after the lamb has completed cooking. Stir gently, cover the pot, and let the meat rest for about 10 minutes.

6. Serve with buttered noodles or garlic bread.

ROAST LAMB WITH POTATOES AND PEAS

SERVES 4–6

Because lamb is readily available, we can enjoy it often. Accompanied by potatoes and peas and maybe a plum tomato or two, one can almost picture a baked lamb stew. Be sure the lamb's thin skin (fell) is intact, as this will give the meat a nice roasted texture.

1 4–5-pound leg of lamb with fell and bone

3 tablespoons olive oil

3 cloves garlic, slivered

2–3 tablespoons dried rosemary or a few sprigs of fresh

Salt and pepper to taste

2–2½ pound small new potatoes

2 (15-ounce) cans small peas, drained

1. Preheat oven to 450°F.

2. Wash and dry the lamb. Place flat-side up in a large roasting pan and rub with some of the oil.

3. Make small incisions around the lamb and insert the garlic slices. Sprinkle with rosemary and salt and pepper to taste.

4. Put the lamb in the oven and lower the heat to 350°F. Cook for 20 minutes per pound for rare, 25 minutes per pound for medium, or 30 minutes per pound for well done.

5. Wash and dry the potatoes, coat with the remaining oil, and add to the pan with the lamb 45 minutes before the lamb is cooked. Add peas the last 5 minutes of roasting.

6. Put meat and vegetables on a warm platter and allow lamb to rest for at least 20 minutes before serving.

RACK OF LAMB WITH MUSTARD AND ROSEMARY

SERVES 4–6

Coat baby bliss red potatoes with olive oil and cook alongside the lamb, and steam some fresh green beans to round out the main course. A spinach salad with mushrooms is good, too.

2 tablespoons French Dijon mustard

1 tablespoon fresh rosemary leaves, finely ground

2 tablespoons fresh lemon juice

4 tablespoons olive oil

2 racks of lamb, 7–8 ribs about 2 pounds each, trimmed with about 2" of bone exposed

Sea salt and freshly ground pepper to taste

1. Preheat oven to 500°F.

2. In a small bowl, combine mustard, rosemary, lemon juice, and oil.

3. On the fat side of the racks, make shallow crisscross marks with a knife. Fold a double strip of foil over the rib ends to prevent them from burning.

4. With a pastry brush, coat the tops and sides of racks with the mustard-rosemary mixture.

5. Place racks rib-end down in a roasting pan. Season with salt and pepper.

6. Place pan in the center of the hot oven and roast until meat is well seared, about 10 minutes. The fat should sizzle and the tops of the racks should begin to brown.

7. Reduce heat to 400°F and roast about 20 minutes more for rare.

8. Remove the lamb from the oven and season with additional salt and pepper if desired. Cover loosely with foil and let stand 15 minutes.

9. To serve, carve into single-rib portions.

PARMESAN-CRUSTED SPRING LAMB

SERVES 6

In my Catholic childhood, Easter was an important observation of how we fulfilled our Lenten duties of fasting and abstaining. It was also a renewal of our Christian faith. The same applies today, for Easter is still the most important festival of the Christian calendar. As for food, lamb will always be the star attraction in an Italian home. For a wonderful and easy recipe, try this lamb delight. Of course, you will be using fresh meat from your favorite butcher.

1 fresh cut leg of lamb, with bone (about 6 pounds)

Salt and freshly ground pepper to taste

2 garlic cloves, mashed

2 tablespoons freshly grated Parmesan cheese

2 teaspoons dried rosemary, crushed

⅓ cup dry white wine or red wine

⅓ cup olive oil

1. Preheat oven to 350°F.

2. Sprinkle lamb on all sides with salt and pepper. Place in a shallow roasting pan.

3. Combine garlic, Parmesan cheese, rosemary, wine, and olive oil in a small bowl. Beat until thick and well-blended.

4. Brush some of the wine mixture over the lamb.

5. Roast in the preheated oven for about 1¾ hours for pink lamb, or 2½ hours for well-done lamb. Brush with the wine mixture every 30 minutes during cooking.

6. Allow cooked lamb to rest 15 minutes before carving.

RABBIT SICILIANO

SERVES 4

Chicken can be substituted for the rabbit in this recipe, but since we don't often find a good rabbit recipe, why not give it a try in its authentic version?

1 small rabbit (about 3 pounds), cut in small pieces

⅔ cup olive oil

2 celery stalks, sliced

1 (6-ounce) jar Sicilian dry-cured black olives, pitted and halved

2 garlic cloves, chopped

¼ teaspoon dried oregano

Pinch of dried red pepper flakes

Freshly ground black pepper to taste

1 teaspoon salt

1 teaspoon capers in water, drained

½ cup white vinegar

1. Wash the rabbit well. Soak it in cold salted water for several hours. Dry with paper towels and reserve.

2. Heat the oil in a large heavy skillet and sauté the sliced celery for 5 minutes. Remove the celery from the pan and reserve.

3. Raise the heat and fry the rabbit a few pieces at a time until nicely browned.

4. Lower the heat to medium and add the celery, olives, garlic, seasonings, and capers. Stir gently until the rabbit and seasonings are well blended. Sprinkle with the vinegar and simmer, covered, for about 30 minutes or until the rabbit is tender. Add more of the seasonings if needed.

5. Remove the pan from the heat and let it rest, covered, for about 10 minutes to combine flavors. Serve with noodles and a salad.

This dish can be refrigerated for several days.

FRESH BAKED RABBIT

SERVES 4–6

This is one of my favorite recipes. After months of experimenting and combining different vegetables, I feel it is the best-tasting rabbit dinner ever—a five-star meal. Polenta makes a good accompaniment.

2½ pounds fresh whole rabbit, cut in serving-size pieces

1 large onion, cut in large chunks

3 carrots, cut in chunks

6–8 stalks young celery, cut in chunks

Salt and freshly ground pepper to taste

Turmeric to taste

½ pound salt pork, diced in small pieces

1 whole bud garlic, cloves separated with skins left on

2 large shallots, coarsely chopped

1 cup chopped fresh fennel, or 1 tablespoon fennel seeds

¾ cup white wine

½ cup marsala wine

1. Preheat oven to 550°F.

2. Wash rabbit while rubbing with coarse salt. Wipe dry with paper towels.

3. Spread onion, carrots, and celery on the bottom of a large baking pan. Spread rabbit pieces over vegetables. Sprinkle rabbit and vegetables generously with salt and pepper and turmeric.

4. Scatter diced salt pork evenly on rabbit pieces. Sprinkle garlic cloves, chopped shallots, and fennel over rabbit.

5. Bake in the preheated oven for 30 minutes. Turn pieces over, lower heat to 350°F, and continue baking 15 minutes more.

6. Raise heat again to 550°F and pour in white wine. Bake 10 minutes longer.

7. Add marsala and bake 10 more minutes or until golden brown.

8. Place rabbit on a large platter and top with vegetables and wine sauce from bottom of pan.

The addition of salt pork distinguishes this recipe from all others. The total cooking time is 1 hour, 15 minutes.

OLGA'S RABBIT CACCIATORE

SERVES 4–6

When I was a child, my grandfather would often come over to our house and request that my mother prepare this recipe. Since he always asked for it in Italian, my brothers, sisters, and I always thought we were eating chicken, and my mother didn't tell us any differently since she thought we might be a little sensitive to eating a rabbit. We used to get a bunny each Easter and raise it as our pet. When it became grown, we were told it had to be given away. Little did we know it was to become a Sunday dinner. Only in later years did we find out how lucky we were to have such delicacies as Rabbit Cacciatore as part of our ethnic tradition.

1 small rabbit (about 3 pounds), cut in small pieces

⅔ cup olive oil

2 large green peppers, sliced

3 medium onions, sliced lengthwise

½ pound button mushrooms, cut in chunks

6 garlic cloves, halved

Salt and freshly ground pepper to taste

3 ripe red tomatoes, peeled and chopped

Dried red pepper flakes to taste

1 (6-ounce) can small peas (reserve juice)

1. Wash the rabbit well and soak it in cold salted water for several hours. Dry with paper towels and reserve.

2. Put the oil in a large heavy skillet and sauté the peppers until tender. Remove them from the oil and set aside. Sauté the onions until tender, then remove them from the oil and add to the peppers. Sauté the mushrooms and 3 garlic cloves until slightly browned, then remove them and add to the peppers and onions.

3. Put the rabbit and the remaining garlic cloves in the skillet and fry until browned. Salt and pepper the meat. Add the tomatoes, stirring gently. Cover.

4. Let the rabbit boil slightly to dry out any remaining water. Add red pepper flakes, more salt and pepper, and other seasonings, if desired. If the mixture becomes too dry, add juice from the can of peas.

5. Remove the cover after 20 minutes and add the pepper-onion-mushroom mixture. Let simmer 10 minutes, then add the peas. Remove the skillet from the heat and let rest for a few minutes to allow flavors to combine.

This dish may be refrigerated for a couple of days.

ITALIAN SAUSAGES, VINEGAR PEPPERS, AND POTATOES

SERVES 4–6

My mother made this meal at least once every two weeks, alternating the sausages with pork chops. We would follow the heavenly aroma all the way up three flights of stairs and patiently sit at the kitchen table with fork and crusty bread in hand.

2 pounds sweet, all-pork Italian sausages

¼ cup olive oil

6 large potatoes, peeled, thickly sliced, and wiped dry

6–8 spicy or hot vinegar peppers (purchase at supermarket or make them yourself; see page 286)

Salt and freshly ground pepper to taste

1. In a large heavy skillet, over medium heat, fry the sausages in hot oil until well browned. Pierce them gently with a fork as they cook. Using a slotted spoon, transfer the sausages to a large platter.

2. In the same skillet, on high heat, add the clean, dried potatoes. (To prevent the potatoes from sticking, add a little salt to the hot oil.) Cook until crispy, turning them often with a spatula.

3. Keep the heat on high and add the cooked sausages, stirring gently.

4. When all the ingredients are well heated, add the vinegar peppers, one at a time. Tear them into bite-size pieces over the skillet, allowing the juices to fall over the sausages and potatoes. Toss gently. The pepper juices will cause the mixture to steam, so be careful. Sauté for about 3 minutes and add salt and pepper as desired.

5. Remove the skillet from the heat and let rest for 5 minutes. Serve with Italian bread and a salad.

If you are on a busy schedule, fry the sausages and prepare all the ingredients early in the day. Keep the sliced, uncooked potatoes in water, however, or they will brown. Then assemble and cook the dish just prior to serving. It is best eaten the same day it is prepared because the potatoes, in particular, will not taste the same after refrigeration.

PORK CHOPS PIZZAIOLA STYLE

SERVES 4

Pork chops are always served in an Italian home, regardless of the weather. There is nothing tastier than a juicy chop with some spaghetti on the side.

4 center-cut pork chops, each about 1¼ inches thick

Salt and freshly ground pepper to taste

2 tablespoons olive oil

1 small onion, thinly sliced

1 large garlic clove, minced

1 cup chopped, canned or fresh tomatoes

1 teaspoon chopped fresh basil leaves, or ½ teaspoon dried basil

½ teaspoon dried oregano

¾ cup chicken broth, canned or fresh

1. Trim fat from the chops. Season with salt and pepper.

2. In a heavy skillet, heat 1 tablespoon olive oil and brown chops on both sides over medium-high heat. Remove chops and keep warm.

3. Discard drippings from skillet, add remaining tablespoon of olive oil, and sauté onion and garlic over medium heat until limp and golden brown.

4. Add tomatoes, basil, oregano, and half the chicken broth. Stir well to deglaze the skillet.

5. Return pork chops to skillet and cover tightly. Cook slowly for about 45 minutes or until chops are tender. Turn chops once or twice during cooking and add more broth if needed.

6. Serve chops smothered with the sauce, or serve the sauce on top of spaghetti, with the chops on the side.

Cutting onions with a very sharp knife helps keep your eyes from tearing.

PORK RIND BRACIOLE

SERVES 4

Pork rind is the skin of the pig. It is considered a treat in an Italian home, but a lot of people don't know how to prepare it. This recipe was made mainly by the Sicilian people and, unfortunately, was never written down. It will be lost forever if it is not recorded. I have tried to re-create the traditional recipe to the best of my knowledge. Like other braciole meats, this is added to tomato sauce. Use the recipe for Sunday Gravy (page 63), with or without the other meats.

2 pounds pork rind, thinly sliced

¼ cup chopped fresh parsley

¼ cup grated Romano cheese

2 small garlic cloves, chopped

Salt and freshly ground pepper to taste

2-ounce chunk of Romano cheese, cut in small pieces

Tomato sauce

¼ cup Sicilian dry-cured black olives, pitted and halved

1. Boil some hot water, shut off the heat, and wash rind by dipping it in the boiled water for a minute. Remove to cool.

2. Spread rind on a work surface and cover with parsley, grated cheese, garlic, salt and pepper, and pieces of Romano cheese.

3. Roll pork rind and tie with a string or secure with toothpicks.

4. Fry in a large heavy skillet, over low heat, until browned on all sides.

5. Pour tomato sauce into the skillet. There should be enough to cover the rind completely. Cook until rind is tender, about 1½ to 2 hours.

6. Place on a serving platter, remove string or toothpicks, and carve into thin slices. Serve with more sauce and pitted dry-cured olives on top.

PORK ARISTA

ROAST LOIN OF PORK

SERVES 6–8

This is a dish that dates back to the Renaissance. Arista is a way of seasoning and cooking. You can successfully substitute a boned veal roast or a leg of lamb for the pork.

4-pound loin of pork, cut to form chops but not cut through backbone (French style)

4 large garlic cloves, peeled and cut in quarters

3 tablespoons fresh rosemary, or 1–2 tablespoons crumbled dried rosemary

4 whole cloves

Salt and freshly ground pepper to taste

Olive oil

Dry white wine

1. Preheat oven to 325°F.

2. Trim all excess fat from the meat. Wet the garlic pieces in water and roll them in the rosemary leaves to coat.

3. Insert some of the garlic quarters between the chops, together with the cloves.

4. With a sharp knife, cut pockets into the meat and stuff each pocket with the remaining garlic pieces.

5. Rub the meat with salt and pepper to taste. Rub with a thin film of olive oil.

6. Place the meat on a rack in a fairly deep roasting pan. Add about 2 inches of wine and cook uncovered in the preheated oven, basting occasionally. Allow 45 minutes of roasting time per pound, or cook more if a less pink color is desired.

7. Transfer roast to a warmed dish or pan, loosely tent with foil, and let cool in its own juice.

8. Slice and serve with some applesauce or a vegetable salad.

STUFFED HONEY-GLAZED CORNISH HENS

SERVES 2–4

Cornish hens are a great company meal. When served with stuffing and some mashed pota-toes and a vegetable salad, it will seem like a special holiday feast—food that will leave every-one going away happy. A meal they will talk about until turkey time! This recipe is easy and requires ingredients usually on hand. Wondra flour comes in a cylinder and works well for easy dissolving when making sauces. For extra hens, just double the recipe as needed.

STUFFING

1 cup crumbled day-old bread (croutons)

Pinch of Bell's Seasoning

Salt and white pepper to taste

1 stick (½ cup) unsalted butter

1 shallot, finely chopped

1 garlic clove, finely chopped

3 scallions, chopped

3 small stalks celery hearts, chopped

1 teaspoon chopped fresh parsley

Pinch of tarragon

1 small apple, skin removed and diced

2 tablespoons crush pignoli nuts (or walnuts)

1 (14½-ounce) can chicken broth, divided

1. In a large bowl, add croutons, Bell's Seasoning, and salt and pepper to taste.

2. In a small skillet, heat butter and sauté shallots, garlic, scallions, celery, parsley, and tarragon until softened.

3. Add mixture to bread crumbs and toss lightly with diced apple and crushed nuts, slightly moistening with warmed chicken broth. Adjust seasonings and let rest 5 minutes.

GLAZE

2 tablespoons unsalted butter

¼ cup honey

¾ cup orange juice

1. Melt butter in a small skillet. Add honey and let thicken.

2. Add orange juice and whisk until sauce has caramelized, tilting skillet to evenly distribute.

TO PREPARE HENS

2 hens (approximately 1–1½ pounds each)

2 tablespoons soy sauce (1 tablespoon for each or enough to cover both hens)

Butter

1. Preheat oven to 550°F.

2. Clean and wash hens in salted water. Pat dry with paper towels.

3. Loosely fill hens' cavities with stuffing; rub with soy sauce and soft butter. Place hens in a baking pan large enough to accommodate them without crowding. Bake uncovered in the preheated oven on the middle rack for 30 minutes or until dark golden brown.

4. Remove pan from oven, lower heat to 350°F, and baste hens generously with warmed glaze.

5. Return pan to oven, frequently basting hens with drippings. Bake approximately 45 minutes, depending on size. Drumsticks should move easily (do not overcook). Tent hens with foil if browning too fast.

6. Remove hens from oven; spoon out stuffing and reserve. Place hens on a warmed large platter, basting for the last time. Loosely cover with foil and let rest in a warm place until needed.

SAUCE

Wondra flour (optional)

Kitchen Bouquet (optional)

1. Drain drippings from roasting pan. Return pan to top of stove.

2. Add ½ cup chicken broth and let come to a boil. Using a wooden spoon, scrape all particles in pan. Continue cooking until broth turns a caramel color. Sprinkle with flour and some Kitchen Bouquet for a thicker and darker color if desired.

3. Strain into a deep saucepan and keep hot.

4. Serve immediately with remaining hot gravy.

Wondra flour comes in a cylinder and works well for easy dissolving when making sauces.

RICE-STUFFED CORNISH HENS

SERVES 4

Cornish hens or Rock-Cornish hens as they are sometimes described are a big favorite to many. I know you will enjoy this recipe using a rice stuffing. The whole process will take about three hours. Wash hens well; drain and dry thoroughly using paper towels. Remove the giblets and necks, and just throw them into the same pan with the hens. A rubbing of soy sauce helps give a nice browned color.

STUFFING

3 sticks (1½ cups) unsalted butter

1 garlic clove, minced

3 medium mushrooms, chopped

1 stalk celery, finely chopped

3 shallots, minced

1 small red bell pepper, finely chopped

1 cup long grain rice, cooked

Salt and pepper to taste

1 tablespoon chopped fresh parsley

1. In a medium skillet, heat butter on slow heat and sauté garlic, mushrooms, celery, shallots, and red pepper until softened.

2. Add mixture to bowl with rice, toss gently and sprinkle with salt and pepper to taste. Top with parsley and let cool.

TO PREPARE HENS

4 hens (approximately 1 pound each)

4 tablespoons soy sauce (1 tablespoon for each or enough to cover the hens)

¼ cup butter

Green peas (canned or fresh)

1. Preheat oven to 350°F.

2. Clean and wash hens in salted water. Pat dry with paper towels.

3. Rub the hens inside and out with soy sauce. This will help give them a nice brown appearance while baking and add color to the drippings at bottom of pan. Loosely fill hens' cavities with stuffing and cover stuffing with any loose skin.

4. Place hens breast-side up in a baking pan large enough to accommodate them without crowding, and brush with melted butter (¼ cup).

5. Roast in hot oven, basting often with the drippings in the pan, and bake 1¼ hours or until legs move easily and hens are nicely browned (tent with foil if browning too quickly).

6. Remove hens from oven; spoon out stuffing and reserve. Place hens on a warmed large platter, basting for the last time. Loosely cover with foil and let rest in a warm place until needed. Serve with green peas for color.

POLLO ALLA CACCIATORE

CHICKEN CACCIATORE, PEASANT STYLE

SERVES 4–6

If you don't want to use a chicken with bones, you can substitute boneless chicken breasts cut into chunks. However, I prefer the chicken on the bone, feeling that it enhances the flavor of the sauce, and besides, my family loves gnawing on the bones.

1–2½-pound chicken, cut into small parts

¾ cup olive oil

2 green peppers, cut in thick strips

2 red peppers, cut in thick strips

2 medium onions, sliced thick

Salt and freshly ground black pepper to taste

Pinch each of dried red pepper flakes and oregano

3 garlic cloves, crushed

2 tablespoons tomato paste

1 (28-ounce) can plum tomatoes, squeezed, with juice

½ pound fresh mushrooms (quartered if large or left whole if button)

1 (12-ounce) can sweet peas

Chopped fresh parsley for garnish

1. Wash chicken parts and wipe dry with paper towels. Set aside.

2. Heat olive oil on medium-high heat in a large, deep, heavy skillet with cover. Add peppers and onions and sauté until tender but still crisp. Transfer to a warm platter.

3. Return the pan to high heat and when the oil is fairly hot, add chicken parts. Sauté until chicken is nicely browned, turning as needed. Add salt and pepper to taste and a pinch each of red pepper flakes and oregano. Place chicken on the platter with the pepper and onion mixture.

4. Return pan to medium heat and sauté crushed garlic. Add tomato paste and stir well. Add squeezed tomatoes and their juices and, using a wooden spoon, stir well.

5. Add the chicken and the pepper and onion mixture to the pan and mix well. Adjust seasonings.

6. Place the cover on the pan and let the chicken simmer on low heat until tender and a nice sauce is formed (about 20 minutes).

7. Turn off heat. Add mushrooms and peas and their juices to the pan. Toss gently and let cacciatore rest, covered, for about 20 minutes.

8. Using tongs, transfer chicken to a warm platter. Spoon on sauce and sprinkle with chopped fresh parsley. Serve with salad and crusty Italian bread.

You may add hot peppers and/or a couple potatoes cut in chunks while chicken is simmering.

CHICKEN CUTLETS PARMIGIANA

SERVES 4

For this recipe you will need to make my Simple Marinara Sauce first. Veal may be substituted for the chicken.

1 pound chicken cutlets

2 eggs

Salt and freshly ground pepper to taste

3 cups bread crumbs, or more if needed

2 tablespoons grated cheese

¼ cup chopped fresh parsley

Olive oil

Simple Marinara Sauce (page 62)

Sliced mozzarella cheese

1. Have your butcher pound boneless chicken breasts into thin cutlets.

2. In a medium bowl, beat eggs with salt and pepper to taste.

3. In a semi-flat dish, mix bread crumbs, grated cheese, and parsley.

4. Dip cutlets in egg wash and roll in bread crumbs, bearing down to allow the crumbs to stick to the chicken. Place on a platter and let rest about 10 minutes.

5. Heat the olive oil on medium heat, using a large heavy skillet.

6. When oil is good and hot, add the chicken cutlets without crowding. Lower heat and cook until well browned on both sides, turning only once. Continue until all the chicken pieces are cooked, adjusting the heat so that chicken is always sizzling, but not burning.

7. Place the chicken cutlets, in one layer, in a shallow baking pan. Top each cutlet with a scoop of marinara and a thin slice of mozzarella cheese.

8. Bake in a preheated 350°F oven for 15 minutes or until mozzarella turns golden brown and cutlets are cooked. Serve immediately with extra sauce.

CHICKEN CACCIATORE EN BIANCO

CHICKEN WITH WHITE WINE SAUCE

SERVES 6

I often make this recipe when I have guests over for dinner. Needless to say, it is a hit. Let the mixture rest for about five minutes before serving, and you will have a luscious sauce with the chicken. Any cacciatore recipe is tastier after it has set for a while. Try serving the cacciatore atop some buttered noodles.

Olive oil

3 green or red bell peppers, sliced

1 onion, sliced

1 stick (½ cup) unsalted butter

6 boneless, skinless chicken breasts, cut in bite-size pieces

Salt and freshly ground pepper to taste

1 shallot, chopped

Pinch of tarragon

½ pound mushrooms, sliced

2 tomatoes, blanched and skin removed

½ cup dry white wine

Chopped fresh parsley

1. In a large heavy skillet, heat enough oil to cover the bottom of the pan.

2. Add peppers and sauté a few minutes, then add onion and cook until slightly transparent. Cook quickly but carefully so that the vegetables retain their color and crispness. Remove from skillet and reserve.

3. Remove oil from skillet. Melt the butter in the skillet.

4. Add boneless chicken chunks and sauté until lightly browned. While chicken is cooking, add salt and pepper, shallot, tarragon, and mushrooms.

5. When meat is cooked, add reserved vegetables, tomatoes, and white wine.

6. Boil briefly to evaporate alcohol. Garnish with fresh parsley.

CHICKEN LIMONE

SERVES 6

This dish is best made right before serving. Be sure to have all your ingredients prepared and on hand. As with most chicken breast dishes, veal may be substituted for the chicken.

6 boneless chicken breasts

2 eggs

¼ cup milk

1 cup flour

1 stick (½ cup) unsalted butter

¼ cup olive oil

2 lemons

Salt and freshly ground pepper to taste

1 tablespoon chopped fresh parsley

1. Slice the chicken breasts into very thin medallions (or buy small chicken cutlets).

2. In a large bowl, beat the eggs with the milk. Put the flour on a shallow plate.

3. Heat ½ stick butter and olive oil in a heavy skillet over medium heat. At the same time, dredge the chicken in the flour, then dip it quickly in the egg wash.

4. Sauté the chicken for a few minutes on each side until golden brown. Transfer the chicken to a serving platter and keep warm. Pour off any oils that remain in the skillet.

5. Add remaining butter to the skillet. With a wooden spoon, loosen all the particles on the bottom of the pan.

6. Raise the heat under the skillet. Squeeze the juice of 1 lemon into the skillet. Add salt, pepper, and chopped parsley.

7. Slice the second lemon. Overlap the chicken and the lemon slices on the serving platter. Pour the sauce on top and serve immediately with hot buttered linguine or noodles.

ROASTED CHICKEN WITH LEMON AND PARSLEY SAUCE

SERVES 4

Chicken was a staple in my home while I was growing up. I remember my mother putting tons of parsley all over it, and lots of salt and pepper. It was so good that for one of my birthdays I asked for a whole roasted chicken as my gift. This recipe calls for chicken breasts only and can be made so quickly that I think you will love it.

2 whole chicken breasts with skin, halved

2 lemons

¼ cup butter or margarine

Salt and freshly ground pepper to taste

½ cup chopped fresh parsley

Fresh parsley sprigs for decoration

1. Preheat oven to 425°F.

2. Put chicken breasts in a baking dish to fit comfortably.

3. Squeeze the lemons until you get at least ¼ cup lemon juice; reserve.

4. Melt the butter or margarine and lemon juice in a small saucepan.

5. Sprinkle chicken with salt and pepper on both sides. Drizzle 2 tablespoons of lemon butter over it.

6. Bake in the preheated oven until the skin is crisp and golden brown, about 25–30 minutes. Remove and transfer chicken to a decorative serving platter. Keep warm.

7. Briskly stir remaining lemon butter into pan juices, scraping the pan with a wooden spoon to deglaze. Add parsley and adjust seasonings.

8. Pour sauce over chicken, garnish with parsley springs, and serve immediately.

CHICKEN BRACIOLETTINI
WITH MUSHROOM AND WINE SAUCE

SERVES 6

Braciolettini never fails to complement a family dinner. It has been a longtime favorite of mine.

6 large boneless chicken breasts

1 large garlic clove

Freshly ground black pepper to taste

¼ cup freshly grated Parmesan or Romano cheese

¼ pound shredded mozzarella or Fontina cheese

¼ bunch fresh parsley, chopped (reserve 1 tablespoon for garnish)

6 thin slices prosciutto or ham

¼ cup olive oil

1 stick (½ cup) unsalted butter

1 cup Madeira or marsala wine

½ pound whole button mushrooms or thinly sliced large mushrooms

1. Have your butcher pound the chicken slightly to break the tendons, or use the flat side of a heavy meat cleaver to do so yourself.

2. Lay the flat pieces of chicken on a smooth, clean surface. Using a garlic press, squeeze the garlic clove. With your fingertips, transfer these particles to the cutlet pieces. Sprinkle black pepper, grated cheese, shredded cheese, and parsley all over the chicken. Cover each breast with a

slice of prosciutto or ham. Roll each breast jelly-roll style, carefully tucking in all loose ends. Secure with toothpicks (use the same number for each breast).

3. Heat the oil and butter in a large skillet over medium heat. Add the chicken breasts and brown well all over. With a slotted spoon, transfer the chicken to a baking pan. Bake for 20 minutes in a preheated 350°F oven or until the chicken is cooked moist-tender.

4. To make the sauce, drain the fat from the skillet and return the unwashed pan to the stove on medium heat, scraping all browned bits from the bottom of the pan with a wooden spoon.

5. Raise the heat to high and pour in the wine, stirring well. Add the mushrooms and cook 1 more minute, shaking skillet. If the sauce appears too thin, sprinkle with some flour and cook, stirring well, until it reaches your desired thickness. If more sauce is desired, add some chicken broth and more wine.

6. Remove the chicken from the oven, carefully remove all toothpicks, and transfer to a warm serving platter. Pour the hot sauce on top. Sprinkle with the

reserved tablespoon of chopped parsley. To serve, cut meat in thick slices and coat with sauce and mushrooms.

It's a good idea to put the same number of toothpicks in each breast. This way, when it's time to remove them, you'll be sure not to miss any.

Note: If using small pieces of chicken breasts, it will not be necessary to bake the chicken. Simply cook in skillet as directed, transfer to a warm platter, and prepare sauce.

CHICKEN ANGELO

SERVES 12

During a fund-raising luncheon at the North End Union (a settlement house), I salvaged all the leftovers, added chicken and sausages with the correct seasonings, and produced this unusual and hearty meal. I still get raves from friends who make it at home. Add your own leftovers and enjoy!

2 chickens

1 pound sweet Italian sausages

½ cup olive or vegetable oil

Salt and freshly ground pepper to taste

2 sticks (1 cup) butter or margarine

4 garlic cloves, chopped

2 large onions, sliced

2 shallots, crushed

12 medium ripe tomatoes (6 cut in chunks,
    6 cut in large slices)

Pinch of dried oregano

½ cup plus 2 tablespoons chopped fresh
    parsley, plus more for garnish

2 cups homemade or canned chicken stock

Flour

2 cups dry white wine

1 pound whole button mushrooms

1 (8-ounce) can artichoke hearts in water,
    drained (reserve water) and quartered

1 pound medium shells or ziti

1 bunch broccoli, cut into florets
    (save the stems for another use)

1. Cut the chickens into small pieces. Cut the sausages into bite-size pieces.

2. Heat the oil in a large skillet. Fry the chicken and sausages until nicely browned. Sprinkle generously with salt and pepper. Place all the fried pieces in a large baking pan.

3. In the same skillet, melt half of the butter or margarine. Add 2 garlic cloves, the sliced onions, and the crushed shallots. Sauté gently. Add the 6 chopped tomatoes, salt, pepper, oregano, and ½ cup chopped parsley. Toss lightly a few times, then pour over the meat in the baking pan.

4. In a large jar, shake the chicken stock with enough flour to make a thin paste. Pour into a small saucepan and cook over medium heat until slightly thickened. Add salt and pepper to taste.

5. Reserve ½ cup of the thickened stock. Pour the remainder over the chicken and sausages, tossing lightly to coat all the pieces. Bake in a preheated 350°F oven for about 25 minutes. Sprinkle with 1 cup of white wine and continue baking for another 15 minutes.

6. In a large skillet, melt the remaining butter. Add the mushrooms, the 6 sliced tomatoes, the artichoke hearts, 2 tablespoons fresh parsley, salt, and pepper. Sauté for 3 minutes and add the reserved ½ cup of thickened stock. When heated through, add more wine as needed to keep the sauce from thickening too much. Simmer gently for about 10 minutes.

7. Meanwhile, boil the pasta according to package directions. Drain, then toss in a little butter so that it will not stick.

8. At the same time, sauté the broccoli with 2 garlic cloves in enough oil to cover the bottom of the pan, mixed with the juice from the artichokes. Combine the broccoli and the cooked pasta. Sprinkle with salt and pepper.

9. Put the broccoli and pasta on a large platter. Spoon the baked chicken and sausages on top. Cover with the sauce. Sprinkle with chopped parsley and serve.

You can make this recipe through step 6 early in the day. Cook the pasta and sauté the broccoli immediately before serving.

CHICKEN WITH BROCCOLI AND ZITI

SERVES 4

Richard Travaglione, owner/chef of Riccardo's Ristorante in the North End of Boston, loves to prepare this easy, delicious meal. The combination of milk or cream and grated Parmesan cheese renders a light, flavorful sauce that greatly enhances the chicken and ziti. Customers love it! At Riccardo's you can be totally relaxed and happy eating Italian comfort food, after which you might enjoy a promenade on the city streets.

¼ **cup olive oil**

2 large boneless chicken breasts, cut into strips

1–2 garlic cloves, slivered

Salt and freshly ground pepper to taste

2 cups broccoli florets

¼ **cup milk**

½ **cup freshly grated Parmesan cheese**

½ **pound ziti**

2 tablespoons unsalted butter

Dried red pepper flakes (optional)

1. Heat the olive oil in a large skillet over medium heat. Sauté the chicken with the garlic, salt, and pepper until chicken is lightly browned.

2. Add the broccoli florets. Toss with the chicken and adjust seasonings. Cook and stir for 1 minute.

3. Add the milk and ¼ cup grated Parmesan cheese. Over high heat, quickly toss all the ingredients until a nice milky sauce has formed (1–2 minutes).

4. Cook the ziti according to package directions. Drain, but do not rinse.

5. Toss the ziti with the butter. Add to the chicken and broccoli mixture and toss gently. Sprinkle with the remaining grated Parmesan cheese, red pepper flakes, and more salt and pepper to taste and serve.

If you wish, this dish can be refrigerated for 1 or 2 days and then reheated gently before serving.

JARRED PICKLED PIGS FEET

SERVES 2–4

This is a really old favorite. We used to love leaving the feet on the bone and biting off the meat.

4 pigs feet (split)

4 cups water

4 cups cider vinegar

2½ teaspoons whole cloves

2 bay leaves

6 whole peppercorns

1 medium onion, chopped

2 garlic cloves, halved

1 tablespoon salt

1. Cover the pigs feet with the water. Boil until the meat is soft and tender but not ready to fall off the bone. Check frequently.

2. Remove cooked pigs feet from liquid and reserve.

3. Skim liquid of any scum.

4. In a separate pan, combine cider vinegar, cloves, bay leaves, peppercorns, onion, garlic, and salt.

5. Add to pot, cover, and slightly boil mixture for 30 minutes. Remove pan from heat and let cool.

6. In a jar just large enough to accommodate them tightly, layer the pigs feet, alternately covering each layer with some broth mixture and tightly bearing down after each layer. The broth should completely cover the feet.

7. Seal and refrigerate for at least 7 days before using.

Pigs feet should be jarred with a tight cover and preferably refrigerated at least a week so the liquid can gel and acquire the pickle flavor.

FISH
AND
SHELLFISH

SHRIMP SCAMPI AGLIO E OLIO

SHRIMP WITH OIL AND GARLIC SAUCE

SERVES 4

Whenever I see shrimp on sale, I know immediately how I will cook them. I buy a nice, crusty loaf of Italian bread, get out my cast-iron skillet, and fire away. Of course, I will use plenty of garlic and never remove the shells from the shrimp. Leave them on to keep the shrimp from shrinking when cooking and to preserve those wonderful juices. Great served over thin spaghetti or linguini fini.

1 pound large shrimp, shell on

¼ cup butter or margarine

½ cup olive oil

3 garlic cloves, chopped

Pinch of red pepper flakes

Salt and freshly ground pepper to taste

3 tablespoons freshly squeezed lemon juice

1 tablespoon grated lemon zest

¼ cup chopped fresh parsley

1. Rinse shrimp and set aside.

2. Melt butter and olive oil in a heavy skillet. Add garlic and red pepper flakes and sauté on low heat, about 5 minutes.

3. Raise heat to high and when oil is hot, immediately add shrimp in shell. Toss the shrimp around constantly, until they turn pink.

4. Remove pan from heat. Add salt and pepper to taste, lemon juice, lemon zest, and chopped parsley.

5. Return pan to high heat and sauté for a minute or two until butter sauce is slightly thickened.

6. Serve immediately in bowls with the juices poured over the shrimp.

QUICK SCAMPI WITH CREAM SAUCE

SERVES 2

We use a lot of shrimp during the holidays, and this is one recipe we all enjoy. It may be served over fresh, thin noodles (about ½ pound) and accompanied by garlic bread.

8 large red scampi, peeled

Flour

Olive oil

1 garlic clove, crushed

1 shallot clove, chopped

Salt and freshly ground black pepper to taste

1 heaping tablespoon lemon juice

Dash of Tabasco

Dash of white wine

½ cup heavy cream

1. Dust the scampi with flour. Shake off the excess.

2. Pour olive oil into a heavy skillet, just enough to cover the bottom of the pan. Add the crushed garlic and shallot and cook until tender.

3. Add the flour-dusted scampi, salt, pepper, lemon juice, and Tabasco. Cook over medium heat for 5 minutes.

4. Add a dash of wine and bring the mixture to a boil. Remove from heat and slowly add the cream.

5. Return the skillet to the burner and let the mixture boil for a minute or two. Serve bubbling hot.

BAKED STUFFED SHRIMP ITALIAN STYLE

SERVES 4–6

I have been making this recipe for years, and I think it is one of the best ever. Try this stuffing also with lobsters or clams. It is excellent!

1½ pounds large shrimp, unpeeled

2½ cups coarse bread crumbs

12 salted crackers, crumbled

3 ounces canned crabmeat (optional)

½ cup freshly grated Parmesan cheese

½ cup chopped fresh parsley

¼ cup melted butter

¼ cup lemon juice

A few shakes of Tabasco

1 garlic clove, chopped

Pinch of dried tarragon

Salt and freshly ground black pepper to taste

1 tablespoon olive oil

Lemon slices for garnish

1. Leave the shells on the shrimp. Remove all legs. Lay each shrimp flat on the counter. Slice open, devein, and spread open butterfly style.

2. In a large bowl, mix the bread crumbs, crumbled crackers, crabmeat (optional), grated cheese, parsley, melted butter, lemon juice, Tabasco, garlic, and tarragon. Add salt and pepper to taste. At this point, stuffing should be moist. Add extra melted butter and lemon juice if needed.

3. Stuff each shrimp until it is well packed. Place the stuffed shrimp on a cookie sheet, each one nestled into another, in a half-moon curve, so the stuffing stays secure.

4. Drizzle olive oil lightly over the shrimp. Bake the shrimp in a preheated 400°F oven on the middle rack for about 20 minutes or until golden brown. Serve with plenty of lemon slices.

SEAFOOD DIAVOLO

SERVES 4–6

This fish medley is a feast in itself. You need only some hot garlic bread and maybe a salad. Use any or all the shellfish listed in this recipe, and the results will still be pleasing.

½ cup olive oil

1 garlic clove, chopped

1 bunch scallions, chopped

Pinch each of dried red pepper flakes and oregano

A few drops of Tabasco

¼ pound mushrooms, chopped

2 cups canned tomatoes, or 3 fresh, blanched, and peeled tomatoes, chopped, with juices

¼ cup dry white wine

12 littleneck clams, scrubbed clean

12 mussels, scrubbed clean and debearded

6 fresh shrimp, or 1 can (any size) shrimp, or frozen shrimp, rinsed and left whole

½ pound whole bay scallops, or sea scallops, quartered

½ cup bottled clam juice

Salt and freshly ground pepper to taste

½ pound of any firm whitefish (sole, haddock, etc.)

1 pound linguine or thin spaghetti

2 tablespoons butter or margarine

Chopped fresh parsley

1. Heat the olive oil in a large kettle over medium heat. Add the garlic, scallions, red pepper flakes, oregano, Tabasco, and mushrooms.

2. When the mixture starts to brown, add the tomatoes and their juices. Simmer for 2 minutes.

3. Raise the heat to high. Add the white wine and let the sauce come to a boil. Add the clams, mussels, shrimp, scallops, and clam juice. Sprinkle with salt and pepper to taste.

4. Cook, covered, on medium-low heat until the clams start to open. At this point, add the whitefish. Salt and pepper again to taste, if desired. Cover again and cook for 3 minutes.

5. Meanwhile, cook linguine or thin spaghetti according to package directions. Drain well and toss with the butter. Place in a large serving platter.

6. Cover the pasta with half of the sauce and sprinkle with parsley. Place the shellfish around the outside of the platter. Pour the remaining sauce into a serving bowl for use by the family as desired.

CIOPPINO

SERVES 6

This is not exactly a soup, and not exactly a stew. It is a combination of flavors that are light and nutritious.

⅓ cup olive or vegetable oil

3 garlic cloves, chopped

1¼ cups chopped onions

¾ cup sliced scallions

½ cup chopped green pepper

1 (6-ounce) can tomato paste

1 (28-ounce) can plum tomatoes

½ bunch parsley, chopped

1 teaspoon dried oregano

1 teaspoon dried basil

1 teaspoon dried red pepper flakes

1 teaspoon dried tarragon

Salt and freshly ground pepper to taste

1¼ cups burgundy wine

1 (10-ounce) jar whole clams, undrained

1½ pounds haddock, sole, or halibut (no bones)

1½ pounds medium shrimp, unpeeled

3 (6½-ounce) cans crabmeat, drained

1. Heat the oil in a 6-quart kettle. Sauté the garlic, onions, scallions, and green peppers for about 10 minutes or until tender, stirring often.

2. Add the tomato paste and stir until well blended. Add the can of tomatoes, including the juice. Stir gently until the mixture comes to a boil. Add parsley, oregano, basil, pepper flakes, tarragon, and salt and pepper to taste.

3. Simmer for about 5 minutes, then add the wine. Simmer for 10 minutes, then add the clams, fish of your choice, shrimp, and crabmeat. (You can cut the fish into chunks if the pieces are too large, but they are likely to break apart in the cooking process.) At this point you may need more salt and pepper.

4. Simmer, covered, for about 15 minutes, then uncovered for 15 minutes more.

5. Remove the kettle from the heat and let it rest for about 10 minutes.

6. Serve in large bowls, accompanied by garlic bread and salad. Put a large empty bowl in the middle of the table to receive the shells. Have plenty of napkins available.

Cioppino can be refrigerated, but it is best served the same day that it is made.

FRIED SOFT-SHELL CRABS

SERVES 2–3

From April to December hard-shelled crabs are harvested just after molting. Crabs molt in order to grow before the new shell hardens, and during this time they are called soft-shelled crabs. How do you eat them? The answer is you eat the whole thing, shell included. The contrast of the crispy crust and the sweet, moist meat is a special experience.

6 small to medium soft-shell crabs

1–2 garlic cloves, mashed

3 tablespoons unsalted butter, slightly warmed

¼ cup all-purpose flour, or combination 3 tablespoons flour and 1 tablespoon yellow cornmeal

Pinch of paprika

3½ tablespoons olive oil

Salt and freshly ground pepper to taste

12 parsley sprigs, leaves only, minced

Tabasco

Lemon wedges

1. Cut the backs of the crabs and lift out the spongy gills and sand bags. Cut out the face. Lift the small apron at the lower end. Replace the soft top shell over the body. Gently wash the crabs and dry well.

2. Stir the mashed garlic into the warm butter and let stand until needed, then discard the pieces of garlic.

3. Mix the flour with the paprika on a shallow plate. Dredge the crabs on both sides, shaking off any excess.

4. Heat the olive oil in a skillet large enough to accommodate the crabs. When the oil is hot, add the crabs and sauté on each side for 5 minutes or until crust is nicely browned.

5. Pour the garlic-flavored butter over the crabs and add salt and pepper to taste. Cover slightly and cook slowly for 10 minutes.

6. Sprinkle parsley over the top and lightly shake the skillet to distribute flavorings.

7. Arrange the crabs on warm serving plates. Spoon butter drippings, as much as desired, over all the crabs. Serve immediately with Tabasco and lemon wedges.

COOKED CRABS CIOPPINO

SERVES 4

This is a dish you find in lots of restaurants along the wharves of many towns and cities. You can make it with a variety of seafood, but I prefer using only crabs.

1 cup olive oil

1 small onion, chopped

1 teaspoon chopped fresh parsley

4 large cleaned live crabs

1 (6-ounce) bottle clam juice

1 (28-ounce) can crushed Italian tomatoes

2 tablespoons tomato paste

2 teaspoons chopped basil

2 shakes Tabasco, or to taste

Salt and freshly ground pepper to taste

1. Heat olive oil in a large kettle and sauté the onion and parsley.

2. Place crabs into kettle and add clam juice. Cover and steam for at least 10 minutes.

3. Meanwhile, heat the tomatoes and tomato paste in a separate pan. Sprinkle with basil, Tabasco (if using), and salt and pepper to taste.

4. Pour sauce over crabs, cover, and cook until they have turned bright orange (about 20 minutes), stirring gently with a wooden spoon. Taste again and add more spices if needed.

5. Place nutcrackers alongside dishes, crack the shells, and enjoy the succulent meat inside. Serve with crusty French bread or poured over spaghetti.

SCALLOPS MARINARA

SERVES 2–3

Watch out for overcooking the scallops because they will become rubbery. Cooking them in marinara sauce helps keep them tender and juicy.

1 stick (½ cup) butter or margarine

1 pound fresh sea scallops

2 garlic cloves, chopped

3 scallions, chopped

1 small onion, chopped

1 (16-ounce) can whole tomatoes, chopped (reserve juice)

¼ pound fresh button mushrooms, quartered

¼ cup dry white wine

1 tablespoon lemon juice

Salt and freshly ground pepper to taste

Pinch of tarragon

¼ cup chopped fresh parsley

1. In a large heavy skillet, melt the butter or margarine. Add the scallops, garlic, scallions, and onion. Sauté for about 3 minutes, stirring gently.

2. Add the tomatoes and mushrooms and sauté for about 2 minutes.

3. Add the wine and lemon juice, salt, pepper, and tarragon. Cook briskly on medium-high heat for about 2–3 minutes.

4. Add the reserved tomato juice and cook on high heat for about 5 minutes. Add the parsley and serve immediately. You may wish to serve spaghetti or linguine on the side.

Tarragon and shallots work especially well with seafood. They produce a different and interesting flavor.

ITALIAN-STYLE STEAMED MUSSELS

SERVES 6–8

Once you prepare this tried-and-true recipe, you will find it hard to cook mussels differently ever again.

3 quarts mussels

12 shallots, thinly sliced

1 onion, thinly sliced

2 tablespoons olive oil

2 tablespoons unsalted butter

4 garlic cloves, chopped

½ cup bottled clam juice

½ cup dry white wine

1 bay leaf

3 heaping tablespoons chopped Italian parsley

1 teaspoon dried thyme

1 teaspoon freshly ground black pepper

1. Scrub the mussels well. Scrape off the beards, using your fingers or a rough brush. Rinse under cold running water and drain. Discard any mussels with shells that remain open when tapped. Keep the mussels refrigerated until ready to use.

2. In a large heavy pot, sauté the shallots and onion in the oil and butter over low heat until translucent, not brown. Add the garlic during the last 2 minutes of sautéing.

3. Add the clam juice, white wine, bay leaf, parsley, thyme, and pepper. Cook, covered, over low heat for 10–15 minutes.

4. Raise the heat and add the mussels. Cook, covered, just until all the shells are opened. Discard any unopened mussels. Remove the bay leaf.

5. Serve hot in soup bowls, accompanied by crusty Italian bread. Provide extra plates for the empty shells.

These mussels are great served as an appetizer.

QUICK MUSSELS MARINARA

SERVES 4–6

This is an appealing appetizer in which the fish and tomatoes combine to produce a light, traditional flavor.

4 quarts mussels

Olive oil (enough to cover the bottom of the pot)

2 garlic cloves, finely chopped

Pinch each of dried oregano, tarragon, and red pepper flakes

2 teaspoons chopped fresh parsley

1 (14-ounce) can peeled and crushed tomatoes

Salt and freshly ground pepper to taste

1 cup dry white wine

1. Scrub the mussels well. Scrape off the beards, using your fingers or a rough brush. Rinse under cold running water and drain. Discard any mussels with shells that remain open when tapped. Keep the mussels refrigerated until ready to use.

2. In a pot large enough to hold the mussels, combine the olive oil, garlic, oregano, tarragon, red pepper, and parsley. Sauté on low heat for about 5 minutes.

3. Add the tomatoes, salt, and pepper. Let the mixture come to a gentle boil, then cook on low heat for about 15 minutes to blend the flavors.

4. Add the wine and mussels. Cover and cook for 5–8 minutes, shaking the pan so the mussels cook evenly. Discard any unopened mussels.

5. Serve in heated soup bowls with crusty Italian bread, or pour over linguine.

BAKED STUFFED CLAMS

SERVES 6

This is our basic style of baking clams—simple but so tasty that I know you will enjoy them.

12 large clams

2 garlic cloves, chopped

1 tablespoon finely chopped fresh parsley

Salt and freshly ground pepper to taste

2 tablespoons olive oil

2 tablespoons butter

1 cup Italian-style dry bread crumbs

1 whole lemon, plus lemon wedges
    for garnish

Paprika

1. Scrub the clams thoroughly. Open them carefully and pour the juices into a bowl. Chop the clams into small pieces and add to the juices. Reserve 12 shells on a baking sheet.

2. Sauté the garlic, parsley, salt, and pepper in the olive oil and butter for about 2 minutes, stirring constantly.

3. Put the bread crumbs in a medium bowl. Add the garlic mixture and the clams and their juices. Toss lightly until mixture becomes soft and moist but not soaked with juices.

4. Spoon the mixture into the clam shells until they are filled. Sprinkle lightly with the juice of the lemon and top with a light dusting of paprika.

5. Bake the clams in a preheated 375°F oven for 20–25 minutes or until a crust forms on the stuffing. Serve with lemon wedges.

I like to add a dash or two of Tabasco to the stuffing mixture. As another option, I pour enough water or wine in the bottom of the pan to keep the clams on the moist side.

BAKED RAZOR CLAMS

SERVES 2–4

Razor clams are not easily available at all times. They can usually be found at our local fish store at Eastertime, but you must be there on the spot, for the supply is limited and they disappear quickly. My mother prepared them this wonderful, tasty way. I remember biting on the shell to scrape off the delicious crusty tomato-and-cheese mixture. You must be careful not to overcook the clams or they will be tough (5–8 minutes). They should be submerged in wine at least halfway so that they can bake without drying.

2 dozen razor clams

1 cup white wine

½ cup olive oil

1 (16-ounce) can plum tomatoes

1 cup grated Parmesan cheese

Salt and freshly ground pepper to taste

1½ tablespoons dried oregano

5 garlic cloves, chopped

1 tablespoon dried red pepper flakes

2 tablespoons chopped fresh parsley

1 bunch scallions (with narrow ends), chopped

½ pound linguine or thin spaghetti

1 tablespoon butter

1. Preheat oven to 500°F.

2. Wash clams thoroughly in several changes of cold water until all the grit is gone. Arrange clams in a large baking pan in one layer.

3. Add the white wine to the bottom of the pan, plus enough water to submerge the clam flesh as it cooks. Do not submerge the top shell.

4. Sprinkle clams with ¼ cup olive oil, then squeeze the plum tomatoes and their juice generously over the clams. Add grated Parmesan cheese, salt and pepper to taste, oregano, garlic, red pepper flakes, parsley, and scallions. Drizzle with remaining olive oil and sprinkle with additional salt and pepper if desired.

5. Bake for 20 minutes, adding additional wine if needed to keep the clams from drying out. Serve immediately over linguine or spaghetti that has been tossed with butter.

STEAMED CLAMS IN GARLIC SAUCE

SERVES 4–6

This is the only way to make perfect and delicious steamed clams. Instead of using plain water, I make a savory sauce that can be poured over linguine or spaghetti, making it a double treat. You can also put the clams in a bowl and serve them with the flavorful sauce. Either way, you will be pleased with the results.

5 pounds clams (littlenecks or steamers)

1 stick (½ cup) butter

½ cup olive oil

3 garlic cloves, chopped

½ bunch fresh parsley, chopped

1–2 bunches scallions, chopped

3 shakes Tabasco (optional)

Pinch of tarragon

1 lemon, halved

1–2 cups white wine

1. Soak the clams in cold, salted water to remove any sand.

2. Using a medium pot with a cover, heat the butter and olive oil together. Add the garlic, parsley, scallions, Tabasco, and tarragon.

3. Squeeze lemon halves into the butter mixture, then toss the halves into the pot. Sauté the sauce over medium heat for 5 minutes.

4. Add whole clams (in shell) and toss gently until clams are covered with spices. Turn heat up to high, cover the pot, and add wine when mixture starts to boil.

5. Lower the heat to medium-high and let clams cook, covered, until all the clams have opened, about 10 minutes. Discard any unopened clams after cooking time is over.

6. Serve immediately in individual bowls, or pour garlic sauce and opened clams over pasta.

LEMON AND PARSLEY CLAM SAUCE

SERVES 2–3

The tangy flavor of lemon gives character to this quick clam sauce for linguine.

3 (6½-ounce) cans minced clams

1 small onion, chopped

3 large garlic cloves, minced

½ cup olive oil

3 tablespoons butter or margarine

1 teaspoon oregano

Salt and pepper to taste

2 tablespoons chopped fresh parsley

2 teaspoons grated lemon rind

2–3 tablespoons freshly squeezed
    lemon juice

1. Drain clam juice from clams; reserve.

2. In a large saucepan, sauté onion and garlic in olive oil and butter or margarine until tender, but not brown, about 5 minutes.

3. Add reserved clam juice, oregano, and salt and pepper to taste. Bring to a boil until reduced to 2 cups, about 5 minutes.

4. Lower the heat and add reserved clams, parsley, lemon rind, and lemon juice.

5. Heat thoroughly and serve over hot linguine or thin spaghetti.

LITTLENECKS AND SHALLOTS IN BROTH

SERVES 4–6

This broth can also be served over freshly made pasta such as thin linguine. Neatly arrange the clams on the sides of the pasta, which has been sprinkled with herbs and seasoned with salt and pepper.

3 dozen littleneck clams, scrubbed well and rinsed

6 tablespoons butter

1 cup coarsely chopped shallots

3 garlic cloves, slivered

2 cups dry white wine

4 cups canned chicken broth or clam broth

½ cup chopped fresh parsley

Pinch of dried tarragon

Salt and freshly ground pepper to taste

1. Discard any clams that are open.

2. In a large pot, heat butter and sauté the chopped shallots until translucent.

3. Add slivered garlic and white wine and cook briskly for about 10 minutes or until wine is reduced to a third.

4. Add broth and bring to a boil.

5. Add clams and cover pot. Steam until the clams open (about 3–5 minutes). Do not overcook or they will be tough and rubbery. Discard any that remain closed, even when you have given them an extra minute or so to open.

6. Divide clams among individual soup bowls, cover with broth, and sprinkle with chopped parsley, tarragon, and salt and pepper to taste.

7. Serve with some nice crusty Italian bread, such as a bastone, to dip into the broth.

STUFFED CALAMARI IN TOMATO SAUCE

SERVES 6–8

In classical times, inkfish were thought to be the finest "fish" of the sea. Today, Italians still feel that way. We prepare squid (calamari) in a great many ways, as appetizers, with pasta, as meatballs, marinated, fried in olive oil, and more.

It is a "must" for us to have some in our freezers at all times. Squid freezes well, uncooked or cooked, so they are always available when we want a quick, exciting meal. Stuffed Calamari is a favorite.

CALAMARI SAUCE

½ cup olive oil

2 medium onions, chopped

2 large garlic cloves, chopped

Pinch each of dried basil, oregano, and red pepper flakes

3 ounces tomato paste

1 (28-ounce) can crushed and peeled tomatoes

Salt and freshly ground pepper to taste

1. In a large heavy saucepan, combine the oil, chopped onions, garlic, basil, oregano, and red pepper flakes. Sauté until the onions are golden brown (do not burn).

2. Add the tomato paste and stir gently until the mixture is well blended. Add the can of tomatoes and stir until the sauce comes to a light boil. Add salt and pepper to taste and a pinch more of red pepper, basil, and oregano. Let the sauce simmer on lowest heat while you prepare the squid. Stir the sauce often as it cooks.

TO CLEAN SQUID

To clean the squid, separate the head and tentacles from the body. Cut the tentacles apart from the body at the eyes. Discard the head and eyes. Remove the quill and ink sac from the body. Wash out the body; it should be completely empty. Peel off the skin as you wash the body and tentacles under running water. Reserve the tentacles (they may be chopped and added to the stuffing mixture). Drain well and pat dry with paper towels.

FINAL PREPARATION

3 cups soft fresh bread crumbs (use day-old Italian bread)

½ cup freshly grated Parmesan cheese

½ cup chopped fresh parsley

1 teaspoon salt

1 teaspoon freshly ground pepper

2 small garlic cloves, pressed

½ cup olive oil, or enough to coat bread crumbs evenly without soaking them

3 pounds medium whole squid, cleaned (see facing page)

1 pound thin spaghetti or linguine

Freshly grated Parmesan cheese (optional)

1. Toss the first seven ingredients to mix well.

2. Stuff the squid bodies very loosely with the stuffing, about ⅔ full or less, as the squid will shrink when cooked. Secure the top of each squid with a toothpick. Gently drop the stuffed squid into the tomato sauce, which is at a soft boiling stage. They will take about 20 minutes to cook.

3. Bring 6 quarts of salted water to a boil to cook the pasta. When the water is rapidly boiling, add the pasta and cook according to package directions. Drain and place on a large serving platter.

4. Cover pasta with some sauce. Place the stuffed calamari around the pasta (be sure to remove the toothpicks). Put extra sauce and grated cheese on the table and serve.

RICOTTA-STUFFED CALAMARI

SERVES 6

Calamari can be baked as directed or dropped in a meatless tomato sauce. Either way, they are just as delicious. Choose only fresh, young calamari for better flavor. You will need my Simple Marinara Sauce (page 62) for this recipe. You can serve this alone or as a sauce for linguine.

1 pound ricotta cheese, firm

2 egg yolks, slightly beaten

1 garlic clove, chopped

½ cup shredded mozzarella cheese

¼ cup grated Parmesan cheese

1 tablespoon chopped fresh parsley

½ cup freshly ground bread crumbs

Salt and freshly ground pepper to taste

2 pounds medium whole squid, cleaned (see page 212)

½ cup olive oil

2 cups marinara sauce

1 cup white wine (optional)

1. In a wide medium-size bowl, mix ricotta with egg yolks, garlic, shredded mozzarella, Parmesan cheese, parsley, bread crumbs, and salt and pepper to taste.

2. Using a teaspoon, loosely stuff bodies of calamari until about half full. Secure edges with toothpicks.

3. Brown quickly, uncrowded, in hot olive oil, until the calamari start to turn pink. Some stuffing may ooze out, but that's normal.

4. Using a slotted spoon, carefully lift calamari from pan. Drop them into the prepared tomato sauce, and simmer slowly over medium-low heat until cooked, about 20–30 minutes.

5. Calamari can also be cooked by placing them in a deep baking dish or pan in one layer. Cover with marinara sauce and white wine. Season with salt and pepper to taste and fresh parsley. Cover with foil and bake in a preheated 350°F oven until tender, about 20 minutes. Remove from oven and allow to rest at least 15 minutes for better flavor.

RISOTTO E CALAMARI

RICE WITH SQUID

SERVES 4

Squid is one of the tastiest species to be found in our seas and can be used in a variety of preparations. For this recipe, I have combined squid with rice, but you can feel free to add any other shellfish without altering the delicious flavor. Of course, you will need to adjust the amount of liquid and seasonings accordingly.

1 pound long-grain rice

1 ¼ pounds whole baby squid, cleaned (see page 212)

1 tablespoon chopped fresh parsley

2 garlic cloves, chopped

Olive oil

¼ cup sweet white wine

½ teaspoon turmeric

2 cups (or more if needed) chicken broth, boiling

1 tablespoon butter

1. Wash rice, carefully removing any stones. Reserve.

2. Wash and drain squid.

3. In a heavy skillet, sauté parsley and garlic in olive oil, tossing gently, until garlic is golden brown.

4. Add squid and, tossing gently, cook over a low flame for about 5 minutes.

5. Add wine and slowly simmer, allowing liquid to be slightly absorbed.

6. Add rice to the squid mixture and sprinkle with turmeric. Toss mixture gently.

7. Add boiling chicken broth one ladle at a time, stirring constantly so that the rice absorbs the broth gradually. Broth should cover risotto no more than ½ inch over the surface.

8. Cook approximately 25 minutes over low heat. Add more boiling broth if mixture appears too dry.

9. Sample the risotto for doneness, then add butter 1 minute before risotto is ready and mix well.

10. Remove from heat and allow to rest at least 20 minutes before serving.

CALAMARI FREDDO

COLD STUFFED SQUID

SERVES 4–6

In my childhood we always ate calamari, so it was necessary to design different ways of preparing it to keep everyone interested. This is an exciting favorite.

3 pounds baby squid, cleaned (see page 212)

1 pound squid tentacles

¾ cup olive oil

2 garlic cloves, chopped

Salt and freshly ground pepper to taste

3 tablespoons chopped fresh parsley

2 cups soft fresh bread crumbs

⅓ cup freshly grated Romano cheese

2 lemons

1. Rinse squid and tentacles; pat dry with paper towels.

2. Using a heavy skillet, sauté tentacles in ¼ cup warm olive oil until tentacles are slightly pink.

3. Add chopped garlic, a pinch of salt and pepper, and 2 tablespoons chopped fresh parsley. Sauté until garlic is translucent.

4. In a medium bowl, add bread crumbs, Romano cheese, and tentacle mixture. Toss well.

5. Lightly stuff baby squid with this mixture, securing edges with toothpicks.

6. Poach in softly boiling water about 3–5 minutes until tender.

7. Using a slotted spoon, remove squid from water and place in a decorative bowl. Drizzle with ½ cup olive oil and ¼ cup freshly squeezed lemon juice. Sprinkle with remaining tablespoon chopped parsley. Refrigerate overnight.

CALAMARI FRITTI

FRIED CALAMARI

SERVES 4

During our festivals, fried calamari are sold off pushcarts. The lines of people waiting to buy these calamari are usually longer than those at other stands. There are many styles in which to prepare fried calamari, but I think you will like my way just fine.

1 pound whole squid, cleaned (see page 212)

½ cup unbleached flour (King Arthur preferred)

½ cup fine cornmeal

Pinch of paprika

Sprinkle of garlic powder

Salt and freshly ground pepper to taste

½ cup milk

1 teaspoon freshly squeezed lemon juice

3 cups vegetable oil

Lemon wedges

1. Score diagonal slashes in a diamond pattern on squid bodies but do not cut through. Cut calamari into 1-inch rings; leave tentacles whole.

2. Using a wide, deep bowl, mix the flour and cornmeal together. Add paprika, garlic powder, and salt and pepper to taste.

3. Put milk in a deep, small bowl and add lemon juice.

4. Dip the rings and tentacles in the milk a few pieces at a time. Toss pieces around in the flour thoroughly until all moisture is absorbed.

5. Put floured pieces in a sieve and shake them well over the flour bowl until all excess flour is removed.

6. Place on waxed paper and continue the process until all the rings and tentacles are coated.

7. Put oil in a pot and bring it to a boil. Fry the calamari in batches, without crowding, until golden brown and crisp.

8. Drain on paper towels, salt to taste, and serve immediately with lemon wedges.

This calamari also tastes great with a few drops of Tabasco sprinkled on it.

CALAMARI CON VINO

SQUID WITH WINE

SERVES 3–4

The wine in this recipe helps keep the calamari soft and tender. The flavor of this dish is delicate, so be careful not to overcook.

2 tablespoons olive oil

2 garlic cloves, chopped

1 pound whole cleaned squid (see page 212), cut into 2-inch rings

¼ cup dry white wine

Salt and freshly ground pepper to taste

1 tablespoon chopped fresh parsley

Pinch of dried tarragon

Pinch of dried red pepper flakes (optional)

1. Using a heavy skillet, heat the olive oil and lightly brown the garlic.

2. Add the squid and sauté 3 minutes, tossing frequently.

3. Add the wine, salt, pepper, parsley, tarragon, and optional red pepper flakes. Cook over high heat until the wine has slightly evaporated.

4. Turn off the heat and let the mixture rest 5 minutes. Serve as an appetizer or over cooked thin spaghetti.

MONEY IN A BASKET

We had an iceman, a milkman, a farmer who brought us fresh eggs, an oil man, and a laundry man. We had the Fuller brush man, and a Jewish merchant who brought us clothes. As we lived up three flights of stairs, their visits made things easier for my mother. If she needed anything else, she would put money and a list of what she wanted in a basket and yell "Hi-ho!" to the nearest passerby (always a young boy). When she caught his attention, she would ask him to run an errand for her and lower the basket down. Those were trusting days. The boy always ran the errand, and she would happily tip him a nickel or two. No one ever ran off with the money.

CALAMARI WITH FRESH TOMATOES SAUTÉ

SERVES 4

This recipe will give you a light, delicate meal. It is a spicier, shortcut version of stuffed calamari. As with all calamari dishes, this recipe may be made in advance and refrigerated or frozen.

1½ pounds squid, cleaned (see page 212)

¼ cup plus 1 tablespoon olive oil

1 bunch scallions, chopped

1 shallot, chopped

2 garlic cloves, chopped

¼ teaspoon dried red pepper flakes, plus more to taste

Tabasco to taste

3½ cups peeled and diced fresh tomatoes (seeds discarded)

Fresh or dried basil, tarragon, mint, and oregano to taste

Salt and freshly ground black pepper to taste

½ cup finely chopped fresh parsley

Lemon wedges for garnish

1. Wash squid and pat dry with paper towels. Cut the bodies into rings about ½ inch wide. Cut the tentacles into bite-size pieces. There should be about 2½ cups. Set aside.

2. Heat the ¼ cup olive oil in a heavy skillet and sauté the scallions, shallot, garlic, and red pepper flakes for about 5 minutes on low heat.

3. When the scallions are cooked, raise the heat to high and add the cut squid. Toss lightly and quickly, sprinkling with a dash or two of Tabasco. Cook 2 minutes. With a slotted spoon, take the squid out of the pan and set aside.

4. Dry out all the water from the skillet by boiling rapidly for a few minutes, then add the tablespoon of olive oil and the fresh tomatoes. Sauté the tomatoes, adding basil, more red pepper flakes, tarragon, mint, oregano, salt, and pepper to taste. Cook 5 minutes.

5. Add the cooked calamari and chopped parsley. Simmer for 5 minutes, adding more seasonings if needed. Let the mixture rest for 10 minutes so the flavors can meld. Serve with lemon wedges, alone or with spaghetti.

CALAMARI STEWED IN WINE AND TOMATOES

SERVES 4

This stew is easy to prepare, and if using pre-cleaned squid, it will not take long to make. The wine will help tenderize the fish. As with all calamari, this recipe can be made in advance and frozen.

2 pounds fresh squid, cleaned (see page 212) and cut into large rings (reserve tentacles)

⅓ cup olive oil

2 garlic cloves, chopped

1 cup canned plum tomatoes, undrained

Pinch each of tarragon, oregano, and red pepper flakes

Salt and freshly ground pepper to taste

½ cup white wine

1. Wash the calamari and pat it dry with paper towels.

2. Heat the olive oil in a heavy skillet and lightly brown the garlic (garlic can then be removed if desired).

3. Add the tomatoes and juices, thoroughly mashing with a large fork, along with the tarragon, oregano, red pepper flakes, and salt and pepper to taste. Cook for 10 minutes over medium heat, stirring often with a wooden spoon.

4. Raise heat to high and add the white wine and calamari. Boil rapidly for at least 3 minutes, stirring often.

5. Lower heat, cover, and cook until calamari is tender, about 10 minutes. Do not allow stew to dry out; add some hot water if needed. Adjust seasonings.

6. Turn off the heat and let rest for 5–10 minutes to blend flavors nicely.

7. Serve over spaghetti or white rice.

Fresh cleaned squid can be bought in any fish store or supermarket. Be sure it is of a white color (the tentacles are nice if available).

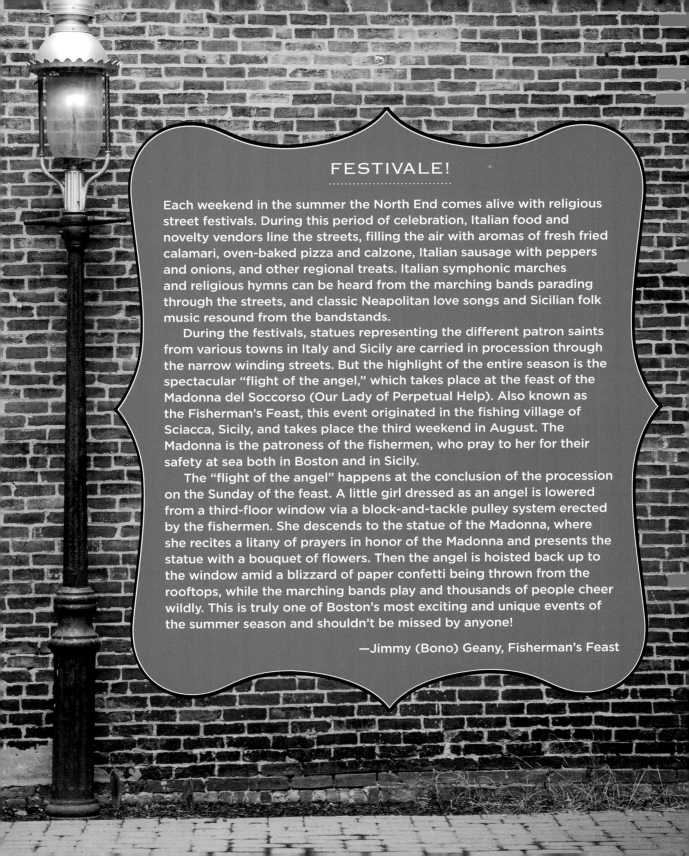

FESTIVALE!

Each weekend in the summer the North End comes alive with religious street festivals. During this period of celebration, Italian food and novelty vendors line the streets, filling the air with aromas of fresh fried calamari, oven-baked pizza and calzone, Italian sausage with peppers and onions, and other regional treats. Italian symphonic marches and religious hymns can be heard from the marching bands parading through the streets, and classic Neapolitan love songs and Sicilian folk music resound from the bandstands.

During the festivals, statues representing the different patron saints from various towns in Italy and Sicily are carried in procession through the narrow winding streets. But the highlight of the entire season is the spectacular "flight of the angel," which takes place at the feast of the Madonna del Soccorso (Our Lady of Perpetual Help). Also known as the Fisherman's Feast, this event originated in the fishing village of Sciacca, Sicily, and takes place the third weekend in August. The Madonna is the patroness of the fishermen, who pray to her for their safety at sea both in Boston and in Sicily.

The "flight of the angel" happens at the conclusion of the procession on the Sunday of the feast. A little girl dressed as an angel is lowered from a third-floor window via a block-and-tackle pulley system erected by the fishermen. She descends to the statue of the Madonna, where she recites a litany of prayers in honor of the Madonna and presents the statue with a bouquet of flowers. Then the angel is hoisted back up to the window amid a blizzard of paper confetti being thrown from the rooftops, while the marching bands play and thousands of people cheer wildly. This is truly one of Boston's most exciting and unique events of the summer season and shouldn't be missed by anyone!

—Jimmy (Bono) Geany, Fisherman's Feast

ANNA B.'S POLPI

OCTOPUS SICILIAN STYLE

SERVES 8–12

My mother-in-law claims this is the best! Octopus has a rich, sweet flavor, similar to that of squid. This dish is wonderful for Christmas Eve or during Lent. It can be served warm or cold as an appetizer or as a side dish with thin linguine and butter sauce.

2 2½- to 3-pound fresh octopuses

Salt

4 garlic cloves, chopped

½ cup olive oil

1 small onion, chopped

1 small bunch celery, chopped

1 (8-ounce) jar capers, drained and rinsed

1 (6-ounce) jar Sicilian dry-cured black olives (soaked and pitted)

2–3 hot vinegar peppers, sliced (optional)

1 (6-ounce) can tomato paste

¾ cup red wine vinegar

Salt and freshly ground pepper to taste

½ cup chopped fresh parsley for garnish

1. Clean each octopus body by continuously pouring salt on it and scrubbing with both hands in a back-and-forth motion. Using your fingers, reach inside the opening in the head and remove any loose particles. Invert the head and wash it inside and out with more salt. Pull out the inner sac. Cut away the eyes. Leave the octopus in one piece.

2. Put the cleaned octopus in a large bowl filled with cold salted water and soak for 30 minutes.

3. Fill a large pan with enough water to cover the octopus. Bring the water to a boil. When it reaches the boiling point, add 6 tablespoons of salt.

4. Pick up the octopus with a fork in the back of the neck. Dip the tentacles into the briskly boiling water 3 times. (Ma B. says this is an old custom and a very important step to prevent shock to the fish, which would immediately toughen it.) On the third time, slide the octopus off the fork into the water. Cover the pan after both octopuses have been added.

5. Cook until tender, using a fork to determine doneness. Figure on 45 minutes or more, according to their size. Do not overcook.

6. Drain in a large colander and cool to room temperature. Using a sharp, thin knife, cut the meat into 2-inch or bite-size pieces, being very careful not to let the meat tear. Reserve.

7. In a large skillet, fry the garlic in the olive oil until tender. Add the onion, celery, capers, olives, vinegar peppers, and chopped octopus. Simmer for about 15 minutes at a very low temperature.

8. Add the tomato paste and mix well. Simmer for 5 more minutes. Sprinkle red wine vinegar over the mixture, stir well, and cover. Simmer at the lowest temperature for 20 minutes more. Add salt and pepper to taste.

9. Transfer to a large serving platter and sprinkle with chopped parsley.

This can be refrigerated for a week, if necessary.

SATURDAY WESTERNS

Once a week after dinner we listened to the radio show *The Shadow Knows.* We would be filled with suspense while listening and discussed who we thought had committed the crime. At the end of the show, some dark, scary voice would shout out, "Who did it? Only the Shadow knows!" When we finally saved enough money to buy a new Andrea television, we started watching the ball games, western movies, and boxing. My father, his father, and my brother would cheer and razz and enjoy each other's company. Sometimes on Saturdays they went to the movies and watched westerns. Strangely, my brother was not allowed to play with toy guns, which were forbidden in our house. We all played a lot of games like Scrabble, Monopoly, Bingo, and one called Go to the Head of the Class. The aunts and cousins who lived nearby joined in, so we had lots of competition. Poker, however, was our number one pastime. I cried every time I lost my pennies, and they were always given back to me. A certain aunt, however, would storm out, yelling we had cheated and stolen her money. She was older and never got her losings back.

MARINATED BABY SQUID SALAD

SERVES 4

Many of our seafood restaurants specialize in calamari salad, and all have their own style. This recipe is a standard one, which allows you to add a few ingredients you may remember your mother using when you were a child.

1 pound whole baby squid, cleaned and rinsed (see page 212)

3 stalks celery hearts, chopped

2 garlic cloves, chopped

2 tablespoon chopped fresh parsley

Pinch of dried red pepper flakes

1 tablespoon olive oil

3 tablespoons vegetable oil

3 tablespoons red wine vinegar

Salt and freshly ground black pepper to taste

1. Cut cleaned squid in thin rings.

2. Put in cold water (enough to cover the rings) and softly boil, about 5 minutes or until tender.

3. Drain well and put in a medium-size serving bowl. Add remaining ingredients and toss gently.

4. Refrigerate at least a day or two to allow flavors to blend. Serve as an appetizer with wonderful round Italian bread.

BAKED STUFFED WHOLE SALMON

SERVES 4–6

Because salmon is such a wonderful fish, I cook it often. After trying many recipes, I decided this one, with the addition of soy sauce and fresh ginger, worked the best.

1 whole salmon (about 5 pounds)

Soy sauce

15 saltines, crushed

½ cup fresh bread crumbs

¾ stick (6 tablespoons) butter

2 bunches scallions, chopped

1 large shallot, chopped

2 garlic cloves, chopped

¼ cup chopped fresh parsley

1 teaspoon dried tarragon

2 lemons

Salt and freshly ground pepper to taste

Thick stalks of carrots and celery (to use as a rack)

1 large onion, thickly sliced

Large piece fresh ginger, slivered

Olive oil

Turmeric

Dry white wine

Tabasco

1. Preheat oven to 450°F.

2. Cover salmon generously with soy sauce, inside and out.

3. Place crushed crackers and bread crumbs in a medium-size bowl. Set aside.

4. In a small skillet, melt butter and sauté scallions, shallot, garlic, parsley, and tarragon. Add to crumb mixture and toss well.

5. Add squeezed lemon juice until bread mixture is moist, and salt and pepper to taste. Reserve lemon halves.

6. Line the bottom of a baking pan with stalks of carrots and celery, and onion slices.

7. Place salmon on top of vegetables and stuff cavity with crumb mixture. Tuck slivers of ginger inside the fish. Scatter more ginger under and around fish.

8. Rub fish with olive oil and sprinkle with turmeric and salt and pepper. Decorate with slices of lemon and smother with ginger slivers.

9. Throw the used lemon halves into the bottom of the pan and add white wine to cover the bottom.

10. Bake 20 minutes, then add more wine as it evaporates, a few shots of Tabasco, and some soy sauce to bottom of pan. Bake about 20 minutes more, until golden brown.

POACHED FISH

You need not use your oven to prepare this healthy, light, and wholesome dish. Lemons will enhance the flavor, and a little Tabasco on the side will add an extra zip. Trout or sea bass steaks work well with this recipe.

4 cups water

3 tablespoons lemon juice

2 tablespoons olive or vegetable oil

2 celery stalks, chopped finely

½ cup coarsely chopped fresh parsley

Pinch of turmeric for color (optional)

Pinch of dried tarragon

Salt and freshly ground pepper to taste

6–8 1-inch-thick pieces of fish

1. In a large, deep skillet with a cover, combine water, lemon juice, oil, celery, parsley, turmeric (if using), tarragon, and salt and pepper to taste. Bring to a soft boil.

2. Arrange each piece of fish in a single layer in the liquid. Cover skillet, reduce heat to low, and simmer until fish flakes easily (about 15 minutes).

3. Remove fish from pan and place it on a warm large serving platter.

4. Boil the liquid in the skillet until it is reduced by half.

5. Pour sauce over fish and serve with quartered fresh lemons. Serve hot or at room temperature.

HOW TO STEAM FRESH LIVE LOBSTERS

SERVES 4

This recipe explains the most perfect and best way to steam lobsters. Placing the lobster in cold water prevents it from being shocked and leaves the meat tender and juicy soft. You may use the cooked lobsters for Lobster fra Diavolo, lobster casserole, or any other lobster favorite.

4 live whole lobsters,
    about 1–1½ pounds each

1 cup beer

1 bunch scallions, trimmed

8 sprigs parsley

½ large onion, thickly sliced

2 lemon halves

Salt and freshly ground pepper to taste

1–2 shots Tabasco

1. Using a large pot with a cover, add cold water to fill pot at least 4 inches.

2. Place live lobsters in the pot of cold water. Add beer, whole scallions, parsley sprigs, sliced onion, lemon halves, salt and pepper to taste, and Tabasco.

3. Place covered pot on medium-high heat and bring to a boil. Lower heat and steam lobsters approximately 25–30 minutes, or until all the lobsters are bright red.

4. Turn lobsters around a few times while steaming, alternating the top ones to the bottom for even cooking. Check liquid for evaporation, and add more beer or water if needed.

5. Place on a platter and serve immediately with melted butter to which Tabasco and freshly squeezed lemon juice have been added.

When eating a whole lobster, avoid eating the upper part where the sac and antennae are located.

BAKED LOBSTER IMBOTTITO

STUFFED LOBSTER

SERVES 2

This is a perfect recipe for baked stuffed lobster using garlic and fresh bread crumbs. The lobster is so succulent and tasty, you will hesitate to prepare it any other way. All ovens vary, so you might have to watch that the bread crumbs do not burn before the lobster is cooked. If they begin to brown, cover with a foil tent. Fresh live lobster is best for this recipe, but squeamish cooks may want to boil the lobsters in advance.

2 large lobsters (about 1½ pounds each), live or boiled

1½ sticks (¾ cup) butter or margarine, melted

2 garlic cloves, finely chopped

1 shallot clove, finely chopped

1 bunch scallions, finely chopped

Pinch of tarragon

1 or 2 shots Tabasco (optional)

1½ lemons

1 cup freshly grated bread crumbs

1 strip (a single rolled package) Ritz crackers, crumbled

¼ cup chopped fresh parsley

1 (8-ounce) bottle clam juice (or more if needed—enough to keep pan from drying)

Salt and freshly ground pepper to taste

Paprika

Additional melted butter, fresh lemon juice, and Tabasco for sauce

1. Cut lobsters down the middle without breaking through bottom shell and spread wide open (be sure the rubber bands are on claws). Place in a baking pan large enough to fit lobsters; remove bands.

2. Melt 1 stick butter in a small saucepan. Add garlic, shallot, scallions, tarragon, Tabasco, the juice of ½ lemon, and a few pieces of lemon peel. Sauté for about 5 minutes.

3. In a large bowl, combine bread crumbs, crumbled crackers, chopped parsley, and the juice of 1 lemon. Toss well. Add melted butter mixture and combine thoroughly.

4. Slowly pour clam juice into bread crumb mixture until stuffing is well moistened but not soaked. Add salt and pepper to taste.

5. Stuff lobsters from cavity to tail until well filled.

6. Melt remaining ½ stick butter. Drizzle it on lobsters and sprinkle with enough paprika to lightly color.

7. Pour remaining clam juice into bottom of pan. Bake lobsters, uncovered, in a preheated 450°F oven on the middle rack for 20 minutes.

8. Lower heat to 350°F and cook for about 30 minutes more for live lobsters or 15 minutes more for boiled ones.

9. When lobsters are cooked and stuffing is crusty brown, remove from oven and baste with remaining juices from bottom of pan.

10. Cover tightly with foil and let sit for about 20 minutes (I also like to put a heavy towel over the foil) to keep the steam in, thus making for a juicier lobster. Serve with melted butter that has been seasoned with fresh lemon juice and Tabasco.

Add some white wine to the bottom of the pan if lobster juices dry out during cooking.

LOBSTER FRA DIAVOLO

SERVES 4–6

When you buy lobsters you should know that generally in winter the lobsters are hard-shelled and packed full of meat, so you may need fewer lobsters for a pound of meat. Soft-shelled lobsters, generally available in summer, are sweeter. Serve boiled or steamed lobsters whole, but first drain water and remove elastics from claws. Lobsters can be cooked ahead of time, but not too long or meat will get tough.

2¼ pounds steamed lobsters, left whole

¾ cup olive oil

1 large onion, chopped

2 garlic cloves, chopped

2 shallot cloves, chopped

Pinch each of dried red pepper flakes, dried tarragon, fresh parsley, and dried basil

1 (8-ounce) can chopped mushrooms (reserve liquid)

2 shakes Tabasco

1 (6-ounce) can tomato paste

1 (28-ounce) can crushed tomatoes

Salt and freshly ground pepper to taste

14 ounces water (fill half the can that contained the crushed tomatoes)

1 pound thin linguine, cooked according to package directions

1 tablespoon butter

1. Reserve tomalley from lobster bodies.

2. Cover the bottom of a deep, heavy saucepan with olive oil. Sauté onion, garlic, and shallots in the oil and gently simmer until golden.

3. Add red pepper flakes, tarragon, parsley, and basil and stir well. Add drained mushrooms and Tabasco. Simmer until mushrooms are slightly crisp.

4. Add the reserved tomalley and stir until it melts down.

5. Add the tomato paste and blend well. Add the crushed tomatoes and stir until blended with the tomato paste and oil. Add salt and pepper to taste and a pinch more of any of the dry seasonings, stirring well.

6. When the sauce starts to boil slightly, add the reserved mushroom juice and water.

7. Let sauce come to a boil and add the lobsters. Gently mix sauce with lobsters and bring the mixture to another boil, stirring often. Adjust seasonings.

8. Simmer on low heat, covered, for 10 minutes. Uncover, stir gently, and cook another 10–15 minutes until sauce is of desired consistency. Remove lobsters from sauce. Put on a large platter and reserve.

9. Serve sauce over 1 pound cooked linguine that has been tossed with butter.

BROILED LOBSTER WITH LEMON AND GARLIC VINAIGRETTE

SERVES 4

In our home, lobster is served the night before Christmas. We usually cook it in a tomato sauce and serve it over linguine. However, for those who would like a change or are strapped for time, this recipe will keep everyone happy and satisfied.

6 tablespoons sweet red wine vinegar or raspberry vinegar

1 tablespoon freshly squeezed lemon juice

Salt to taste

1¼ cups olive oil

3 tablespoons chopped scallions

3 tablespoons minced fresh parsley

Dash of Tabasco, or ½ teaspoon red pepper flakes

4–4½ pounds fresh lobsters halved lengthwise (tomally and other parts may be removed if desired)

¼ cup dry bread crumbs

4 lemons, quartered, for garnish

1. In a small bowl, combine red wine vinegar, lemon juice, and salt to taste. Slowly whisk in the olive oil in a thin stream. Add scallions, parsley, and Tabasco. Reserve.

2. Position rack 4 inches from broiler and turn on heat.

3. Arrange lobsters, cut-side up, on a broiler pan and spoon 3 tablespoons of the stirred vinaigrette over each half.

4. Sprinkle with the bread crumbs and broil until the lobster meat is opaque and the topping is golden brown, about 10 minutes.

5. Place lobsters on 4 decorative plates and garnish with lemon quarters. Serve immediately, with the remaining vinaigrette on the side.

LOBSTER BODIES IN TOMATO SAUCE

SERVES 6–8

This recipe was a favorite in our home. We could buy a bagful of lobster bodies and make a delicious sauce. It was wonderful to nibble on the legs and suck out all the meat. This sauce with spaghetti is a very special one, equally delicious and cheaper than whole lobsters in cost. The tomally (the green pulp in the body) is easier to get at and helps give an added taste to the sauce, but you can spoon it out before cooking if you wish to eliminate it.

¼ **cup olive oil**

1 medium onion, chopped

2 garlic cloves, chopped

2 shallots cloves, chopped

Pinch each of red pepper flakes, dried tarragon flakes, chopped fresh parsley, and dried basil

1 (4-ounce) can chopped mushrooms (reserve liquid)

2 dashes Tabasco

1 (6-ounce) can tomato paste

1 (28-ounce) can crush tomatoes

Salt and pepper to taste

14 ounces water or clam juice

8–10 lobster bodies

1 pound linguine, cooked according to package directions

1 tablespoon butter

1. In a pan large enough to accommodate all the ingredients, add the olive oil and sauté the onion, garlic, shallots, red pepper flakes, tarragon, parsley, and basil, using medium heat. Do not let burn.

2. Add the chopped mushrooms and Tabasco and fry for 5 minutes, turning often.

3. Add the tomato paste and blend well. Add the crushed tomatoes and stir until blended with the tomato paste and oil. Add the salt and pepper and another pinch of seasonings, stirring well.

4. When the sauce starts to lightly boil, add the mushroom liquid and water or clam juice. Bring to a boil.

5. Add the lobsters and turn with the sauce. Let the mixture come to another boil, stirring often. Add more salt and pepper if needed.

6. Simmer uncovered for 30 minutes, turning the lobsters 4 or 5 times during the cooking period.

7. Serve over 1 pound of cooked linguine that has been tossed with butter.

CRABS AND SPAGHETTI

SERVES 4–6

What fun we had going to the fish market for crabs and crab bodies when I was a child. At that time you could buy them so cheaply. There was also a man who drove a pickup truck and went around the North End shouting, "Cawadi! Cawadi!" which meant you could buy wonderful boiled crabs, cooked right in the pots on the truck, for maybe five cents each. We would eat them while sitting on our doorsteps and put the empty shells in the paper bags they came in. Besides boiling them, here is a special way my mother cooked fresh, raw crabs.

⅓ **cup olive oil**

3 garlic cloves, chopped

1 medium onion, chopped

1 tablespoon dried red pepper flakes

1 tablespoon dried oregano

1 (6-ounce) can tomato paste

1 (28-ounce) can crushed peeled tomatoes

Salt and freshly ground pepper to taste

8 fresh, whole crabs, rinsed slightly

½ **cup dry white wine or water**

1 pound spaghetti or thin linguine (linguini fini)

Grated Parmesan or Romano cheese

1. Heat olive oil in a large saucepan over medium heat. Add chopped garlic, onion, red pepper flakes, and oregano; sauté for about 5 minutes.

2. Add tomato paste and blend in well, stirring constantly with a wooden spoon. Add tomatoes and stir constantly until mixture is blended well. Sprinkle with additional red pepper flakes, oregano, and salt and pepper to taste.

3. Bring sauce to a soft boil and add whole, rinsed crabs. Stir gently, tossing crabs in sauce.

4. Put heat on medium-high and add white wine or water. Bring sauce to a soft boil and adjust seasonings. Simmer, covered, for about 15 minutes, then remove cover and simmer at least until pasta is cooked.

5. While crab sauce cooks, prepare pasta al dente in a large pot of boiling water. Drain well.

6. Place pasta on a very large platter and spoon some of the crab sauce on top. Toss pasta lightly to coat well with sauce (to prevent pasta from sticking).

7. Surround the pasta with crabs and sprinkle with grated cheese.

8. Serve immediately with lots of napkins and additional sauce. Have some empty bowls available for shells.

EEL MARINARA

SERVES 2–4

Serve this dish as an appetizer or as a main course with pasta and vegetables.

2 pounds fresh eel

⅓ cup olive oil

1 small onion, minced

2 garlic cloves

1 small piece lemon peel

⅛ teaspoon dried sage

2 tablespoons tomato paste,
    diluted in ½ cup water

½ cup dry white wine

Salt and freshly ground pepper
    to taste

1. Have the eel cleaned by the fish merchant and the heads removed and discarded. Rinse thoroughly in cold, salted water and dry. Cut eel into 3-inch pieces.

2. Pour the olive oil into a large, deep skillet. Add the onion, garlic, lemon peel, and sage. Sauté gently until the garlic is golden brown. Discard the garlic.

3. Add the pieces of eel and fry over medium heat for about 5 minutes. Turn often, gently, using a spatula.

4. Add the diluted tomato paste and wine. Simmer, uncovered, for 10 minutes. Add salt and pepper and simmer for 8–10 minutes more.

5. When the liquid is almost evaporated, transfer to a warm serving platter.

Cooked eel refrigerates well for 2 or 3 days.

EEL WITH PEAS ALLA ROMANA

SERVES 4

When buying eel, make sure they have a fresh odor and are not slimy. Allow three pounds of eel for six people.

1½ pounds fresh small eel

3 tablespoons olive oil

½ garlic clove, minced

4 scallions, sliced

Salt and freshly ground pepper to taste

Pinch of dried red pepper flakes

½ cup dry white wine

¼ cup tomato sauce

2 cups shelled fresh or frozen peas

2 tablespoons warm water or clam broth

1. Have the eel cleaned by the fish merchant and the heads removed and discarded. Rinse thoroughly in cold, salted water, and dry. Cut the eel into 3-inch pieces.

2. Pour the olive oil into a heavy saucepan. Sauté the garlic and scallions until slightly browned.

3. Add the eel, salt, pepper, and red pepper flakes. Cook on medium-high heat until the liquid from the eel has evaporated, turning only once or twice.

4. Add the wine, tomato sauce, and peas and mix well. Add the water or stock and lower the heat to medium. Cook, uncovered, for 15–20 minutes or until the peas are tender. Stir gently a couple of times only. Taste for more salt and pepper.

5. Serve in soup bowls with crusty bread.

FRIED SMALL EEL

SERVES 4

Because baby eel are available for such a short time each year, they are considered a great delicacy, especially in Italian homes. When I was growing up, at Eastertime they could be seen swimming around in large pails out on the sidewalks of our local fish markets. They were sold by the pound, then the vendors would remove the entrails and heads and wrap them in heavy-duty white paper, to be cooked the day before Easter. The cooking styles varied, according to region. Sometimes the eel were dipped in flour and pan-fried; others were marinated with a vinegar and oregano dressing and baked or cooked in a light tomato sauce with only pure olive oil.

Whichever way you decide to cook eel, they are something you have to acquire a taste for. Youngsters may not appreciate them, but as they grow older and more knowledgeable about food, they will change their minds.

3 pounds fresh small eel

1 cup flour

1 teaspoon paprika

Salt and pepper to taste

1 cup olive oil (or more as needed)

1 lemon, quartered, for garnish

1. Have the eel cleaned by the fish merchant and the heads removed and discarded. Rinse thoroughly in cold, salted water and pat dry with paper towels. Cut them into 2-inch pieces.

2. Season the flour with paprika, salt, and pepper. Put the flour in a brown paper bag. Shake the pieces of eel in the bag, a few at a time, to evenly distribute the flour mixture. Set aside.

3. Heat the olive oil in a medium-size heavy skillet over medium-high heat. When the oil is hot, add some of the pieces of eel so they can fry uncrowded until brown on both sides. The frying time will be about 10–15 minutes on each side. Drain on paper towels. Add more oil to the skillet as needed. When all the pieces have been cooked, transfer them to a warm platter.

4. Sprinkle with more salt and pepper, if desired, and serve with lemon quarters.

COSCE DI RANNO A FRITTE

FRIED FROGS LEGS

SERVES 2

Frogs legs have a delicate flavor and texture similar to chicken. They are generally sold in connected pairs. They are available fresh during the warmer months and frozen year-round—look in the fish section of specialty shops. Allow 7 pairs per person.

2 pounds fresh or frozen frogs legs (connected), about 7 pairs per person

⅓ cup milk

⅔ cup corn flour

1 teaspoon salt

1 teaspoon ground red pepper (paprika) or cayenne

Vegetable oil for deep frying

4 lemon wedges for garnish

3 sprigs parsley, chopped, for garnish

Many Italians still support themselves by frog fishing. They scour at night with an oil lamp that radiates a strong light, and a long rod to whose end is tied a brilliant red cloth. The frog is lured by the light, which excites his wonder, then fascinated by the cloth intriguingly dropped near the wily hunter. The scarlet suggests a succulent morsel, making the reptilian's mouth water. He swallows it greedily, and before he realizes his gluttonous mistake, he is in an osier basket ready for market.

1. If frozen, thaw legs in milk until thawed. If fresh, soak in milk for 1 hour.

2. In a medium-size paper bag combine corn flour, salt and red pepper. Remove legs from milk, shaking off excess, then add them to paper bag, secure tightly, and toss briskly until legs are well coated.

3. In a saucepan or deep fryer, heat about 2 inches of vegetable oil. Fry coated frogs legs a few at a time quickly in deep hot oil for 1½–2 minutes or until golden brown and done. A nonstick skillet works best since the legs tend to stick.

4. Place on a warm dish lined with a paper towel and keep warm in a 200°F oven while frying remaining legs.

5. To serve the frog's legs, mound them attractively on a heated platter and arrange the lemon wedges around the edge. Sprinkle with fresh chopped parsley if desired.

6. Serve at once, accompanied by cocktail or tartar sauce.

OLGA'S FISH CAKES

YIELD: 15 CAKES

My mother never had any idea that this recipe would follow her granddaughter to Georgia, where it would become a big hit with all of her friends.

3 large boiling potatoes, peeled

3 pounds fish fillets or other skinless pieces (pollock, scrod, or any inexpensive boneless fish will do)

½ cup freshly grated Parmesan cheese

2 garlic cloves, finely chopped

1 cup chopped fresh parsley

3 eggs

Salt and freshly ground black pepper to taste

Fresh bread crumbs (enough to hold mixture together)

1 cup olive oil

Lemon slices, parsley, and tartar sauce (optional)

1. Cut the potatoes into large cubes and boil for 20 minutes. Drain them thoroughly by shaking the colander well. Then put the potatoes in a large bowl and mash until fluffy.

2. Put the fish in a saucepan (cut it to fit, if necessary). Add water to cover the fish and boil gently for 5 minutes.

3. Drain the fish and add to the potatoes. Add the grated cheese, garlic, parsley, eggs, salt, and pepper. Gently toss the mixture until well blended.

4. Add the bread crumbs a little at a time until the mixture becomes firm to the touch but not dry. Keep the potato-fish mixture light and not laden with crumbs.

5. Bring the mixture to the stove area along with a dish of bread crumbs and a small bowl of water. Take a fistful of the fish mixture and roll it into a ball. When the ball is smooth, gently flatten it to form a patty. Use the water to keep your hands moist (this will prevent the fish cake from sticking to your palms and help keep a smooth shape). Lightly dust the fish cake with bread crumbs to dry excess moisture (this will also stop it from sticking to the skillet). Place the fish cake on a large tray. Repeat with the rest of the mixture, then let them sit for 5 minutes.

6. Heat the olive oil in a large heavy skillet on medium-high heat. Gently add the fish cakes to the hot oil without crowding. Fry on both sides until golden brown or until a nice crust forms. Use a spatula to turn the cakes over gently. Transfer to a paper-lined dish to absorb excess oil. Continue until all the fish cakes have been fried.

7. When all the fish cakes have cooked and drained, arrange on a platter with lemon slices, parsley, and tartar sauce and serve.

SOGLIOLA ALLA LIMONE GRATO

LEMON BREADED SOLE FILLETS

SERVES 4

You may use store-bought bread crumbs or use a blender to grate day-old Italian bread finely enough so that the crumbs will adhere to the fish without sliding off. Remove the crusts from the bread before grating.

1 egg, beaten

¾ cup plain bread crumbs

1½ teaspoons finely chopped fresh parsley

Salt and freshly ground pepper to taste

¾ teaspoon grated lemon peel

12 ounces sole fillets (4 pieces)

3 tablespoons butter

½ cup olive oil, or more if needed

4 lemon wedges for garnish

1. In a shallow dish, beat the egg until smooth and frothy. In another shallow dish, combine the bread crumbs, parsley, salt and pepper to taste, and lemon peel, mixing well.

2. Dip the sole fillets in the beaten egg. Place on bread crumb mixture and pat down until crumbs adhere, turning to coat both sides.

3. In a large heavy skillet, heat the butter and olive oil over medium-high heat.

4. When hot, add the breaded fish and cook for 3–4 minutes or until golden brown and fish flakes easily with a fork, turning only once. Serve immediately with lemon wedges.

PESCE ALL'ACQUA PAZZA

FISH FILLETS IN WINE

SERVES 2

Acqua Pazza is Italian for "Crazy Water." The Italians like to dramatize because the fish is cooked in wine, and so they chose to give this peasant dish an interesting name. Filets of sole or flounder will do fine. We are using haddock in this very easy-to-cook recipe. Be gentle when turning fish over. It is delicate and needs to be handled as little as possible. Do not overcook. Using unsalted butter will help keep fish from burning.

4 tablespoons unsalted butter

1 pound haddock fillets (medium-thick)

1 teaspoon lemon juice

1 tablespoon golden raisins (optional)

Salt and pepper to taste

Pinch of tarragon

¼ cup sherry or any sweet wine

1 teaspoon parsley, finely chopped

1. Using medium-low heat, melt butter in a heavy skillet to accommodate fish. Lay fish on the melted butter.

2. When butter is thoroughly heated, add the lemon juice and raisins and cover. Let fish steam for 10–15 minutes or until opaque in texture.

3. Uncover and gently turn fish over, using a wide spatula. Sprinkle with salt and pepper to taste and a pinch of tarragon.

4. Add sherry and bring liquid to a rapid boil. Reduce heat and simmer for 2 minutes.

5. Place fish on a warmed, decorative platter, and spoon the juices on top. Sprinkle with parsley and serve immediately.

This dish goes well with broccoli, fresh green beans, or rice.

HADDOCK ALLA PIZZAIOLA

SERVES 4

A thick piece of sole may be substituted for the haddock in this recipe.

2 pounds haddock fillets

1 pound fresh tomatoes, skins on, seeds removed, and chopped

1 tablespoon chopped fresh parsley

1 large garlic clove, finely chopped

Pinch each of dried tarragon and mint

Salt and freshly ground black pepper to taste

5 tablespoons olive oil

¼ cup freshly grated Parmesan cheese

Lemon wedges for garnish (optional)

1. Place the fish in a buttered baking dish.

2. Combine the tomatoes, parsley, garlic, seasonings, olive oil, and cheese. Toss gently until well mixed. Spread evenly over fish fillets.

3. Bake the fish in a preheated 350°F oven for 20 minutes, until cheese is nicely melted and tomatoes are soft.

4. Serve very hot with lemon wedges and pan drippings.

ALWAYS BEING THERE

I feel so grateful for all I witnessed growing up in the North End. I feel especially indebted to my parents for always being there, waiting for us. And the delicious dinners my mother prepared, using the recipes our grandparents brought from their peasant towns in Italy. Now when I think about all these things, they bring a smile to my heart.

MACKEREL IN TOMATO SAUCE

SERVES 4

This tomato sauce is generally used with a full-bodied fish such as mackerel. You can buy mackerel whole, filleted, or cut as steaks. Just be gentle with it when handling, and try to lift it only once while cooking.

3 pounds mackerel

2 tablespoons olive oil

1 small onion, sliced

1 garlic clove, chopped

1 tablespoon chopped fresh parsley

1 (14-ounce) can peeled and crushed tomatoes

Salt and freshly ground pepper to taste

½ teaspoon dried red pepper flakes

½ teaspoon dried basil

½ teaspoon dried oregano

2 tablespoons water

1. Remove the bones from the mackerel. Cut the fish into 4 pieces.

2. Heat the olive oil in a large heavy skillet. Add the onions, garlic, and parsley and cook until the onions become translucent.

3. Add the tomatoes and seasonings. Cook for 5 minutes on medium heat, stirring often.

4. Add the water and let it come to a boil. Add the mackerel and cook for 5 minutes, uncovered. Turn the fish over and cook an additional 10 minutes.

5. Serve the mackerel on flat plates with the sauce, or serve over spaghetti.

This may be refrigerated for 2 or 3 days.

PAN-FRIED SMELTS OR SARDINES

SERVES 6–8

A quick and easy Lenten favorite. We like to cook our smelts whole for easier handling. Cooked this way, they look very appealing when served on a decorative platter, accompanied by lemon and parsley. When ready to eat, simply lift the meat off the bone; it will come off very easily.

2 pounds fresh whole smelts or sardines (small size, if possible)

Semolina flour

Paprika

Salt and freshly ground pepper to taste

Olive oil

Lemon wedges and chopped fresh parsley for garnish

1. Rinse the smelts or sardines under cold water and dry with paper towels.

2. Put 1 cup of flour in a paper bag (adding more as you go along, if needed) along with a sprinkle of paprika, salt, and pepper. Shake 3 or 4 fish at a time in the bag to coat them with flour.

3. When all the fish have been floured, quickly fry in hot olive oil until golden brown. Be careful not to crowd the fish in the pan. Continue until all the fish are used. Drain on paper towels.

4. Serve immediately, garnished with lemon wedges and parsley. These are best eaten the same day they are made.

Semolina is a nice, soft, refined flour that Italians use often.

BROILED MARINATED SWORDFISH

SERVES 4–6

The marinade used in this recipe also complements halibut, snapper, or cod. The lemony sautéed mushrooms are great, too.

2 pounds swordfish steaks, each cut about ¾ inch thick

3 tablespoons lemon juice

¼ cup dry white wine (or water)

2 garlic cloves, chopped

½ teaspoon each crushed oregano, tarragon, salt, and pepper

¼ teaspoon fennel seeds, crushed

½ pound fresh mushrooms, sliced

2 tablespoons olive oil

¼ cup scallions, thinly sliced

1. Cut the swordfish into serving-size pieces. Place in a deep bowl with the lemon juice, wine, garlic, oregano, tarragon, salt, pepper, and fennel. Cover and refrigerate at least 2 hours, turning often.

2. Remove the fish from the marinade (reserve marinade) and broil about 4 inches from heat for 5–8 minutes each side, or until fish is nicely browned and flakes easily with a fork.

3. Meanwhile, sauté the mushrooms in olive oil until limp. Stir in reserved marinade and simmer for about 2 minutes.

4. Transfer fish to a serving plate, top with the mushroom sauce, and sprinkle with chopped scallions. Serve immediately.

BAKED BACCALÀ WITH POTATOES AND TOMATOES

SERVES 3–4

Be sure to buy boneless baccalà, since it takes only twenty-four hours to soften. Keep refrigerated, changing the water frequently. Drain, rinse, and cut into 2-inch chunks. Prepared fish will take about an hour and a half to cook. See "How to Pre-Soak Boneless Baccalà" on page 247.

2½ cups fresh or canned seedless tomatoes, drained (reserve juice) and coarsely chopped

1½ pounds softened baccalà chunks

4 baking potatoes, peeled and cut lengthwise into 6 pieces each

1 large onion, thickly sliced

4 garlic cloves, halved

½ cup Sicilian dry-cured black olives

½ cup chopped fresh parsley

Pinch of oregano

Salt and freshly ground pepper to taste

¾ cup bread crumbs

¾ cup extra-virgin olive oil

1 cup water

1. Place half of the tomatoes in a 10 × 14-inch heavy baking pan. Place the baccalà, potatoes, and onions in a single layer over the tomatoes. Arrange the remaining tomatoes, garlic, and olives on top.

2. Sprinkle with parsley, oregano, and salt and pepper to taste, then cover with bread crumbs.

3. Drizzle olive oil evenly over fish. Gently pour reserved tomato juice and water over the top, being careful not to disturb the bread crumbs.

4. Bake in a preheated 375°F oven until potatoes are tender and bread crumbs are golden brown. Make a foil tent if crumbs brown too quickly.

5. Serve with crusty Italian bread and a salad.

BACCALÀ WITH FRESH TOMATOES

SERVES 6–8

Baccalà, or salt cod, has always been one of the "must" dishes of Florence because of the proximity of the fishing port of Livorno. Use nice, ripe red tomatoes that are still firm to make this delicious sauce. See "How to Pre-Soak Boneless Baccalà" below.

2 pounds boneless dried salt cod

Flour

2 eggs, beaten

Olive oil

1 garlic clove

2 pounds ripe tomatoes, peeled and cut in chunks

Salt and freshly ground pepper to taste

Chopped fresh parsley for garnish

1. Dry the fish well and cut into 3-inch squares. Flour the fish, dip into beaten eggs, and flour again.

2. Using a deep heavy skillet, add enough olive oil to fry the fish. Fry evenly on both sides until golden brown. Remove from the pan and drain on paper towels.

3. In a large, wide frying pan or saucepan, sauté the garlic clove in ¼ cup olive oil until golden brown. Remove clove from pan.

4. Add the peeled tomatoes and their juices. Cook for 10 minutes, stirring often with a wooden spoon. Add salt and pepper to taste.

5. Place the baccalà in the tomato mixture, making sure it is covered with some of the sauce. Cook slowly for another 10 minutes.

6. Serve hot with lots of chopped fresh parsley on top.

HOW TO PRE-SOAK BONELESS BACCALÀ

Baccalà is a dried form of cod which has been heavily salted to extract moisture and thereby preserve the fish. Before cooking, it must be soaked to remove the salt. The stiffer the fish, the longer the soaking time required. Salted cod should be soaked in cold water for at least twenty-four hours. Drain the fish, cover it again with cold water, and bring it gently to a boil. Skim off the foam, reduce the heat to a gentle simmer, and poach for fifteen to twenty minutes, according to the thickness of the fish. When the fish is cooked, it can be flaked and used in your chosen recipe.

Note: Whole pieces of dried salted cod need at least 2 or 3 days to soften and remove salt.

BACCALÀ WITH VINEGAR PEPPERS

SERVES 6–8

This is another of my mother's delicacies. How I enjoy her talents! This recipe should be prepared up to twenty-four hours in advance to enhance the flavors. Serve with crusty Italian bread as an appetizer or with other main dishes for dinner during Lent. See "How to Pre-Soak Boneless Baccalà" on page 247.

2 pounds boneless dried salt cod

6 large vinegar peppers, hot or sweet

Olive oil

Salt and freshly ground black pepper to taste

3 large garlic cloves, chopped

Chopped fresh parsley

10 Sicilian dry-cured black olives, pitted and sliced

1. When you are ready to cook, drain and rinse baccalà well in cold water.

2. Put the fish in a large pot and cover with water. Gently boil on medium heat until the fish is tender. (The fish should not become so soft that it breaks apart in the water.) Rinse under cold running water and drain well.

3. Tear the fish into bite-size pieces and spread them attractively on a large serving platter. Tear the vinegar peppers over the fish, letting the juices fall on the cod.

4. Sprinkle the cod and peppers with a little olive oil, salt (only if needed) and pepper, chopped garlic, chopped parsley, and sliced olives. Gently lift the fish with a spatula to let these ingredients fall through so everything marinates evenly. Do this several times before serving, but try not to disturb the arrangement.

5. Refrigerate, covered, for at least overnight.

BACCALÀ AND POTATOES

SERVES 4

Codfish, dried in the sun and wind, was once considered a poor man's fish. The poor man always knew what a tasty food he had. See "How to Pre-Soak Boneless Baccalà" on page 247.

1½ pounds boneless dried salt cod

Olive oil

3 garlic cloves, chopped

1 tablespoon dried oregano

1 teaspoon dried red pepper flakes

4 fresh basil leaves, or a huge pinch of dry basil

1 (14-ounce) can plum tomatoes

5 medium potatoes, peeled and quartered

¼ pound Spanish green olives, pitted

Salt and freshly ground pepper to taste

1 tablespoon chopped fresh parsley

10 Sicilian dry-cured black olives, pitted

1. When you are ready to cook, drain and rinse baccalà well in cold water. Cut into 3- or 4-inch squares.

2. Heat enough oil to cover the bottom of a heavy saucepan, and sauté garlic, oregano, red pepper flakes, and basil. After the garlic has slightly browned, add the plum tomatoes and cook for 15 minutes. Gently crush the tomatoes with a large fork and stir often.

3. Add the fish, potatoes, and green olives. Stir well, using a wooden spoon. Add salt and pepper to taste, and more red pepper if desired.

4. Cover and simmer on low heat for 45 minutes or until the potatoes are tender and the fish is cooked. Remove from the heat. Sprinkle with chopped parsley and black olives. Let rest for 10 minutes. Serve with Italian bread.

This dish refrigerates well.

BACCALÀ FRITTO

FRIED SALT COD

SERVES 4–6

This salt cod dish is best eaten the day it is cooked. Serve it as an appetizer or a side dish. See "How to Pre-Soak Boneless Baccalà" on page 247.

1 pound boneless dried salt cod, cut in 3 x 5-inch pieces

¼ cup olive oil

2 tablespoons vegetable oil

3 garlic cloves, crushed

¼ cup diced salt pork

Flour (enough to coat fish)

¼ teaspoon freshly ground black pepper

3 tablespoons freshly squeezed lemon juice

Chopped fresh parsley and lemon wedges for garnish

1. When you are ready to cook, drain and rinse well in cold water. Pat dry with paper towels.

2. Heat both oils in a large heavy skillet over medium-low heat. Add the garlic and salt pork. Cook about 10 minutes or until the garlic is lightly browned and the fat has melted.

3. Using a slotted spoon, remove the garlic and any unmelted fat. Discard. Raise the heat to medium-high.

4. Combine the flour and pepper on a plate. Dip the fish in the flour to coat lightly.

5. Using tongs, add the fish to the skillet. Cook until the fish is golden on both sides or until it begins to flake, about 10 minutes. Turn it only once.

6. Using a spatula, gently transfer the fish to a heated serving platter.

7. Discard all but ¼ cup of the drippings in the pan. Stir the lemon juice into the skillet. When hot and bubbly, pour it over the fish. Garnish the platter with parsley and lemon wedges.

MERLUZZI IN WHITE SAUCE

SICILIAN-STYLE WHITING

SERVES 4–6

My Uncle Tony, now deceased, taught me how to cook this wonderful "poor man's repast." Because whiting is a bony fish, we usually strain the juices and discard the fish unless it has previously been deboned.

⅓ cup olive oil

1 large onion, sliced

1 garlic clove, chopped

1 shallot, chopped

3 scallions, sliced

1 tablespoon chopped fresh parsley, plus more for garnish

Pinch each of dried tarragon, red pepper flakes, and oregano

2 pounds whiting, cleaned and dressed

Salt and freshly ground pepper to taste

Water (enough to cover the fish)

⅓ cup dry white wine

1. Heat the olive oil in a medium-size heavy saucepan over medium heat. Sauté the onion, garlic, shallot, scallions, parsley, tarragon, red pepper flakes, and oregano.

2. When the onion is transparent, add the fish and salt and pepper to taste. Brown lightly for a few minutes, turning often.

3. Raise the heat to high and add enough water to cover the fish. Add the white wine. Let the mixture come to a rapid boil and boil for 5 minutes, or until the fish is cooked and the sauce turns milky white. Taste for more salt and pepper. Check the fish carefully to remove all bones.

4. Serve very hot in soup bowls with more fresh parsley on top and accompanied by garlic bread. Or use as a sauce for ½ pound spaghettini.

This dish can be refrigerated for 1 or 2 days.

FISH SALAD A LA PAPA

SERVES 4

My beautiful friend Jeannete Bennett, now deceased, contributed this recipe many years ago for our fund-raising North End Union Italian Cookbook. *She said it was brought here from Italy by one of her Sicilian friends.*

It was customary to soak store-bought fish in milk to refresh it before cooking. You may want to try this yourself. For added flavor you should precook the mushrooms the day before. Boil them for a couple of minutes and marinate them in enough red wine to cover. It is not necessary to refrigerate them. Marinating the mushrooms gives a wonderful zip to the salad.

2 pounds cod or haddock fillets

1 cup milk

½ cup water

1 head Boston lettuce

1 garlic clove, chopped

1 cup Sicilian dry-cured black olives, pitted

½ cup sliced almonds

1 large red onion, sliced in rings

¼ cup olive oil

Juice of 2 lemons

Salt and freshly ground pepper to taste

1 cup button mushrooms, marinated in red wine

1 teaspoon chopped fresh parsley

1. Boil the fish in a mixture of the milk and water for 5–8 minutes, or until the fish is flaky.

2. Cool the fish and cut it into 2-inch squares. Carefully place on a decorative platter garnished with lettuce leaves.

3. Add the chopped garlic, olives, and almonds. Top with the onion rings.

4. Pour the olive oil and lemon juice evenly over fish. Sprinkle with salt and pepper to taste.

5. Arrange the mushrooms around the fish and sprinkle the whole dish with parsley.

PERIWINKLES ALLA PALERMO

PERIWINKLES IN SAUCE

SERVES 6

This is an old, rare recipe, one that has been in our family for quite some time. It is adaptable to any shellfish but is especially good with periwinkles. You will likely find these critters in old fish markets, climbing in huge barrels, especially around holiday time. Buy only live snails with the heads out of the shell. When I was very young, we used to buy our periwinkles freshly boiled and served in paper bags. Of course, we always had our safety pins with us to pry them from their shells. This dish is served as an appetizer and will keep everyone busy while you're preparing other foods.

3 pounds fresh periwinkles (or snails)

Salt

Olive oil

1 small onion, chopped

1 garlic clove, chopped

½ cup tomato paste

1 pint hot water

Salt and freshly ground pepper to taste

Pinch of dried red pepper flakes

1 tablespoon chopped fresh parsley

1. Place snails in a medium-size deep pot and cover with water. Rub salt around inside of pot above the water line to keep snails from crawling out. Soak for 30 minutes, then wash thoroughly several times in fresh water. Drain well in a plastic colander to prevent shells from cracking.

2. Using the same deep pot, heat enough olive oil to cover the bottom. Add chopped onion and garlic and cook on low heat for 5 minutes. Add tomato paste, stirring constantly with a wooden spoon. Add a pint of hot water and mix well.

3. Gently add snails to sauce and simmer for 10 minutes.

4. Add salt and pepper to taste, a pinch of red pepper flakes, and parsley; stir well and cover. Simmer for another 20 minutes.

5. Remove to deep bowls and serve hot with sauce. To remove meat from shells, use toothpicks or oyster forks.

SCUNGILLI

SERVES 6

Conches are big snails. The meat has a sweet taste similar to scallops. Conches are usually cooked for salads, but they may also be served cooked in a sauce and eaten from their shells, similar to periwinkles.

4 large conches

1 garlic clove

Juice of 1 lemon, or 3 tablespoons white wine vinegar

¼ cup extra-virgin olive oil

Salt and freshly ground pepper to taste

1 tablespoon chopped fresh parsley

Pinch of oregano (optional)

1. Select fresh conches and scrub with a vegetable brush until all sand is removed.

2. Place conches in a large pan and cover with briskly boiling water. Cover the pan tightly and cook slowly over low heat for 1 hour or until half the body protrudes from the shell.

3. Remove from the heat and run cold water into the pan.

4. Take the meat out of the shells with a large fork, and cut off the hard outer cover. Cut the meat into ½-inch slices and cover with dressing made from the remaining ingredients. Toss until the meat is well-covered. Serve hot or cold.

SCUNGILLI EN BIANCO

SCUNGILLI SALAD

SERVES 4–6

Scungilli are usually prepared at Lent or at other times that a meatless meal is desired. Simply serve them as an appetizer or atop an antipasto. All you need is some delicious Italian bread and a fine wine to complete the menu. Don't forget that the meat has to be removed from the shell. Simply pull it out with a large safety pin or another pointed utensil. You may use canned scungilli (sometimes labeled as conch) if you prefer.

8 scungilli in shells or 2 (8-ounce) cans conch

2 garlic cloves

2 celery stalks, thinly sliced

2 teaspoons chopped fresh parsley

½ cup olive oil

¼ cup lemon juice

Sprinkle of paprika

Pinch of dried red pepper flakes

10 Sicilian dry-cured black olives, pitted and halved

Salt and freshly ground pepper to taste

2 hot or sweet vinegar peppers

Lettuce

1. Scrub conch shells thoroughly with a stiff brush under hot water.

2. Place in a large pot of boiling water, enough to cover, and cook on medium heat for about 1 hour, adding more water if needed.

3. Remove the pot from the heat and rinse the shells with cold water until cooled.

4. Pull the meat from the shells with a large pin, pointed knife, or fork. Slice meat lengthwise, using a small sharp knife or razor blade.

5. Place meat in a bowl and toss with remaining ingredients, except for the lettuce, adjusting seasonings if needed. Cover and refrigerate overnight.

6. Arrange salad on a serving platter lined with lettuce, and drizzle with additional olive oil if needed.

VEGETABLES

CAULIFLOWER WITH ANCHOVY SAUCE

SERVES 4–6

When you shop for cauliflower, avoid loose, spread-out heads. That is a sign of overmatura-tion. Choose compact white heads with fresh-looking green leaves and creamy white or purple curd. This recipe is a Sicilian dish—very popular and very economical. It is customary to undercook cauliflower to enhance its unique flavor.

1 head cauliflower, rinsed, trimmed, and left whole

Freshly squeezed lemon juice

1 stick (½ cup) unsalted butter

1 small garlic clove, crushed

3 anchovy fillets, well drained and patted dry

1 hard-boiled egg

1 teaspoon small capers, rinsed and drained

1 teaspoon finely chopped fresh parsley

1. Using a deep pot with a cover, steam whole cauliflower in 1 inch of boiling water. Add 1 tablespoon lemon juice to water to help keep cauliflower white. When water comes to a boil, simmer 10 minutes uncovered, then cover and simmer about 15 minutes more. Drain well and reserve to a deep serving dish.

2. Heat butter in a small saucepan over medium-low heat. When foam subsides, add garlic and sauté for 1 minute.

3. Stir in anchovy fillets and mash with a wooden spoon until dissolved. Remove from heat and drain. Reserve.

4. Separate yolk from white of hard-boiled egg. Finely chop white and set aside. Press yolk through a sieve with a wooden spoon and reserve.

5. Just before serving cauliflower, quickly reheat anchovy sauce over low heat. Stir in chopped egg white, 1 teaspoon lemon juice, and capers.

6. Pour hot anchovy sauce over top of reserved cauliflower. Sprinkle with egg yolk and parsley.

7. Serve immediately. For individual serv-ings, cut flowers down to stem, put on plates, and spoon with sauce.

BAKED STUFFED FINGER PEPPERS

DITIELLI

SERVES 2–3

Serve with lasagne or manicotti, chicken or turkey. These peppers also make a delicious sandwich the next day with any white poultry meat.

6 green Italian finger peppers

1 cup fresh soft bread crumbs

2 garlic cloves, chopped

1 tablespoon chopped fresh parsley

¼ cup freshly grated Parmesan cheese

Salt and freshly ground pepper to taste

Olive oil

1. Remove the stems and seeds from the peppers, leaving a small opening.

2. Mix together the bread crumbs, garlic, parsley, cheese, salt, and pepper. Drizzle olive oil lightly over the mixture until it is well coated.

3. Using fingers, gently push the bread stuffing into the pepper cavity.

4. Place the peppers on a baking sheet. Drizzle with more olive oil and sprinkle with salt.

5. Bake in a preheated 450°F oven (use the middle rack) for about 20 minutes or until nicely browned. Do not let the bread stuffing burn during the cooking process. If it gets too brown, lightly tent the pan with foil until the peppers are cooked and tender.

6. Let the peppers rest at least 30 minutes before transferring them to a serving platter. They will keep 2–3 days in the refrigerator.

FRESH BREAD CRUMBS

To make fresh bread crumbs, use day-old Italian bread. Cut any leftover pieces into small chunks. Put in the blender a few chunks at a time, and blend just until you have light and fluffy crumbs. Coarse crumbs are good for stuffings (such as for peppers and artichokes); fine crumbs are good for coating meats or fish. The crumbs can be frozen in a plastic bag.

BAKED STUFFED BELL PEPPERS
SICILIAN STYLE

SERVES 8

This recipe makes a substantial meal for lunch or an appetizer for company. The addition of anchovies and olives makes them quite spicy, so adjust the ingredients to your liking. A scoop of tomato sauce on top of the peppers wouldn't hurt, either.

2 large green bell peppers

2 large red bell peppers

3 cups fresh bread crumbs (use French or Italian bread)

2 garlic cloves, finely chopped

1 (2-ounce) can flat anchovies, rinsed and chopped (reserve oil)

6 tablespoons capers, rinsed in cold water and finely chopped

8 Sicilian dry-cured black olives, pitted and finely chopped

¼ cup finely chopped fresh Italian parsley

¼ cup freshly grated Parmesan cheese

Salt and freshly ground black pepper to taste

Olive oil

1 (4-ounce) can tomato sauce (optional)

1. Cut the peppers in half, lengthwise, and remove stems and seeds.

2. In a large bowl, combine the bread crumbs, garlic, anchovies, capers, olives, parsley, Parmesan, salt, and pepper. Combine ¼ cup olive and anchovy oil. Slowly drizzle over crumb mixture, tossing lightly until the crumbs are slightly moistened but not wet.

3. Spoon the stuffing into the pepper halves and arrange them in a single layer in an oiled baking dish. Pour tomato sauce over peppers if using.

4. Bake in the middle of a preheated 400°F oven for about 30 minutes or until the peppers are tender, but not limp, and the stuffing is golden brown and crusty.

5. Let peppers cool to room temperature before serving.

ZUCCHINI STEW

SERVES 4

You will never see zucchini stew on a restaurant menu. But if you do ask for it, you will be considered a true and traditional lover of Italian peasant cooking.

⅓ cup olive oil

½ pound ground beef *

1 small onion, chopped

2 garlic cloves, chopped

1 small green pepper, chopped

2 celery stalks, finely chopped

2 pounds small zucchini, washed and cut in ¼-inch rounds

2 medium potatoes, thinly sliced

¾ cup canned tomatoes, or 1 tablespoon tomato paste

Salt, freshly ground pepper, and dried red pepper flakes to taste

1½ cups water

Freshly grated Parmesan cheese (reserve)

*Vegetarians may omit the beef and still be pleased with the result. The ingredients may need to be slightly altered to taste.

1. Using a large skillet, heat the olive oil. Sauté the ground beef, onion, and garlic in the oil until browned.

2. Transfer the beef into a large soup pot and add the remaining ingredients (except the cheese).

3. Cover the pot and cook over medium-low heat for 30 minutes or until the zucchini is tender. Be sure not to overcook the zucchini. Serve in soup bowls and sprinkle with Parmesan cheese if desired.

TO ROAST LEFTOVER VEGETABLES

Sprinkle scraps of parsley, lettuce, escarole, onions, or other leftover vegetables with olive oil and salt to taste. Broil until crispy brown but not burned. Serve on top of any cooked meat as a garnish.

ZUCCHINI FRITTATA

ZUCCHINI OMELETTE

SERVES 4

My father loved preparing the eggs for an Italian omelette. He would use an old-fashioned hand-beater and crank and crank until the eggs were so frothy, they almost jumped out of the bowl.

8 eggs

½ teaspoon salt

Freshly ground black pepper to taste

¼ cup freshly grated Parmesan cheese

2 medium zucchini, thinly sliced

2 tablespoons chopped fresh parsley

2 tablespoons chopped fresh basil

3 tablespoons olive oil

1. Beat the eggs with the salt and pepper. Stir in the Parmesan cheese, zucchini, parsley, and basil.

2. Preheat the broiler.

3. Heat the oil in a 10½-inch ovenproof skillet. Add the eggs and cook undisturbed over low heat for about 10 minutes. Carefully lift the edge to check the bottom—it should be golden brown.

4. Place the skillet under the broiler for 30 seconds until top is golden. Cut into wedges. Serve hot or at room temperature.

BATTER-FRIED ZUCCHINI STICKS

SERVES 4–6

Many popular restaurants feature this dish on their menus.

3 6-inch-long zucchini

½ cup semolina or all-purpose flour

2 teaspoons cornstarch

1 large egg

½ cup ice water

Olive oil for deep frying

Salt

Dried oregano

1. Wipe the zucchini with a paper towel. Do not peel. Cut off the ends and discard. Cut the zucchini lengthwise into ¼-inch-thick strips, similar to carrot sticks.

2. In a medium-size bowl, stir together the flour and cornstarch.

3. In a small bowl, beat the egg until foamy. Add the water and beat to blend. Add the egg mixture to the flour mixture and stir just until moistened. The batter will be lumpy, but do not stir it again.

4. Heat 2 inches of olive oil in a heavy skillet. Dip the zucchini sticks into the batter and place them, uncrowded, in the hot oil. When they have nicely browned on one side, turn them over to brown the other side.

5. When the sticks are golden brown on both sides, transfer them to paper towels to drain. Sprinkle with salt and oregano. Serve hot as an appetizer or as a side dish.

BAKED ZUCCHINI CASSEROLE

SERVES 6

This is another delicious appetizer or party dish. It can be assembled ahead of time and baked just before serving.

6 small or 2 large firm zucchini

2 eggs, beaten

¼ cup fresh bread crumbs

1 small onion, grated

Salt and freshly ground black pepper to taste

¼ cup melted butter or margarine

¼ cup freshly grated Parmesan or Romano cheese

1. Wash the zucchini, cut off tips, and slice in ¼-inch rounds. Cook in a small amount of salted water until soft. Drain well and mash coarsely.

2. In a large bowl, combine the beaten eggs, bread crumbs, grated onion, salt, and pepper. Mix well. Toss with the melted butter until the crumbs are coated. Add the zucchini and mix gently.

3. Transfer the mixture to a baking dish and sprinkle with the cheese. Bake in a preheated 350°F oven for 30 minutes.

4. Serve at room temperature.

FRIED ZUCCHINI BLOSSOMS

SERVES 4

If you want to impress your friends with something exotic, here is the recipe for you. And the best part is that the preparation is simple. Your biggest challenge will be finding zucchini blossoms. These are the flowers that grow on a zucchini plant, so find someone who grows zucchini and you'll be all set.

24 zucchini blossoms

1¾ cups flour

Pinch of salt

3 teaspoons baking soda

2 eggs, slightly beaten

¾ cup milk

¼ cup water

6 cups vegetable oil

1. Do not wash the flowers. Clean by carefully removing the pistils.

2. Combine the flour, salt, baking soda, eggs, milk, and water. Stir until a smooth batter is obtained.

3. In a heavy frying pan, heat the oil to boiling. Dip each flower into the batter, then carefully spoon into the hot oil. Fry the flowers until they are golden brown on both sides. Remove with a slotted spoon and drain on paper towels.

4. Sprinkle with salt and serve hot. These blossoms are best when served immediately.

FRIED RICOTTA-STUFFED
ZUCCHINI BLOSSOMS

SERVES 4

Trattoria Il Panino is a famous restaurant of twenty-five years in the North End. Its founder, Frank DePasquale, hails from the San Giuseppe region of Naples, Italy. He brought back this exotic and hard to come by recipe and happily shares it with us.

8 large zucchini blossoms

4 cups all-purpose flour

6 ounces beer or sparkling water

Salt and freshly ground pepper to taste

¼ cup ricotta cheese, well drained

1 tablespoon grated Parmesan cheese

1 egg yolk

6 cups vegetable oil

1. Do not wash the flowers. Clean by carefully removing the pistils.

2. In a medium-size bowl, slowly sift the flour into the beer, beating well with a wooden spoon until the mixture has the consistency of a smooth pancake batter. Add a sprinkle of salt.

3. In a small bowl, mix together the drained ricotta, Parmesan cheese, egg yolk, and salt and pepper to taste.

4. Gently open each blossom and, using a small spoon or small pastry bag, carefully fill the blossoms with a little ricotta mixture, tucking over the petal tops so it won't escape.

5. Dip each flower in batter to coat completely.

6. In a heavy deep pot, heat the oil to boiling. Quickly spoon in the coated blossoms and fry until golden brown on both sides. Using a slotted spoon, remove to paper towels to drain.

7. Sprinkle blossoms with salt and pepper to taste and serve while still hot.

ZUCCHINI FRITTERS

SERVES 4–6

This is a very old recipe that is used often in our homes. Zucchini is always available and is inexpensive.

2 eggs

2 cups coarsely grated zucchini (use large holes of grater)

½ cup flour

½ cup fine, dry bread crumbs

2 tablespoons freshly grated Parmesan cheese

Salt and freshly ground pepper to taste

1 cup olive oil

1. In a large bowl, beat eggs thoroughly with a wire whisk.

2. Add remaining ingredients, except oil, and mix well. Let mixture stand 20–30 minutes.

3. Meanwhile, heat oil in a medium-size, heavy skillet.

4. Drop zucchini batter by the tablespoons into the hot oil, bearing down with a fork until slightly flattened. Fry on each side until golden brown.

5. Remove to a platter lined with paper towels and serve warm.

TOMATOES AND GRAPES

Because my grandparents came from different regions of Italy, my mother was able to combine both regions and developed her own style of cooking. From my grandfather's farm in Revere, Massachusetts, came fresh tomatoes and grapes from which my father enjoyed rich homemade wine. On weekends my grandfather would cultivate his land and grow apples, pears, and tomatoes. This gave him great pleasure and a chance to breathe in the fresh air after working in a dreary shoe factory all week. At harvest time he would generously share his bounty with the entire family. It was the finest of all foods, simple and fresh.

EGGPLANT PARMIGIANA WITH MEAT SAUCE

SERVES 8–10

This dish is a favorite in my home. A duplicate of my mother's, it is a sure hit. Make the best sandwiches in the world with it, use it for an appetizer or with pasta, or carry it along when picnicking. It also makes an exciting housewarming gift. Eggplant has many uses, and once you get a system, you will find it easy to prepare.

2 small, dark, firm eggplants

1½ cups oil, or more as needed

Flour

4 eggs, beaten

1 recipe Quick Meat Sauce (see page 66) or a plain marinara sauce

¾ cup sliced or shredded mozzarella cheese (optional)

1 cup freshly grated Parmesan or Romano cheese

Chopped fresh parsley for garnish

1. Remove the stem from the eggplants. Cut the eggplants crosswise into slices about ¼ inch thick. Do not remove the skin, as this helps to hold the eggplant together.

2. Heat the oil in an electric frying pan on the highest heat, or use a large heavy skillet.

3. Dust each eggplant slice with flour, dip into the beaten eggs (if you prefer a thicker coating, you can dip the slices into coarse bread crumbs after the egg wash), and fry on both sides until golden brown. (I like to use tongs to handle the eggplant.) Use more oil as needed. Drain on paper towels.

4. Line a 2½-quart shallow baking dish with a little of the tomato sauce. Arrange a layer of eggplant slices over it. Cover with a layer of mozzarella cheese, more sauce, and a sprinkling of grated Parmesan or Romano cheese. Repeat the layers until all ingredients are used. Pour leftover egg, if any, around the edges of the eggplant.

5. Bake in a preheated 350°F oven for 30 minutes or until the eggplant is tender and golden on top.

6. Garnish with chopped parsley and serve. For best results, let eggplant rest for at least 30 minutes before you cut it.

CRISPY EGGPLANT SANDWICHES

SERVES 4–5

This recipe allows you to cook the eggplant so it doesn't absorb all the oil it normally would. Serve between two slices of crusty French bread. Be sure to select heavy eggplants with shiny taut skin and flesh that is neither too hard nor too soft. They should yield to soft pressure when pressed with a finger, but not form an indentation.

1 medium eggplant

4–5 slices provolone cheese, about ¼ inch thick

1 teaspoon oregano

2 eggs

2 cups fine bread crumbs

½ cup grated Parmesan cheese

½ cup finely chopped fresh parsley

Olive oil

8–10 slices crusty French bread

1. Preheat oven to 375°F.

2. Slice eggplant into ½-inch rounds; you should have about 8–10 pieces. Do not remove skin.

3. Place a slice of cheese on half the eggplant slices. Sprinkle with oregano and top with remaining eggplant slices to form "sandwiches."

4. Beat the eggs in a wide medium-size bowl. Dip the sandwiches in the egg and reserve.

5. Combine the bread crumbs, Parmesan cheese, and parsley on a wide plate. Dip the sandwiches in the crumb mixture, turning on both sides and slightly bearing down to allow crumbs to firmly adhere (use a large fork to do this).

6. Place on a baking sheet and lightly drizzle each sandwich with about 1 teaspoon olive oil. Bake in the preheated oven for 20–25 minutes or until browned and crusty. Remove from the oven and slice in half.

7. Serve between 2 slices of bread while still warm.

I bet you didn't know that there are male and female eggplants! The males are preferred, as they are less bitter and have fewer seeds. Male eggplants have a rounded bottom with a smooth stem area. Female eggplants have a narrow bottom and an indented stem area.

WARM RED LENTILS

SERVES 4

These lentils are very good with roasted cod or any soft meat dish such as lamb. I like to use white pepper with a lot of my recipes, and this is one of them.

1 cup dry red lentils

1 tablespoon olive oil

¼ cup minced red onion

¼ cup peeled and finely diced celery

¼ cup peeled and finely diced carrots

2 cups chicken stock

Salt and freshly ground pepper to taste

1. Rinse lentils and pick over for stones.

2. Heat olive oil in a saucepan with a cover, using medium heat. Add onion, celery, and carrot and sauté until tender, about 5 minutes.

3. Add lentils and toss well to coat. Add chicken stock and simmer, covered, until lentils are tender, about 20 minutes. (At this point you may add more stock if mixture seems too dry.)

4. Season with salt and pepper to taste. Keep warm until ready to serve.

BROCCOLI AND CAULIFLOWER FRITTATA

VEGETABLES FRIED IN AN EGG BATTER

SERVES 4–6

This recipe makes a great appetizer or side dish.

½ **medium head of broccoli**

½ **medium head of cauliflower**

3 **eggs**

Salt and freshly ground black pepper to taste

1½ **cups fresh fine bread crumbs**

½ **cup freshly grated Parmesan cheese**

Olive or vegetable oil

1 **large garlic clove**

Lemon wedges for garnish

1. Wash and trim the broccoli and cauliflower. Cut them into florets. Blanch them separately in salted boiling water for about 4 minutes or until tender. Drain well and cool.

2. Beat the eggs in a shallow bowl with salt and pepper.

3. Combine the bread crumbs and grated cheese in a pie plate or shallow dish.

4. Dip the florets in the eggs, shaking off the excess. Coat with the bread crumb mixture and shake off the excess. Reserve.

5. Pour oil into a large heavy skillet, to about 1 inch deep. Heat over medium heat. Add the garlic and sauté until golden, about 1 minute. Discard the garlic.

6. Fry the breaded florets in batches. Turn them over as they cook, frying until they are golden brown on all sides, about 3 minutes. Adjust the heat as necessary to keep the oil sizzling.

7. Transfer the florets to a baking pan lined with paper towels to drain. Keep them warm in the oven at the lowest setting until all of them have been fried. Serve with lemon wedges.

TANGERINE PEELS

Our grandparents visited us almost every night. For a nighttime snack, my grandfather would transform any leftover food into a regional peasant treat. With polenta, he would put some olive oil in a cast-iron pan, and when it was red hot, he would plop in and arrange the polenta, using a wooden spoon to press it down until if formed the shape of a pie. When it turned golden brown, he'd flip it over until both sides were brown and crusty. Then it would go onto a plate, where he'd use a string to slice it into wedges. Each wedge he'd coat with butter, grated black pepper, and freshly grated cheese—this we loved!

On other nights he would sprinkle the tops of unpeeled potato halves with lots of salt and pepper, place them on the sides of the open flame of the cast-iron stove, and cook them until dark brown and soft. We would walk around the house nibbling on this hot, tasty treat. On holidays he would roast slit chestnuts in the same manner. Tangerine peels would sit on the back of the stove and release such fragrant smells, our own potpourri.

Grandfather came to our house so often that he became like a second father, watching out for us. When my sister and I went out at night to the local playground, he would follow us. If he saw us talking to any boys, he'd come after us, screaming in Italian for us to get home. I guess this was the only way he knew to keep us good kids, which was all he cared about. Our hearts told us it was because he loved us, but we remained surprised each time he did this, and would hide under any nearby car if our friends warned us he was coming. Lipstick was a no-no, and chewing gum was even worse! How lucky we were to be so very protected.

BROCCI DI RABE CON FAGIOLI

BROCCOLI RABE WITH BEANS

SERVES 3–4

Brocci di rabe, or broccoli rabe, is a slightly bitter vegetable in the broccoli family. It is now a very popular item in our local restaurants, as well as in our homes. Just cook it with the water that remains on the leaves from washing. Although the rabe is wonderful when cooked alone, I like to add beans to the dish. I use canned cannellini or red beans, but even black beans are wonderful.

1 bunch broccoli rabe

7–10 garlic cloves, thickly slivered

Dried red pepper flakes to taste

Olive oil

Salt and freshly ground pepper to taste

1 (19-ounce) can beans (cannellini, red beans, or black beans) (optional)

1. Trim the broccoli rabe by cutting off the thick, dark leaves. Make several slits in the bottoms of the stems. Cut rabe in half, rinse in cold water, and drain.

2. Using a medium-size heavy saucepan, sauté half of the garlic and a pinch of red pepper flakes in enough oil to cover the bottom of the pan. When garlic is slightly browned but not burned, turn the heat on high and add the drained broccoli rabe a handful at a time, turning each batch over before adding the next.

3. Sauté for a few minutes, turning often, adding salt and pepper to taste.

4. Shut off heat, cover, and steam for at least 10 minutes or until tender.

5. Remove broccoli rabe to a warm platter and return pan and its juices to stove. Add remaining slivered garlic and a pinch of red pepper flakes and sauté a couple of minutes.

6. Add a whole can of beans with liquid to pan (optional) and let simmer until heated thoroughly. Adjust seasonings and pour immediately over broccoli rabe.

7. Serve immediately with crusty Italian bread.

FUSILLI CON BROCCI DI RABE

SERVES 4

Once you acquire a taste for broccoli rabe (like my grandchildren have), it will be included in many of your recipes for a wonderful, healthy meal. In this recipe the pasta can be cooked in advance and then tossed with the wonderful lemony garlic and raisin sauce. Naturally you will need plenty of freshly grated Parmesan and fresh black pepper. We like ours on the dry side, but you can add some of the reserved pasta water to your taste.

½ **pound fusilli pasta**

1 bunch broccoli rabe

¾ **cup olive oil**

3 garlic cloves, thickly slivered

Dried red pepper flakes to taste

Salt and freshly ground pepper to taste

½ **lemon**

½ **cup golden raisins**

Freshly grated Parmesan cheese

1. Cook fusilli in boiling salted water according to package directions. Strain, and reserve some of the cooking water.

2. Trim the broccoli rabe by cutting off the thick, dark leaves. Make several slits in the bottoms of the stems. Cut rabe in half, rinse in cold water, and drain.

3. Meanwhile, slowly heat the olive oil in a large heavy skillet. Add garlic slivers and red pepper flakes and simmer until golden. Raise heat and let oil get very hot.

4. Carefully add strained, wet rabe to the hot oil. It is best to do this over the kitchen sink to contain the splatter. Return to high heat and stir constantly until slightly wilted. Add salt and pepper to taste and the juice of ½ lemon and toss well.

5. Shut off heat, cover, and let sit for 10 minutes, or until rabe is tender. Return heat to high and add the golden raisins, tossing well.

6. Add cooked, strained pasta and toss until mixture is hot and well coated with the garlicky sauce. Adjust seasonings. Add some of the cooking water if a soupy sauce is desired.

7. Place pasta in a large serving bowl and sprinkle with lots of freshly grated Parmesan cheese.

LIMA BEANS ITALIAN STYLE

SERVES 3–4

Serve these beans with any meat or fish dish. If you wish, you may refrigerate them for several days.

3 cups fresh, cooked lima beans, or
    1 (16-ounce) package frozen lima beans

1 garlic clove, chopped

¼ cup olive oil

⅔ cup crushed tomatoes or squeezed
    whole plum tomatoes

Pinch each of dried oregano, red pepper
    flakes, and mint

Salt and freshly ground black pepper
    to taste

1 cup hot water

1 celery stalk, chopped

Freshly grated Parmesan cheese

1. Drain the beans well or, if using frozen beans, defrost.

2. In a medium saucepan, sauté the garlic in the olive oil. Add the tomatoes and seasonings and simmer for 5 minutes, stirring often.

3. Add the water and let the sauce come to a boil. Add the beans and celery, stir well, and let boil gently for a minute or two. Taste and add more seasonings, if desired.

4. Cover and gently boil for about 30 minutes or until the beans are tender. (Do not overcook.)

5. Sprinkle with grated cheese and serve.

Before starting this recipe, cook the beans in unsalted water for at least an hour. It would be best to do this well in advance, or even the day before.

VERDURA

DANDELION GREENS

SERVES 4

You can substitute any leafy vegetable, such as cabbage, spinach, or chicory, for the dandelion greens in this recipe.

1 pound tender young dandelion greens

1 large baking potato

Salt

2–3 tablespoons extra-virgin olive oil

1 garlic clove, minced

Freshly ground black pepper to taste

Juice of ½ lemon or to taste

½ teaspoon sugar (optional)

1. Remove the stems from the dandelion greens and wash the leaves. Cut the leaves into ¼-inch strips, cutting across the leaf.

2. Peel the potato and cut it into ½-inch cubes. Place the potato cubes in cold salted water, bring to a boil, reduce the heat, and gently simmer for 3–4 minutes or until tender. Refresh the potatoes under cold water and drain.

3. Meanwhile, cook the dandelion greens in rapidly boiling salted water for 1–2 minutes or until tender. Refresh under cold water and drain. (The recipe can be prepared to this stage up to 12 hours before serving.)

4. Just before serving, heat the olive oil in a skillet over medium heat. Add the garlic and cook for 10 seconds, then add the dandelion greens and potatoes. Add salt and pepper to taste.

5. Sauté the vegetables for 2 minutes or until thoroughly heated. Add lemon juice to taste. If the greens are still bitter, add a small pinch of sugar.

STUFFED ESCAROLE

SERVES 4

Escarole should be thoroughly washed until all dirt particles are removed. For a nice crispness, soak it in hot water for a few seconds, then wash it in cold water, and finish washing under even colder water.

1 whole escarole, well washed

1 cup coarsely ground fresh bread crumbs

6 Sicilian dry-cured black olives, pitted and chopped

4 garlic cloves

¼ cup freshly grated Parmesan cheese

2 tablespoons chopped fresh parsley

Salt and freshly ground pepper to taste

Olive oil

½ cup water

Dried red pepper flakes (optional)

1. Drain well-washed escarole in a colander.

2. Prepare stuffing in a medium bowl. Mix together the bread crumbs, olives, 2 finely chopped garlic cloves, cheese, parsley, and salt and pepper to taste. Slowly drizzle crumb mixture with olive oil until slightly glistening.

3. Stuff bread crumb mixture into each leaf of drained escarole until stuffing is used up. Tie escarole around the middle with string to keep the stuffing from falling out.

4. Using a large pot, add enough olive oil to generously cover the bottom of the pot. Heat oil on medium heat until warm.

5. Place escarole in the pot, pour ½ cup boiling water over it, and salt to taste. Add other 2 cloves of garlic, cut in chunks, and some red pepper flakes (optional). Cover and cook until tender.

6. Remove from pan and let cool; remove string and cut in thick slices. Serve warm as a side dish with any meat or fish.

ESCAROLE SAUTÉ

SERVES 2–4

This is a simple, easy recipe that can be served hot or cold, as a side dish, or with beans for a delicious lunch. In some regions of Italy, cooks like to fry some bread crumbs separately in olive oil until crusty brown and add these to the top of the escarole before serving.

2 pounds escarole

2 tablespoons olive oil

2 tablespoons vegetable oil

3–4 large garlic cloves, chopped

¼ cup fine, dry bread crumbs

Salt and freshly ground pepper to taste

Dried red pepper flakes to taste

1. Trim the escarole and wash it thoroughly but quickly.

2. Bring a large pot of water to a boil and blanch the escarole for 5 minutes. Drain the escarole and chop coarsely.

3. Using a heavy skillet, heat the oils on medium heat. Sauté the garlic until browned, add bread crumbs, and cook until crusty brown.

4. Raise heat to high and add the escarole, turning it over a few times. Add salt and pepper and red pepper flakes to taste.

5. Transfer to a serving platter and pour hot oil on top. Serve hot or warm.

RICE-STUFFED CABBAGE LEAVES

SERVES 6

I have made this recipe on many occasions and it has never failed to be delicious. Serve as an appetizer kept at room temperature, or for a light dinner with some crusty garlic bread.

1 head cabbage

2 cups cooked rice

1 large onion, chopped

1 garlic clove, minced

½ cup chopped celery

1 pound ground beef

¾ cup ketchup

Salt and freshly ground pepper to taste

4 (6-ounce) can tomato juice, heated

½ cup vegetable oil

3 cups canned beef broth, heated

1. Trim cabbage and remove core.

2. Drop the cabbage into a pot of boiling water and separate the leaves. Boil for about 5 minutes or until leaves are slightly limp but not mushy. Drain and gently rinse with cold water.

3. In a medium-size mixing bowl, lightly toss together the cooked rice, onion, garlic, celery, ground beef, ketchup, and salt and pepper to taste.

4. Place a heaping tablespoon of the stuffing in the center of each cabbage leaf, then fold and tuck edges envelope style. Repeat, using all the cabbage leaves and filling.

5. As cabbage bundles are being folded, place seam-side down in a deep pan large enough to snugly accommodate them.

6. Pour in the tomato juice, vegetable oil, and beef broth. Slowly bring to a boil and cook until tender, 20–25 minutes.

7. Place on a serving platter, cover with hot sauce, and serve.

MARINATED MUSHROOMS AND GREEN BEANS

SERVES 4–6

This dish can be served as a side dish or over spinach or lettuce salad, tossed with croutons and grated cheese.

2 garlic cloves, chopped

¼ teaspoon grated lemon peel

¼ cup freshly squeezed lemon juice

¾ cup olive oil

1 tablespoon chopped fresh parsley

Pinch of dried oregano

Salt and freshly ground pepper to taste

½ pound fresh green beans, tips snapped off

2 cups sliced fresh mushrooms

1 tablespoon sliced scallions

1. Combine the first seven ingredients and mix well. Set the dressing aside.

2. Steam the green beans until tender but not soft, then plunge them into cold water. Drain well.

3. Mix the beans with the mushrooms and scallions. Pour the dressing over the vegetables and let them marinate about 2 hours.

COOKING VEGETABLES

When cooking vegetables that grow under the ground, such as onions, potatoes, and turnips, cover the pan with a lid. Cook uncovered all vegetables that grow above the ground.

MARINATED MUSHROOMS

SERVES 2–4

Serve these mushrooms as an appetizer or put them over a fresh garden salad.

¾ pound small, white fresh mushrooms

¼ cup freshly squeezed lemon juice

½ teaspoon Dijon-style mustard

¼ teaspoon salt

¼ teaspoon freshly ground black pepper

½ teaspoon dried oregano

½ cup olive oil

2 garlic cloves, halved

1. Wipe the mushrooms with paper towels. Trim the stems.

2. In a large jar with a tight-fitting lid (a mayonnaise jar will do), combine the lemon juice, mustard, salt, and pepper.

3. Stir until the mustard is blended with the juice and the salt has dissolved. Add the oregano, olive oil, and garlic. Cover the jar tightly and shake well.

4. Add the mushrooms, cover, and shake again. Marinate in the refrigerator for at least 4 hours, shaking occasionally.

5. Drain the mushrooms before serving. If you are serving them as an appetizer, put them in a small bowl and serve with toothpicks.

BAKED RICOTTA-STUFFED MUSHROOMS

SERVES 5

These mushrooms are an excellent appetizer or side dish for a meat meal.

10 large fresh mushrooms

¼ cup fresh bread crumbs

2 garlic cloves, pressed

1 tablespoon chopped fresh parsley

2 medium eggs

½ cup ricotta cheese

2 tablespoons freshly grated Parmesan cheese

Salt and freshly ground black pepper to taste

2 tablespoons olive oil

1. Wipe the mushrooms with paper towels. Remove the stems and finely chop them.

2. Mix the chopped mushroom stems with the bread crumbs, garlic, parsley, eggs, ricotta, grated cheese, and salt and pepper to taste.

3. Fill each mushroom cap with the stuffing. Place in a shallow ovenproof pan.

4. Lightly drizzle olive oil over each mushroom. Bake on the highest rack in a preheated 350°F oven for 20 minutes. Let sit for 10 minutes before serving.

PORTOBELLO MUSHROOM SAUTÉ

SERVES 3–4

Mushrooms are considered a culinary treat. Whether added alongside a meat dish or served over linguine, risotto, or a simple salad, they play an important role in Italian cooking.

6 portobello mushrooms, stems intact

Flour to coat mushrooms

Salt and freshly ground pepper to taste

¼ cup unsalted butter

2 shallots, chopped

Pinch of tarragon

½ cup marsala wine, or more if desired

Chopped fresh parsley

1. Lightly wipe the mushrooms with a damp paper towel. Thickly slice the mushrooms lengthwise.

2. Put some flour on a shallow plate and add salt and pepper to taste.

3. Dredge the mushrooms in the flour, shake excess, and reserve.

4. Melt the butter in a large, heavy skillet over medium heat. Place the mushrooms in the skillet and lightly sauté on one side until nicely golden.

5. Gently turn the mushrooms over and add chopped shallots and tarragon. Cook for 1 minute more and remove to a platter.

6. On high heat, quickly pour the marsala into the skillet and boil briefly until liquor has slightly evaporated. Return the mushrooms to the skillet and cook briefly to blend flavors.

7. Transfer the mushrooms to a platter, pour the sauce over them, and sprinkle with parsley. Serve immediately as a side dish or appetizer along with other vegetables.

RISOTTO AI FUNGHI

RICE WITH FRESH MUSHROOMS

SERVES 4–6

Risotto requires a little more effort than most of my recipes, but it makes a wonderful meal in itself or a side dish to accompany any meats or fish. This risotto recipe is richer than most.

3 tablespoons finely chopped onion

1 garlic clove, peeled

3 tablespoons olive oil

1 tablespoon chopped fresh parsley

1 tablespoon chopped celery

Salt and freshly ground pepper to taste

10 ounces fresh mushrooms, thinly sliced

1 cup milk

1½ cups Italian arborio rice

¼ cup cream

2 (14½-ounce) cans chicken broth, heated

1 tablespoon butter

1 cup freshly grated Parmesan cheese

1. In a casserole dish, sauté the onion and garlic in olive oil over medium-high heat. Add the parsley, celery, and salt and pepper. Discard the garlic when it becomes pale brown.

2. After about 5 minutes, add the mushrooms and cook over low heat. Stir frequently and add the milk to keep the mushrooms tender.

3. Add the rice and cream. Cook the rice by adding the hot chicken broth, a ladleful at a time. Stir constantly and add more broth to the rice mixture as liquid evaporates. Watch carefully to prevent rice from burning.

4. When the rice is cooked (approximately 25 minutes), add the butter and cheese. Serve immediately.

FANNY'S VINEGAR PEPPERS

YIELD: HALF-GALLON JAR

To purchase the type of vinegar peppers needed for home jarring, you will have to wait until the last week of August or the beginning of September. This is the only time of the year this type of pepper is available. They are shipped to produce centers and disappear fast. The type of pepper you will need is called Santa Nicola, or Saint Nicholas. They are the size of a large tomato and come in green or red. The red ones come either hot or sweet. I like to add a hot red one to my jar for an extra zing, though it is best to use the green ones when pickling, for the red peppers tend to get soft and mushy. The peppers can be packed in any size glass jar—quart, half gallon, or gallon. The amount of liquid needed can be determined by following the measurement rule of thumb below. Adjust the seasonings according to the size of jar you will be using. This recipe is for a half-gallon jar.

⅓ **part white vinegar, ⅓ part cider vinegar, ⅓ part water**

1 heaping teaspoon kosher salt (with no iodine)

30–36 peppers

6 large garlic cloves, thickly sliced

1 heaping tablespoon oregano (preferably fresh dried)

1. Combine the vinegars, water, and salt in a large bowl and set aside.

2. Wash and dry the peppers. Cut large peppers in thick slices and smaller ones in half.

3. Place the peppers, garlic, and oregano in the jar in layers. Pack tightly in jar.

4. Add the mixture of vinegars, water, and dissolved salt to the jar, pushing the peppers down constantly, as they will try to rise to the top. Add enough liquid to cover the peppers completely. The peppers will absorb the vinegar, so keep adding the liquid mixture until the jar is completely full, keeping the proportions in mind.

5. Secure the lid tightly and store in a cool place. The vinegar peppers will be ready to eat after 3–4 weeks.

6. As you remove peppers for eating, keep the remaining peppers covered with extra vinegar mixture. Just repeat the vinegars and water combination.

If you first slice the peppers, they will be ready to eat in 2 weeks.

FAVA BEANS WITH OLIVE OIL, GARLIC, AND ROSEMARY

SERVES 4

Fava beans, also called broad beans, are widely eaten in Europe but in America are usually only found in Italian markets. They grow in long, thick, spongy pods: Twist open the pod and snap out the beans. The inner thick skin should be removed, most easily done by blanching, which also shortens the cooking time. When buying favas, allow for some extras to be nibbled on while shelling.

5 pounds fresh fava beans

1 scant tablespoon fresh rosemary leaves

3 tablespoons extra-virgin olive oil

¼ cup water

1 tablespoon chopped garlic

½ teaspoon salt

Freshly ground black pepper to taste

1. Remove beans from pods, blanch in boiling water for 1 minute, and drain in a colander. Run cold water over beans to cool.

2. Using your fingernail, break outer skins and squeeze beans out between your forefinger and thumb.

3. In a 9-inch skillet, warm rosemary in olive oil. Add beans, ¼ cup water, garlic, salt, and a little pepper. Bring mixture to a low simmer, cover, and stew for about 5 minutes, or until the water has evaporated and the beans are slightly softened.

4. Continue cooking beans for about 20 minutes so that the flavors combine and penetrate, stirring often to prevent beans from sticking. Grind some more pepper over the beans just before serving.

SEASONED FAVA BOLLITO

SERVES 4–6

When I was a little girl visiting with my aunts, my grandfather would give each of us a small dish of fava beans sprinkled with extra salt and tons of pepper freshly ground from my grandmother's pepper mill. What a delicious treat it was to sit down together, pick off the skin, and eat the inside hulk.

1 pound dried fava beans, soaked overnight

3 tablespoons olive oil (use a very good-quality oil)

1 small onion, sliced

Salt and freshly ground black pepper to taste

¾ cup water

Chopped fresh parsley for garnish

1. Shell the soaked fava beans and wash them in cold water. Drain well.

2. Heat the olive oil in a large heavy pot and sauté the onion until golden.

3. Add the fava beans and stir until all of them are coated with oil. Add salt and pepper to taste.

4. Add the ¾ cup water and stir. Cover the pot and simmer over low heat until the beans are soft and the water has evaporated. Drain well.

5. Sprinkle with parsley and more salt and pepper to taste. Serve immediately as an appetizer or a side dish.

STEAMED BREAD-STUFFED ARTICHOKES

CARCIOFI ALLA ROMANA

SERVES 4

A must for the holidays! After steaming the artichokes, let them rest for at least 30 minutes to capture their full flavor.

6 medium-size artichokes

1 lemon, halved

1½ cups fresh bread crumbs (use day-old Italian bread)

¼ cup chopped fresh parsley

½ cup freshly grated Parmesan cheese

2 garlic cloves, chopped

Salt and freshly ground pepper to taste

Olive oil

1 tablespoon salt

4 garlic cloves, halved

1. Soak the artichokes in cold water for 30 minutes to release dirt.

2. Cut off the stems of the artichokes with a sharp knife. Carefully cut straight across the top to remove the prickly tips. Stand the artichoke upside down and give it a firm whack to open the leaves slightly for stuffing. Repeat with the other artichokes, then squeeze the insides with fresh lemon juice.

3. In a large bowl, mix together the bread crumbs, parsley, grated cheese, garlic, salt, and pepper. Toss the crumbs with olive oil until they glisten slightly but are not soaked.

4. Fill each cavity of the artichokes (inside the leaves) with stuffing until well packed. Squeeze lemon juice over the artichokes; reserve the used lemon. Lightly sprinkle a little salt over artichoke tops and sides.

5. Put water (enough to cover ¾ of the artichokes) and salt in a deep saucepan. Add the artichokes. Toss the halved garlic cloves and used lemon into the bottom of the pan.

6. Drizzle the tops with olive oil. Cover and let the water come to a boil. Lower the heat and let the artichokes simmer for about 45 minutes or until tender.

7. Serve warm or at room temperature, not hot.

To eat the artichokes, scrape off pulpy ends of leaves between your teeth.

JOANNE'S SPICY WHITE RICE

SERVES 6–8

My dear friend Joanne Frias has a wonderful garden with an abundance of every known vegetable. Her Sicilian father, who lovingly tends the garden, taught her how to cook them. This is the way he flavors plain rice.

Olive oil

1 large soft green tomato, chopped

1 large ripe red tomato, chopped

1 small onion, chopped

1 garlic clove, chopped

2½ cups water

Salt and freshly ground pepper to taste

1 cup converted rice, washed and
   picked over

1. Using a medium saucepan, add enough olive oil to just cover the bottom of the pan. Sauté the chopped vegetables over medium heat until tender.

2. Add the water and salt and pepper to taste. Cover.

3. When the water comes to a boil, add the rice. Stir well and cover.

4. Simmer rice for 15 minutes. Remove the pan from the heat and let sit until the rice is fluffy.

To serve 10–12: Use 5 cups water and 2 teaspoons salt, then add 2 cups rice.

LEEK PATTIES

YIELD: 6–8 PATTIES

These patties are a good accompaniment to fish or meat.

4 leeks, trimmed and thinly sliced

4 slices white bread, cubed

¼ cup milk

1 egg

Salt and freshly ground pepper to taste

½ cup flour (preferably semolina)

1 onion, thickly sliced

Olive oil

1. Cover the leeks in salted boiling water and cook until they are tender.

2. Meanwhile, soak the bread cubes in the milk.

3. Drain the leeks well. Mix them with the soaked bread (thoroughly squeezed), egg, salt, and pepper.

4. Roll into medium patties. Slightly flatten the patties with your hands and quickly coat both sides with flour. Place the patties on a large platter and reserve.

5. In a large heavy skillet, sauté the sliced onion until transparent in enough olive oil to cover the bottom of the pan generously. (Do not burn.)

6. Discard the onion and gently fry the patties on both sides until golden brown. Transfer to paper towels to drain before serving.

LA GIAMBOTTA

ITALIAN VEGETABLE STEW

SERVES 3–4

When I was a child, my mother would collect all the leftover vegetables and cook them into this wonderful stew. We would eat the stew for lunch with lots of cheese and bastone bread.

1 garlic clove, chopped

1 large onion, chopped

½ cup olive oil

1 (8-ounce) can whole tomatoes

2 tablespoons tomato paste

Salt and freshly ground black pepper to taste

Pinch each of dried oregano, red pepper flakes, basil, and mint

½ cup hot water

1 pound zucchini, cubed

2 medium potatoes, peeled and cubed

1 green bell pepper, thickly sliced

2 celery stalks, sliced

1 pound string beans, trimmed and cut in 1-inch pieces

Grated Parmesan cheese (optional)

1. In a large heavy skillet, sauté the garlic and onion in the olive oil for 3 minutes.

2. Add the tomatoes, mashing them slightly with a large fork. Stir well and add the tomato paste, salt, pepper, and a sprinkle of the seasonings. Stir gently about 5 minutes until well blended.

3. Add the hot water and stir well. Let the sauce come to a gentle boil.

4. Add the zucchini, potatoes, green pepper, celery, beans, and additional seasonings to taste. Let the mixture come to a gentle boil, cover, and simmer until the vegetables are tender, but not mushy.

5. Shut off the heat and let the stew rest for about 15 minutes for a better flavor. Serve it in bowls, accompanied by crusty garlic bread and salad. Sprinkle with Parmesan cheese (optional).

PLAN YOUR POINTS
BEFORE
YOU SHOP

WEEKLY BUDGET
BY
SIZE OF FAMILY

PERSONS	TOTAL POINTS	WEEKLY POINTS
2	96	21
3	144	31
4	192	42
5	240	53
6	288	63
7	336	74
8	384	85
9	432	97
10	480	107

YOUR KITCHEN CUPBOARD
MAY LOOK LIKE THIS

5 LARGE CANS FOR
EACH PERSON IN YOUR
FAMILY

Grandma

Mother

Father

Mary

Johnnie

15 PTS.

7 PTS.

21 PTS.

24 PTS.

10 PTS.

MY NONNA'S STRING BEANS AND POTATOES

SERVES 6

One evening my friend Barbara came for a visit. She mentioned her son Richard and how much he desired string beans and potatoes prepared the way his grandmother used to make it. Naturally, I set forth to my mother's house. She gave me the list of ingredients needed, and I sat and wrote down every step while she prepared the vegetables. Sometimes she slipped by and did things automatically—I couldn't take my eyes off her for a second! When the dish was finished, I had this wonderful recipe to pass on to you, straight from our peasant kitchens of years past.

1½ pounds string beans, trimmed

4 medium potatoes, peeled

Olive oil

1 large onion, cut in large chunks

1 garlic clove, chopped

1 (6-ounce) can tomato paste

1 (35-ounce) can peeled plum tomatoes

Salt and freshly ground pepper to taste

Dried red pepper flakes

1 tablespoon chopped fresh parsley

4½ cups water

1. Snap string beans in half and rinse in cold water. Reserve.

2. Wash potatoes, cut in medium cubes, and soak in enough water to cover. Reserve.

3. Using a wide 6-quart pan, add enough olive oil to cover the bottom. Sauté onion and garlic over medium heat until translucent.

4. Add tomato paste and, using a wooden spoon, stir mixture until well blended.

5. Strain tomatoes and put through a blender until coarsely chopped. Add to sauce and stir well.

6. Add salt and pepper to taste, a pinch of red pepper flakes, and parsley. Stir well.

7. Let sauce come to a full boil and add 4½ cups water.

8. Return sauce to a boil and add cut string beans. Stir a couple of times and cook for about 15 minutes or until tender. Remove beans and reserve to a warm place.

9. Bring sauce to a boil again and add potatoes. Stir a couple of times, then cook for about 30–35 minutes or until tender, stirring only once or twice to prevent sticking.

10. Add string beans to potatoes in sauce and bring to a soft boil. Adjust seasonings and simmer for an additional 5–10 minutes just to blend.

11. Let mixture rest 10 minutes, then serve in bowls with garlic bread or crusty Italian bread.

BUDINO DI PATATE

MASHED POTATOES BAKED WITH EGGS AND CHEESE

SERVES 4–6

This simple dish is simply delicious—and a great way to use up leftover mashed potatoes.

4 medium potatoes, unpeeled

2 cups freshly grated Parmesan cheese

2 eggs, slightly beaten

1 cup milk, warmed

Salt and freshly ground pepper to taste

Butter

1. Preheat oven to 400°F.

2. Boil the potatoes whole until tender. Drain and carefully peel the potatoes while hot. Place in a medium bowl and mash.

3. Add the cheese, eggs, milk, salt, and pepper. Mix thoroughly until well blended.

4. Transfer to a baking dish smeared with butter (the potatoes should come halfway up the sides) and bake on the middle rack for 20–25 minutes or until outsides look slightly browned. Serve immediately.

PATATE DEI POVERI

POOR PEOPLE'S POTATOES

SERVES 4–6

I always keep a tube of tomato paste handy for the times I need only a little for a recipe such as this one.

2 pounds potatoes, peeled and cut in large chunks

¼ cup extra-virgin olive oil

3 garlic cloves, crushed

1 tablespoon tomato paste

Salt and freshly ground pepper to taste

Pinch of oregano

1. Rinse the potato chunks under cold water and reserve.

2. Heat the olive oil in a large skillet. Add the garlic and cook over medium heat until it is translucent.

3. Add the tomato paste and stir quickly with a wooden spoon. Cover and cook over low heat for 3–4 minutes until well blended.

4. Place reserved wet potatoes into the skillet and toss well to coat with the sauce. Add salt and pepper to taste and oregano.

5. Lower heat, cover, and cook for 15 minutes, or until potatoes are nice and soft but not mushy.

6. Serve hot with a mixed salad and slices of thick crusty bread to soak up the sauce.

SPINACH AND POTATOES MA'S WAY

SERVES 3–4

Because we were poor when I was growing up, my mother would make our lunches for school by using any leftovers from the night before. We always had spinach in the refrigerator, and so we would bring our oil-sopped crusty Italian bread and garlicky spinach sandwiches to school. How wonderful this tasted, and how lucky I felt to bring something special from our kitchen at home.

2 packages spinach, cleaned and dried

4 medium potatoes, peeled and cubed

Salt and freshly ground pepper to taste

Olive oil

6–8 garlic cloves, thickly slivered

1 tablespoon dried red pepper flakes

1. Using a large pan, bring 1 cup of water to a boil. Add spinach, cover, and steam for 3 minutes, turning only once or twice. Remove from heat, drain thoroughly, and set aside.

2. Boil potatoes in enough salted water to cover. Cook until tender and drain, reserving some water.

3. Combine spinach and potatoes and place on a serving platter. Add salt and pepper to taste.

4. In a small skillet, slowly heat enough oil to cover the bottom of the pan. Sauté chopped garlic and red pepper flakes until garlic is golden brown and almost burned.

5. Immediately pour hot garlic oil over spinach and potatoes. This will sizzle, so be careful.

6. Adjust seasonings. If more sauce is desired, you may add the heated reserved potato water.

7. Let mixture set and serve with strong, crusty Italian bread to sop up the juices.

FRITTATA CON SPINACI

SPINACH OMELETTE

SERVES 4–6

To steam spinach, first soak it thoroughly until all dirt particles are removed. Then plunge it in hot water, turning quickly until it is slightly wilted. Drain well and chop into pieces for this recipe.

2 cups steamed spinach, chopped

2 tablespoons olive oil

Salt and freshly ground pepper to taste

Dried red pepper flakes (optional)

6 fresh eggs

¾ cup milk

¼ cup grated Parmesan cheese

¾ stick (6 tablespoons) butter

1. Quickly sauté spinach in hot olive oil for 1 minute. Season with salt and pepper to taste and red pepper flakes.

2. Using a fork or whisk, beat eggs with milk and salt and pepper to taste until fluffy. Add grated cheese and beat until well blended.

3. Heat butter in a medium-size skillet on medium heat. Slowly add beaten eggs, pushing with a fork, until all the egg is used and slightly puffy. Cook until nicely browned.

4. Cover omelette and let cook for 1 minute. Add cooked spinach to top of omelette and fold over.

5. Cut in serving-size portions and serve immediately.

Eggs and spinach may be cooked in smaller portions for individual servings.

SAUTÉED SPINACH WITH PIGNOLI AND RAISINS

SERVES 2

Pignoli and golden raisins add flavor and nice texture to this quick and easy cooked spinach dish.

1 pound fresh spinach

¼ cup olive oil

¼ cup pignoli nuts

¼ cup golden raisins

Salt and freshly ground pepper to taste

Pinch of dried red pepper flakes (optional)

2 lemon wedges for garnish

1. Rinse the spinach. Remove tough stems and tear any large leaves in half. Place in a colander until needed.

2. Heat the olive oil in a large skillet. Sauté the pignoli until golden.

3. Add the wet spinach to the hot oil and pignoli (watch out for splattering oil). Stir continuously for 1 minute, add raisins, and toss to combine.

4. Season with salt and pepper to taste and red pepper flakes if using. Serve with wedges of lemon.

FRESH MUSHROOM SOFFRITTO

SERVES 4–6

This recipe is so good and easy! The tomato paste gives the mushrooms a sweet, pungent flavor, which gets tastier as it reaches room temperature. Try to use button mushrooms, especially if serving as an appetizer. If you choose large mushrooms, cut them in big chunks. These are great to take on a picnic or use as a side dish with your favorite roast. I love them for lunch with some Tuscan bread and an arugula salad.

Olive oil

5 garlic cloves, chopped

3–4 small hot red peppers, chopped, or 1 teaspoon dried red pepper flakes, (optional)

2 large onions, thinly sliced

3 red bell peppers, thinly sliced

3 green bell peppers, thinly sliced

Salt and freshly ground pepper to taste

2 pounds fresh mushrooms (small button mushrooms left whole, or large ones cut in chunks)

1 (6-ounce) can tomato paste

Pinch of dried oregano

20 Sicilian dry-cured black olives, pitted

1. In a large skillet, add enough olive oil to cover bottom of pan.

2. Sauté garlic and hot peppers (if using) over medium heat. You may substitute 1 teaspoon red pepper flakes if you wish.

3. Add more oil if needed, and sauté onions and bell peppers until tender. Salt and pepper to taste.

4. Add mushrooms and tomato paste. Using a wooden spoon, stir gently until the paste is dissolved and the vegetables are nicely coated with the sauce.

5. Add oregano, pitted olives, and additional salt and pepper if needed. Toss gently and simmer 1 minute until the mushrooms are warmed through but still have their fresh, crisp texture. Serve at room temperature.

EGGPLANT FRITTELLES

SERVES 4

Try this easy recipe if you need to add another quick, delicious appetizer or side vegetable dish to your meal. Don't expect these to taste like eggplant. Excellent either plain or topped with marinara sauce, they are very similar in texture to meatballs and are a great meat substitute for vegetarians. I get nothing but raves over this recipe.

1 pound eggplant

1 cup soft, fresh bread crumbs

¾ cup grated Parmesan cheese

2 garlic cloves, chopped

¼ cup chopped fresh parsley

2 eggs

Salt and freshly ground pepper to taste

Flour for dredging

Olive oil

Marinara sauce for dipping (optional)

1. Peel the eggplant and halve it lengthwise.

2. In a large pot of water, simmer eggplant halves for 40 minutes or until they are tender.

3. Drain eggplant well. Puree in a food mill or processor until texture is smooth.

4. Transfer eggplant to a medium-size bowl and add bread crumbs, grated cheese, garlic, parsley, eggs, and salt and pepper to taste. Mix well, using a wooden spoon.

5. Flour your hands and shape eggplant mixture into little balls. Roll the balls in flour and set aside.

6. Heat about 2 inches of olive oil in a small saucepan. When oil is very hot, deep-fry the eggplant balls, 2 or 3 at a time, until crisp and golden.

7. Drain on paper towels and remove to a warm platter. Serve immediately if possible.

STUFFED EGGPLANT ROLLS

SERVES 4

This recipe is a wonderful variation for eggplant. Serve it as an appetizer or a side dish with pasta or meat. You need not remove the skin; it will help keep the slices from tearing. The Sicilians are noted for using hard-boiled eggs in their cooking, and we are doing the same here.

Olive oil

2 large eggplants, thinly sliced

1 onion, thinly sliced

1 cup soft, fresh bread crumbs

½ cup grated Parmesan cheese

2 cups shredded mozzarella

2 hard-boiled eggs, chopped

2 tablespoons chopped fresh parsley

Salt and freshly ground pepper to taste

Simple Marinara Sauce (page 62)

1. Heat ¼ cup olive oil in a heavy skillet over high heat. Sauté slices of eggplant until they are golden brown on both sides. Drain on paper towels and reserve.

2. Using same skillet, heat 2 tablespoons olive oil over medium heat and sauté the sliced onion until golden brown. Lower heat and add the bread crumbs. Quickly stir mixture until crumbs are golden in color.

3. Turn off the heat and, to the same skillet, add the Parmesan cheese (reserve some for topping), shredded mozzarella, chopped eggs, 1 tablespoon fresh parsley, and salt and pepper to taste. Toss well.

4. Preheat oven to 350°F.

5. Spread each eggplant slice with 1 teaspoon of the bread crumb mixture and 1 teaspoon of marinara sauce. Roll up slices and secure with toothpicks. Place rolls, seam-side down, in an oiled baking dish.

6. Spread remaining bread crumb mixture over eggplant and drizzle each roll with olive oil. Cover with remaining Parmesan cheese and chopped parsley.

7. Bake for 15 minutes or until bread mixture is crusty and browned. You may top cooked eggplant rolls with extra marinara sauce and cheese if desired.

PASTRIES, COOKIES, AND DESSERTS

CANNOLI

Cannoli are made for holidays like Easter and Christmas. The shells store well in covered canisters and can be made at least a week in advance. The filling can be made a day or two ahead, but don't fill the shells in advance, as they will get soggy. You will need to purchase aluminum tubes from a specialty store. Buy a dozen. Aluminum will not sink to the bottom of the pan, so the cannoli shells cannot get oily. Make about 8 cannoli at one time, then remove cooked shells from the pan and start again.

SHELLS

YIELD: 20–25 MINIATURE SHELLS

1¾ cups all-purpose flour

½ teaspoon salt

¼ teaspoon cinnamon

1 tablespoon granulated sugar

1 egg, slightly beaten

2 tablespoons firm butter, crumbled

¼ cup port wine

1 egg yolk, slightly beaten

1 (3-pound) can vegetable shortening

1. Sift flour with salt, cinnamon, and granulated sugar.

2. Make a well in center of flour mixture and add beaten egg and crumbled butter. Work with fingertips to blend well until the flour is moist.

3. Add wine a little at a time, until dough just clings together. Knead for at least 5 minutes, or until the dough is smooth.

4. Form dough into a loaf shape, flatten down, cover, and let rest for at least 20 minutes.

5. Cut dough into 4 portions. Roll one portion at a time, on a lightly floured surface, until paper-thin.

6. Using a biscuit cutter, cut out circles of dough about 3½ inches in diameter. Patch all the scrap pieces and use for additional shells. Continue rolling and cutting until all the dough is used up.

7. Wrap each piece of cut dough loosely around the aluminum tubes, pressing ends of dough to flare slightly. Seal middle edges together with beaten egg yolk. Press lightly with fingertips until middle edges are well sealed. This step is important, or shells will open during cooking and cannot be filled.

8. In a wide, semi-deep, heavy pan, heat shortening until very hot (350°F). Drop 3–4 cannoli, attached to aluminum tubes, in the hot oil (do not crowd) and fry for 2–3 minutes, turning often with tongs, until golden brown but not burned.

9. Drain on paper towels, and let cool a minute.

10. With a clean dish towel, hold shell lightly and, with other hand, pull out tube. Be careful or shell will crumble if you bear down too hard.

11. Continue until all the dough pieces are cooked.

12. Fill the shells with either the ricotta or cooked cream filling (recipes follow).

RICOTTA FILLING

YIELD: FILLING FOR 20–25 MINIATURE CANNOLI

2 pounds ricotta

2 cups confectioners' sugar, plus extra for topping

½ teaspoon cinnamon

4 teaspoons vanilla extract (I use white)

¼ cup semisweet chocolate chips, crushed

2 tablespoons chopped citron

½ cup grated lemon peel

Chopped pistachios or walnuts (optional)

1. Using a large bowl, mix ricotta with 2 cups confectioners' sugar and stir in remaining ingredients, except nuts, until well blended.

2. Chill several hours or overnight.

3. When ready to serve, fill shells with ricotta mixture, using a long thin spoon or a pastry tube.

4. Sprinkle confectioners' sugar generously over cannoli. Garnish ends with chopped nuts if desired, and serve immediately.

PANNA COTTA, OR COOKED CREAM, FILLING

YIELD: FILLING FOR 6–8 CANNOLI

For a combination of fillings, use half the amount of the cooked cream filling, then add the chocolate to the remaining half for a nice presentation. Be sure to sprinkle the cannoli with lots of confectioners' sugar before serving.

2 eggs, slightly beaten

⅔ cup sugar

¼ cup cornstarch

2 cups whole milk

Pinch of salt

1 teaspoon grated lemon zest (optional)

2 teaspoons vanilla extract (optional)

Confectioners' sugar

1. Whisk together the eggs and sugar in a small, heavy saucepan.

2. In a small bowl, whisk the cornstarch with ½ cup milk until slightly pasty. Add salt and remaining milk and mix well.

3. Slowly pour the milk mixture into the saucepan with the eggs and whisk thoroughly.

4. Place over low heat and cook for 10 minutes or more, stirring constantly, until the mixture comes to a soft boil and is shiny and of pudding consistency. Do not allow to burn.

5. Remove the pan from the heat and stir in the lemon zest or vanilla or both, if using.

6. Pour into a small bowl and cover with wax paper, placing the paper directly on the cooked cream to prevent a skin from forming on top.

7. Cool and refrigerate until needed. This will keep 3–4 days.

8. When ready to use, whisk until smooth if the filling has separated.

For chocolate cream, whisk an additional ½ cup sugar with the eggs and add ¾ cup shaved unsweetened chocolate to the hot cooked cream, stirring well.

ZEPPOLE

FRIED DOUGH

YIELD: 1 DOZEN

Anyone who has ever been to an Italian feast will recognize the enticing smell and taste of these fried treats. Once you master the recipe, you can experiment with shapes, as the outdoor vendors do. My grandmother used to stuff the dough with cauliflower, chopped anchovies, or codfish before cooking it. She did this by wrapping the dough around the cooked ingredient before dropping it into the hot oil.

1 (3-pound) can vegetable shortening

2 eggs, beaten

1½ cups milk

2 cups unbleached and unsifted flour (King Arthur preferred)

1 teaspoon baking powder

½ teaspoon salt

Confectioners' sugar

1. Heat the shortening in a deep, wide fryer (a heavy-duty wok works well) until hot but not burning. You will need the shortening to be about 6 inches deep.

2. In a large bowl, combine the eggs, milk, flour, baking powder, and salt. Using a large wooden spoon, mix thoroughly to form a smooth dough.

3. When the dough is pliable, drop it by heaping tablespoonfuls into the hot oil. Do only about 3 at a time so they do not touch each other or the sides of the pan. Fry until golden brown on all sides.

Remove with a slotted spoon and drain on paper towels. The shortening may be cooled, strained, and stored to be used another time.

4. When cool, transfer to a large platter and sprinkle with confectioners' sugar. Serve as a snack or dessert. They are best served the day they are made.

ZEPPOLE DI SAN GIUSEPPE

ST. JOSEPH'S DAY CREAM PUFFS

YIELD: ABOUT 16–18 PUFFS

This recipe was donated by one of our senior citizens. Please enjoy.

1 cup hot water

1 stick (½ cup) butter

1 tablespoon sugar

½ teaspoon salt

1 cup sifted flour

4 fresh eggs

1 teaspoon grated orange peel

1 teaspoon grated lemon peel

1. Bring water, butter, sugar, and salt to a boil in a saucepan.

2. Add flour all at once. Stir vigorously with a wooden spoon until mixture leaves sides of pan and forms a smooth ball, about 3 minutes.

3. Remove from heat and quickly add eggs, one at a time, beating until smooth after each addition. Continue beating until mixture is smooth and shiny.

4. Add grated orange and lemon peels.

5. Drop mixture by tablespoons about 2 inches apart onto a lightly greased baking sheet.

6. Bake in a preheated 425°F oven for 15 minutes. Lower heat to 350°F and bake until golden brown, about 15–20 minutes more.

7. Remove to rack and cool completely.

8. With a sharp knife, cut a slit in the side of each puff. Fill with cream filling (recipe below) or whipped cream.

CREAM FILLING

YIELD: FILLING FOR 10–14 CREAM PUFFS

¾ cup sugar

⅓ cup flour

Pinch of salt

2 cups hot scalded milk

1 teaspoon vanilla extract

2 eggs, slightly beaten

Confectioners' sugar

1. Using a medium bowl, mix sugar, flour, and salt. Gradually add hot scalded milk.

2. Pour into the top of a double boiler, directly over bottom pan of boiling water. Stir constantly over medium heat until mixture thickens, about 2–3 minutes.

3. Remove pan from heat and cool for 10 minutes.

4. Add vanilla and quickly whisk in slightly beaten eggs.

5. Return to top of boiler pan and cook for 2–3 minutes, using low heat.

6. Remove from heat, cover, and let cool.

7. Chill in refrigerator and fill cream puffs as needed. Sprinkle filled puffs with confectioners' sugar.

TO SCALD MILK

Before heating milk in a saucepan, rinse the pan with water. This way it will not scorch as easily.

RICOTTA CREAM PUFFS

YIELD: APPROXIMATELY 2½ DOZEN

These are a lovely dessert and are easier to prepare than you may think. They also are very convenient to make for company. The cream puffs may be baked early in the day and filled a couple of hours before serving.

CREAM PUFFS

½ cup vegetable shortening

⅛ teaspoon salt

1 cup boiling water

1 cup sifted flour

3 eggs

1. Add the shortening and salt to the cup of boiling water and stir over medium heat until the mixture resumes boiling.

2. Lower the heat. Add the flour all at once and stir vigorously until the mixture leaves the sides of the pan.

3. Remove the pan from the heat. Add the eggs, one at a time, beating thoroughly after each addition.

4. Shape on an ungreased cookie sheet, using a tablespoon of batter for each cream puff. You may use a pastry bag if you wish.

5. Bake in a preheated 450°F oven for about 20 minutes. Reduce the temperature to 350°F and bake for 20 minutes longer.

6. Remove the cream puffs from the oven and place on a rack to cool.

RICOTTA FILLING

¼ cup confectioners' sugar

¼ teaspoon grated lemon or orange rind

1 teaspoon vanilla extract

1 pound ricotta cheese, well chilled

Add the confectioners' sugar, lemon or orange rind, and vanilla to the ricotta. Blend. Do not stir too long; just use quick strokes to mix all the ingredients or the ricotta will become too soft and milky and seep through the puffs.

TO FINISH PREPARATION

1. Cut the tops off the cooled cream puffs. Save the tops.

2. Fill the puffs with the filling. Replace the tops and dust with sifted confectioners' sugar. Refrigerate up to 2 hours before serving.

RICOTTA CAKE

SERVES 12

This is a light, pie-like treat. It can be made a day or two before serving and kept refrigerated.

3 pounds ricotta cheese

2 cups sugar

8 eggs, separated

½ cup sifted flour

Grated rind of 1 lemon

1 teaspoon vanilla extract

½ cup cream, whipped

Graham cracker crumbs (enough to coat pan)*

1 cup strawberries or cherries, crushed and sugared (optional)

1. In a large bowl, beat the ricotta with a wire whisk until smooth. Gradually add 1½ cups sugar and the egg yolks, beating after each addition. Beat in the flour, lemon rind, and vanilla.

2. In another bowl, beat the 8 egg whites with the remaining ½ cup sugar.

3. Gently fold the whipped cream and beaten egg whites into the ricotta mixture.

4. Turn the batter into a 12-inch springform pan that has been well buttered and sprinkled with graham cracker crumbs.

5. Bake in a preheated 425°F oven for 10 minutes. Lower the temperature to 350°F and continue baking for 1 hour.

6. Turn off the heat and allow the cake to cool in the oven with the door closed.

7. Refrigerate the cake until serving time. Top it with crushed, sugared strawberries or cherries before serving, if desired.

*For this recipe, you may substitute graham cracker crumbs with Pasta Frolla (a crust of butter and sugar combined with flour; see page 314), the crust for Pizza Rustica (see page 317), or your favorite piecrust recipe.

TO MAKE CREAM WHIP

When cream will not whip, add the white of an egg to it. Refrigerate both the cream and egg white thoroughly, try again, and it will whip easily.

EASTER SWEET RICOTTA PIE

This pie is the star of stars at Eastertime. In my neighborhood, if you don't include it on your Easter menu, then nothing else matters. This recipe is foolproof. If you follow the directions and use only the freshest ingredients, you will make a beautiful pie.

PASTA FROLLA

2 cups all-purpose flour

1 cup confectioners' sugar

½ teaspoon baking powder

½ teaspoon salt

4 egg yolks (reserve whites for filling)

¼ cup vegetable shortening, melted

1 teaspoon vanilla or orange extract

1 tablespoon ice-cold water

1. Using a medium bowl, sift together the flour, sugar, baking powder, and salt.

2. Make a well in the flour mixture and add, all at once, the egg yolks, melted shortening, and vanilla or orange extract. Mix with a large fork until mixture resembles coarse crumbs.

3. Add just enough ice water to make dough just moist enough to stick together. If dough still seems dry, keep hands damp until dough clings together instead of adding more water.

4. Roll into a ball shape and wrap in plastic. Slightly flatten the package of dough and refrigerate while you make the filling.

FILLING

2 pounds ricotta cream cheese, firm

1 cup confectioners' sugar, sifted

1 teaspoon cinnamon

Grated peel of 1 orange

Grated peel of 2 lemons

1 teaspoon vanilla extract

½ cup white chocolate chips, crushed (optional)

4 egg whites, stiffly beaten

1. Place ricotta cheese in a large bowl and stir with a fork until mashed. Add sugar, cinnamon, grated peels, vanilla extract, and crushed chocolate chips.

2. Using a large spatula, gently fold in stiffly whipped egg whites. Blend well.

Milk

Confectioners' sugar

1. When filling is completed, take dough out of refrigerator and break off ⅔ of the piece; keep other ⅓ wrapped.

2. Using a wooden board or counter, place dough between 2 pieces of waxed paper. Roll dough until it will generously overhang a 9-inch Pyrex glass dish or tin plate.

3. Roll out remaining dough between waxed paper into a 9½-inch round. Using a fluted cookie cutter, cut this round into lattice strips at least 1 inch wide.

4. Pour filling into prepared pie shell and form a crisscross pattern with lattice strips to make top crust.

5. Brush with milk and bake in a pre-heated 350°F oven for 50 minutes or until golden brown in color.

6. Cool on a wire rack at least 2 hours.

7. Sprinkle with confectioners' sugar. Serve warm, or loosely cover with plastic wrap and refrigerate until needed. Dust with additional confectioners' sugar before serving.

Because this is a rich pie, you will need a sharp knife that has been dipped in water to cut the pie into thin wedges.

FRIED EGG WITH BACON

Every morning my mother would wake one of us up to go to the bakery for our fresh bread. For breakfast she would squeeze a dozen oranges bought cheaply from the marketplace. Then she would start our breakfast. It was the same ritual every morning: fresh orange juice, a soft-boiled egg, toasted Italian bread, and hot cocoa. How I yearned for a fried egg with bacon! For lunch she made lots of omelettes, using only fresh eggs. We would have peppers and eggs, or potatoes and eggs, or onions and eggs. It was certainly healthy, but very embarrassing to me, especially when the olive oil would leak out of the bread. But we ate everything because we knew my mother really tried to stretch any food that was inexpensive and turn it into something special. Besides, it was so delicious!

BUDINO DI RISO

BAKED ITALIAN RICE PUDDING

SERVES 6–8

Italians favor arborio rice when making any sweet desserts. Because it slightly thickens while cooking, it gives a nice, smooth density to this recipe. Be sure to use only evaporated milk.

2 cups uncooked arborio rice

Vegetable oil

8 eggs, at room temperature

1½ cups sugar

1 tablespoon vanilla extract

2 pounds ricotta cheese

1 (12-ounce) can evaporated milk

1½ teaspoons cinnamon

1½ cups soft golden raisins (optional)

Vanilla ice cream or whipped cream (optional)

1. In a large saucepan, sauté the rice in just enough vegetable oil to coat it. Cook until lightly golden; be sure not to brown.

2. Cover the hot rice with water, with about an inch of water above the rice. Bring to a soft boil and cover. Simmer over low heat for 15 minutes, leaving the cover on while the rice is cooking. Do not allow rice to dry out.

3. In a large mixing bowl, beat the eggs, sugar, vanilla, ricotta cheese, evaporated milk, and cinnamon until smooth and creamy.

4. Stir in the cooked rice and raisins, if using.

5. Pour into a lightly buttered oblong cake pan. Bake in a preheated 325°F oven for about 35–40 minutes, or until top is golden brown. Do not overbake or pudding will be dry.

6. Place in pudding cups and top with vanilla ice cream or whipped cream, if desired.

PIZZA RUSTICA

DEEP-DISH RICOTTA PIE

YIELD: APPROXIMATELY 20 PIECES

This is a truly excellent dessert. It is nice to serve at a party because it makes enough for a large group.

PASTRY

2 cups sifted flour

¾ teaspoon salt

⅔ cup vegetable shortening

1 egg

6–8 tablespoons cold water

1. Sift the flour with the salt into a large mixing bowl. Cut in the shortening until the mixture resembles cornmeal.

2. Add the egg and water. Blend together with quick motions.

3. Roll out the dough to fit a glass or metal baking dish about 12 inches long, 8 inches wide, and 2 inches deep. Press it into the baking dish. Set aside while you prepare the filling.

RICOTTA FILLING

2 pounds ricotta cheese

1½ cups sugar

½ teaspoon salt

4 eggs, separated

2 teaspoons vanilla extract

1 cup milk

1. Put the ricotta, sugar, salt, egg yolks, vanilla, and milk in a large bowl. Using a wooden spoon, blend until smooth.

2. Beat egg whites just until foamy, but not stiff. Gently fold into the ricotta mixture.

TO FINISH PREPARATION

Confectioners' sugar

1. Carefully pour the filling into the pastry shell.

2. Bake the pie in a preheated 400°F oven for 20 minutes. Reduce the heat to 375°F and bake 45 minutes longer.

3. Remove from the oven and cool. Sprinkle with confectioners' sugar.

4. Cut into wedges and serve at room temperature, or refrigerate for several hours and serve cold.

SAVOIARDI

LADY FINGERS

YIELD: 3 DOZEN

I like to serve these with a cup of coffee or use them in any recipe calling for lady fingers.

4 eggs, separated

⅛ teaspoon salt

10 tablespoons sugar

2 teaspoons vanilla extract

⅓ cup sifted flour

1. Cut a brown paper bag to line 2 cookie sheets.

2. Beat the egg whites and salt until foamy. Add 2 tablespoons sugar and beat until soft peaks form. Set aside.

3. In another bowl, beat the egg yolks until thickened, then gradually beat in the remaining sugar and the vanilla. Beat until very thick and lemon colored.

4. Sprinkle the flour over the egg yolk mixture, then fold in the flour carefully.

5. Fold the egg yolk mixture into the egg whites.

6. Using a pastry tube or spoon, make 3-inch-long finger shapes of batter 2 inches apart on the brown paper.

7. Bake in a preheated 350°F oven for 5 minutes or until deep golden brown. Cool 2–3 minutes.

8. When cool and dry, carefully remove the lady fingers from the paper with a spatula. Store in an airtight container.

SICILIAN CASSATA

SERVES 6–8

A cassata is not difficult to make. You can purchase a pound cake or make your own a day or two in advance. If you do make the cake from scratch, it would be a good idea to substitute orange juice for the vanilla.

1 pound cake

1 pound ricotta cheese

4 ounces semisweet chocolate chips, chopped

¼ cup pignoli nuts, chopped (optional)

3 tablespoons vanilla extract or orange juice

Grand Marnier liqueur to taste (optional)

¼ cup sugar

12 maraschino cherries, drained and chopped

1. Using a sharp, serrated knife, cut the pound cake horizontally into 4 equal slices.

2. Put the ricotta into a large mixing bowl and beat until smooth, using a wooden spoon. Fold in the remaining ingredients and mix until well blended.

3. Put one slice of cake on a decorative platter and evenly spread it with a third of the ricotta mixture. Top it with the second slice and spread with ricotta. Continue until the cake and ricotta mixture are used up; the fourth cake layer will be on top. The cake should be compact and even.

4. Cover cake with plastic wrap and refrigerate while you make the frosting.

CHOCOLATE FROSTING

2½ cups confectioners' sugar

⅓ cup butter or margarine, softened

2 ounces unsweetened chocolate, melted

3 tablespoons hot espresso, or dissolve 2 teaspoons instant coffee in 3 tablespoons hot water

1. Beat together the sugar, butter, and chocolate in a small mixing bowl at low speed. Add coffee gradually to chocolate mixture, beating until creamy and smooth. If necessary, stir in additional water, a few drops at a time.

2. Frost top and sides of cake, using a swirling motion. Insert toothpicks into the top of the cake, cover with plastic wrap, and chill 24 hours before serving.

MARGUERITA CAKE

SERVES 6–8

This cake is a sweet, crisp, sponge-type cake with rum frosting. It is great for the holidays or other special occasions.

5 eggs, separated

Confectioners' sugar

1 tablespoon lemon juice

¼ teaspoon almond extract

½ cup cake flour, sifted

½ teaspoon vanilla extract

1. Preheat oven to 375°F.

2. Beat egg yolks until thick and lemon colored. Add ½ cup confectioners' sugar gradually and beat for about 5 minutes. Add lemon juice and almond extract. Fold in sifted flour.

3. Beat egg whites until they hold a peak. Fold them into cake batter.

4. Grease a 10-inch square cake pan and sprinkle with additional confectioners' sugar. Pour batter into pan and top with more confectioners' sugar.

5. Bake for approximately 30 minutes or until cake springs back when touched.

6. Cool on a wire rack and sprinkle cake with vanilla extract.

CHIACCIATA AL RUM (RUM FROSTING)

1 cup butter

2 cups cocoa powder

4 cups confectioners' sugar, sifted

2 egg yolks

2 tablespoons rum

1. Cream butter, cocoa, and sugar until well blended.

2. Beat egg yolks until thick and lemon colored, and add to butter mixture. Add rum and beat thoroughly.

3. Frost cake and serve.

VINCENZO'S ZUCCHINI BREAD

SERVES 14

Vincent, a former employer of the North End Union, was very interested in health food. His zucchini bread was so rich and moist, it was like eating a complete meal. It became one of our favorite recipes.

3 eggs

2¼ cups sugar

2 cups shredded zucchini

1½ teaspoons vanilla extract

1 cup vegetable oil

3 cups flour

½ teaspoon baking powder

4 teaspoons cinnamon

1 teaspoon baking soda

1 teaspoon salt

1 cup chopped nuts

1. Mix the eggs, sugar, zucchini, vanilla, and oil in a large bowl.

2. Mix the flour, baking powder, cinnamon, baking soda, and salt in a second bowl.

3. Mix the dry ingredients into the zucchini mixture. Add the chopped nuts.

4. Grease and flour two 9 x 5-inch loaf pans. Pour in the batter.

5. Bake in a preheated 350°F oven for 1 hour. (They may take a little longer, so test with a toothpick.) Cool and serve at room temperature.

This bread may be frozen.

LA PASTIERA DOLCE

SWEET SPAGHETTI PIE

SERVES 8–10

A much sought-after recipe, this is to be treasured! You will see this wonderful dish in most Italian homes, mainly at Eastertime. There are many recipes for la pastiera. This one is made with milk and sugar, which makes it like a dessert. Use freshly cooked or leftover pasta. Enjoy this wonderful meal not only at Eastertime, but on any fasting day when meat is not allowed. This also makes a great lunch or snack and can be eaten either hot or cold.

¾ pound spaghetti

1 pound ricotta cheese

3 eggs, slightly beaten

½ cup sugar

¼ cup grated Parmesan cheese

1 cup whole milk

¼ stick butter

Cinnamon

1. Preheat oven to 450°F.

2. Break pasta into irregular-size pieces. Cook pasta in boiling, salted water until al dente; drain well and reserve.

3. Place ricotta in a large bowl and stir until smooth. Add beaten eggs, sugar, Parmesan cheese, and milk and mix well. Add spaghetti and toss until well coated with cheese mixture.

4. Pour into a well-buttered 10 x 8 x 2-inch baking pan. Dot with slices of butter and sprinkle with cinnamon.

5. Bake in the preheated oven for 30–35 minutes or until puffy and golden brown.

6. Remove from oven and set in a warm place for at least 1 hour before serving. If you want to serve the pie at another time (or save its leftovers), it can be kept in the refrigerator, covered with foil.

7. Cut in squares with a sharp, wet knife.

For a sweeter pie, sprinkle with confectioners' sugar before serving.

PASTIERA GRANO

EASTER WHEAT PIE

SERVES 8–10

To make this pie, you will need to buy skinless grano wheat in a specialty store, and you will need to make my Pasta Frolla for the crust (see page 314). If any of the filling is left over, serve it cold in pudding cups topped with whipped cream.

TO MAKE FILLING

1 cup skinless grano wheat

3 cups water

1 cup scalded milk

1½ cups granulated sugar, plus ½ teaspoon

1 teaspoon salt

1 teaspoon freshly grated orange peel, rind only

1 teaspoon freshly grated lemon peel, rind only

2 teaspoons vanilla extract

1½ pounds ricotta cheese, drained

4 egg yolks, beaten (reserve whites)

1. Wash well grano and soak overnight in 2 cups water.

2. The next day, drain grano and simmer in a large saucepan with 1 cup water, scalded milk, ½ teaspoon sugar, and salt. Cook for at least 30 minutes, or until soft and pasty. Add more water, if needed, to prevent wheat from sticking to pan. Grano will triple in amount.

3. Remove grano from heat and add orange and lemon peels and vanilla extract. Reserve.

4. In a large bowl, combine ricotta, 1½ cups sugar, and 4 beaten egg yolks. Use a large wooden spoon to mix until well blended. Add grano and mix thoroughly.

5. Refrigerate while you make pie crust.

Pasta Frolla (page 314)

6 egg whites

1. Divide the Pasta Frolla in half; handle dough carefully. Using a well-floured board, roll one of the dough halves to form a round that is slightly larger than your pie pan (you will need a large, deep pie pan for this). Line pie pan, leaving a slight overhang around the edge.

2. Roll out remaining dough and cut into latticed strips, about 1 inch wide, using a fluted pastry wheel. Reserve.

3. Beat 4 egg whites until stiff and gently fold into grano and ricotta mixture, using a large spatula.

4. Pour mixture into lined pie plate and spread evenly.

5. Arrange lattice strips in a crisscross pattern over filling.

6. Lightly beat the 2 remaining reserved egg whites and brush them over the lattice crust.

7. Bake in a preheated 350°F oven for at least 1 hour or until filling is slightly firm but moist (it will set while cooling) and crust is golden brown.

8. Cool in oven with door open.

For a sweeter pie, sprinkle with confectioners' sugar before serving.

AIR RAID DRILLS

I remember air raid drills with the sirens blaring. We would all jump with terror and run under the bed in case there was a bombing. I remember noticing how most of the men in our area wore a black band around their arm. When I grew older, I learned it signified the death of a loved one who had served and died in the war. Our immigrants were people who had not come here to make their fortunes and go back. They came to stay. They worked diligently and proudly. They brought their crafts, workmanship, and artistic talents and used these skills, which helped give the North End its special character. They were not afraid of hard work. These people, our Italian immigrants, contributed so much to our country.

BISCOTTI

YIELD: ABOUT 2 DOZEN LARGE COOKIES
OR 3½ DOZEN SMALL COOKIES

I have been making this recipe for so long, and yet my friends still rave about it. My friend Nancy first helped me with the recipe, then I made a few changes to suit my style. Biscotti are dry, plain cookies enhanced by the flavor of anise. They are excellent with coffee, cappuccino, or espresso. They make a nice snack and help curb your appetite before meals.

2 cups flour (King Arthur preferred)

2 teaspoons baking powder

½ teaspoon salt

3 eggs, well beaten

1 cup sugar

1 stick (½ cup) butter or margarine, melted

2 teaspoons vanilla extract

1½ tablespoons anise extract

1 cup chopped walnuts (optional)

½ cup dried cranberries (optional)

½ cup miniature chocolate chips (optional)

1. Preheat oven to 350°F.

2. In a small bowl, sift together flour, baking powder, and salt.

3. In a large bowl, using an electric mixer on medium speed, beat together the beaten eggs, sugar, melted butter, and the 2 extracts.

4. Blend the flour into the egg mixture and beat on slow speed until smooth and firm. Add more flour if dough is too soft to handle.

5. Remove from bowl onto a floured board or counter. Gently knead dough, using floured hands. If the dough is too soft to handle, add more flour as needed.

6. Knead in the walnuts, cranberries, and chips, if using.

7. Cut dough in 3 parts. Put dough pieces on ungreased cookie sheet and form dough into log shapes, each about 6 inches long. Flatten slightly. If smaller cookies are desired, make 6 smaller loaves instead.

8. Bake in the preheated oven for about 25 minutes for large loaves or 20 minutes for small loaves. It is best to keep the cookie sheet on the middle rack and away from the sides, or loaves will burn on the bottom. You will have to check them periodically to prevent burning. Remove from oven when slightly browned. If bottoms burn, scrape with the smallest part of a cheese grater.

9. Cool loaves on a rack for 5 minutes, then, while still warm, slice them diagonally into ½-inch slices using a long, small, serrated knife.

10. Place the slices cut-side down on the ungreased baking sheet and return to the oven to toast until they turn a light golden color, about 10–15 minutes.

11. Remove from oven, cool, and store in a covered container. They will keep fresh at least 3 weeks.

Instead of anise extract, I use full-strength anisette for a more pronounced flavor.

It is important to cook biscotti thoroughly to prevent raw middles, as they will tear apart when cut.

CHOCOLATE WALNUT BISCOTTI

YIELD: ABOUT 3 DOZEN

I love this recipe! Make the plain biscotti, and if you have the time, make this chocolate one also. These biscotti recipes are so easy to make, and the combination of the two of them looks inviting when served on a doily-lined decorative platter.

2 cups unbleached flour (King Arthur preferred)

½ cup cocoa powder (Hershey's preferred)

1 teaspoon baking soda

½ teaspoon cinnamon

1 teaspoon salt

¾ stick (6 tablespoons) unsalted butter

1 cup sugar

2 large eggs, slightly beaten

1 teaspoon orange extract

1 teaspoon vanilla extract

1 cup chopped walnuts

1 cup semisweet chocolate chips

Confectioners' sugar

1. Preheat oven to 350°F.

2. Butter and flour a large baking sheet.

3. In a small bowl, using a wire whisk, mix flour, cocoa powder, baking soda, cinnamon, and salt.

4. In a large bowl, using an electric mixer, cream butter and sugar. Add eggs, orange extract, and vanilla.

5. Stir flour mixture into bowl with egg mixture to form a stiff dough.

6. Remove dough from bowl and, using a floured board, gently knead walnuts and chocolate chips into the dough. If dough is too soft to handle, add more flour.

7. Cut dough into 3 parts. Place all 3 pieces onto the baking sheet.

8. With floured hands, form 3 long log shapes, slightly flattening each one. (By keeping the shapes long, cookies will cook well inside and will cut easily.)

9. Sprinkle tops with a generous amount of confectioners' sugar.

10. Bake for 25–30 minutes on middle rack of oven. Remove from oven and let cool for 5 minutes.

11. Remove to a cutting board and cut the loaves diagonally into ½-inch slices while still warm. You will need a long, small, serrated knife. Work quickly or the cookies will break.

12. Return cookies, cut-side down, to the ungreased baking sheet and bake in the oven until crisp, about 10 minutes.

13. Remove from oven and cool biscotti completely. Store in an airtight container. Cookies will stay fresh at least 2 weeks; they also freeze well.

STRUFOLI

SERVES 8–10

We usually make this dessert for Easter and Christmas. Use your prettiest platter and shape the strufoli into a cone or Christmas tree or even an Easter bunny if you're artistic. So pretty, and delicious, too!

2 cups peanut oil

2 cups sifted flour

¼ teaspoon salt

3 eggs

½ teaspoon vanilla extract

1 cup honey

1 tablespoon sugar

1 tablespoon multicolored sprinkles

1. Heat the oil in a deep saucepan to 365°F. Meanwhile, mix the flour and salt in a large bowl.

2. Make a well in the center of the flour. Add the eggs, one at a time. Mix slightly after each addition, using a fork or tossing the eggs with your fingers, squeezing slightly. Add the vanilla. Mix well to make a soft dough.

3. Turn the dough onto a lightly floured surface and knead for 5 minutes. Divide the dough in half. Lightly roll each half into a ¼-inch-thick rectangle. Cut the dough with a sharp knife or pastry cutter into ¼-inch-wide strips. Use the palm of your hand to roll the strips to pencil thickness. Cut into pieces about ¼ inch long.

4. Add the pieces to the hot oil, being certain they can float uncrowded. Fry 3–5 minutes or until lightly browned, turning often during the cooking time. Transfer with a slotted spoon to paper towels to drain. Finish frying all the pieces.

5. Meanwhile, cook the honey and sugar in a separate skillet over low heat for about 5 minutes.

6. Remove from the heat and add the deep-fried pieces. Stir constantly until all the pieces are coated with the honey-sugar mixture.

7. Remove the strufoli with a slotted spoon and set on a pan in the refrigerator to chill slightly. Transfer to a large serving platter and arrange in a cone-shaped mound. Sprinkle with multicolored sprinkles. Chill in the refrigerator to set the shape desired and cool the syrup.

8. Strufoli may be kept in a cake box for up to 2 weeks. Serve by breaking off individual pieces.

SWEET WINE STRIPS

STRICCIA

YIELD: 2½ DOZEN

Wine strips are an excellent, fancy Italian cookie. They are so crisp and light, your guests will never stop eating them.

2 cups all-purpose flour

½ teaspoon baking powder

3 tablespoons sugar

¼ cup butter

½ cup Italian red wine

2 cups vegetable oil

½ cup confectioners' sugar

1 teaspoon cinnamon

1. Sift the flour, measure, and resift with the baking powder and sugar.

2. Cut the butter into the flour with your fingers until the mixture resembles cornmeal. Make a well in the flour and pour the wine into it. Mix the wine into the flour. Knead the dough until smooth, about 5 minutes.

3. Wrap the dough in waxed paper and set aside for 2 hours. Do not chill.

4. Roll the dough into a rectangle, ¼ inch thick. Cut into strips 1 inch wide and 4 inches long.

5. In a deep heavy skillet or pan, heat the oil on medium-high heat.

6. Drop about 4 strips of dough at a time into the hot oil, and fry until they are golden brown. Turn them over as they rise to the surface (using a pair of tongs makes this easy).

7. Remove the strips from the oil with tongs or a slotted spoon and drain on absorbent paper. Repeat until all the strips are fried.

8. Combine the confectioners' sugar and cinnamon. Sprinkle it over the strips when they are cool. Arrange on a pretty platter and serve.

These will keep in a covered container for a while. Put a paper towel on the bottom of the container to absorb any moisture. Do not sprinkle with confectioners' sugar until just before serving.

CENCI

FRIED BOWKNOTS

YIELD: 3–4 DOZEN

These are light and delicate, oddly shaped cookies. They are very interesting for an afternoon tea or a special luncheon dessert. Some people like to drizzle them with honey and sprinkle on multicolored candies for a colorful effect.

4 egg yolks

1 egg white

½ teaspoon salt

¼ cup confectioners' sugar, plus more for dusting

1 teaspoon vanilla extract

1 teaspoon rum

1 cup flour

1 (3-pound) can vegetable shortening

1. Combine the egg yolks and egg white. Add the salt and beat 8–10 minutes on high speed with an electric mixer, or use a wire whisk and beat rapidly.

2. Add the sugar, vanilla, and rum and beat until well blended, about 2 minutes. Add the flour a little at a time, lightly folding it in.

3. Transfer the dough to a well-floured surface and knead until the dough blisters, about 5 minutes. If no blisters form and the dough seems quite smooth, cover it with a towel and let it rest for about 20 minutes.

4. Divide the dough into 4 parts. Roll out one part at a time on a lightly floured board to paper-thinness.

5. Cut into strips ½ inch wide and 6 inches long. Tie each strip into a loose bowknot or twist. Let dry for about 5 minutes or until the oil is ready.

6. Using a large, deep, and heavy pan, heat the shortening to 375°F. Fry the bow-knots, uncrowded, until golden brown, turning once. Using a slotted spoon or tongs, carefully lift them out of the oil. Drain on paper towels. (The oil can be strained and stored for a future use.)

7. Transfer to a large serving platter and sprinkle with confectioners' sugar.

CHRISTMAS FROSTED ANISETTE COOKIES

**YIELD: 3–4 DOZEN LARGE COOKIES OR
6–7 DOZEN SMALL COOKIES**

My friend Nancy worked in her family's pastry shop for many years. She gladly shared this recipe for these S-shaped cookies with me.

Have all ingredients at room temperature.

1 cup granulated sugar

12 heaping tablespoons butter-flavored vegetable shortening (Crisco preferred)

6 fresh eggs

½ cup milk, at room temperature

5 cups unbleached flour (King Arthur preferred)

6 heaping teaspoons baking powder

1¾ tablespoons anise or lemon extract

1. Preheat oven to 400°F.

2. In a large bowl, using an electric mixer, cream together sugar and shortening for about 5 minutes.

3. Add eggs, one at a time, mixing well after each addition.

4. Using the mixer at low speed, add ½ cup milk, 3 cups flour, baking powder, and extract.

5. Stir slowly for a few minutes as you add the remaining 2 cups flour (or more if needed) until dough is soft and pliable and not stiff. Dough should be a little on the sticky side.

6. Using a large spatula, scrape dough from bowl onto a well-floured board. Knead slightly with floured hands until dough is firm (about 2 minutes).

7. Break off small pieces to form 1-inch balls, keeping in mind that the dough will double in size while cooking. Roll between hands to form a pencil-like shape.

8. Twist pencil-shape dough into a mound to form a pyramid shape. Seal the ends by pinching the dough. The dough can also be twisted into the letter S or the figure 8. All these shapes are traditional for these cookies.

9. As each cookie is made, place on an ungreased cookie sheet at least 2 inches apart.

10. Bake in the preheated oven for 8–10 minutes or until light on top and slightly browned on bottom. Check baking cookies periodically.

11. Remove from oven and, when cool, brush with anise frosting.

ANISE FROSTING

1 pound confectioners' sugar

1 teaspoon anise extract

¼ cup milk (plus a little extra), at room temperature

Multicolored sprinkles

1. Combine the sugar with extract and mix well.

2. Add ¼ cup milk to form a smooth paste. If mixture is too thick, add more milk. If too thin, add more powdered sugar.

3. Frost cookies and immediately sprinkle with candies. Set on waxed paper until frosting is firm.

4. When completely cooled, about 1 hour, place on a decorative platter and serve.

STORYTELLER

My father's father was born in Avellino; my mother's mother was born in Rome, and both only spoke Italian. We were able to understand them mostly by gestures. For example, my grandfather would sit in the rocking chair (when grandma wasn't on it), and rock back and forth as we gathered on the floor at his feet. He would tell us all kinds of parables in Italian, always about doing wrong, like stealing and lying. Because he repeated the same stories over and over, we understood almost every word. He was a very dramatic storyteller, speaking softly and then loudly when he came to the punch line so we would jump with fright tinged with glee, even though we knew what was to come. In this way we understood his lessons and took them to heart in our everyday lives.

ANISEED COOKIES

YIELD: 4 DOZEN

Enjoy this old-fashioned, easy dessert when you need a relaxing change. Be sure to have all ingredients at room temperature. These cookies need to be stored at least a week before you can eat them. They are great to give as gifts during the holidays or as hostess gifts.

1 stick (½ cup) unsalted butter, softened

1½ cups firmly packed brown sugar
   (or granulated sugar)

3 eggs

Few drops of anise oil

3 cups sifted all-purpose flour

Freshly toasted aniseeds

1. Preheat oven to 350°F.

2. Using a food processor on low speed, cream the butter with the sugar.

3. Add eggs one at a time and beat well after each addition. Add anise oil at a point during this process.

4. Pour 2 cups flour into this batter and gently blend at low speed.

5. Remove bowl from appliance and stir in remaining flour. Mix well.

6. Drop teaspoonfuls of finished dough onto a greased cookie sheet and sprinkle with the toasted aniseeds. (Use a toaster oven for toasting the seeds.)

7. Bake in the preheated oven for about 12 minutes, until bottoms are golden and tops are pale.

8. Cool and store in an airtight container for a week to allow flavors to develop before eating.

ITALIAN CLOVE COOKIES

YIELD: APPROXIMATELY 4 DOZEN

For easier handling, add as much flour as needed to slightly hold dough together and not be too sticky to handle. Use only unsweetened cocoa powder.

¾ cups vegetable oil

3 eggs

¼ cup milk

1¼ cups dark brown sugar

1 teaspoon vanilla extract

1½ teaspoons oil of orange

4 cups flour (Gold Medal preferred)

3 teaspoons baking powder

1 teaspoon cinnamon

1 teaspoon cloves

½ cup cocoa powder (Hershey's preferred)

½ cup chocolate chips, crushed

1 cup walnuts, crushed

1. Beat together the oil, eggs, milk, brown sugar, vanilla, and oil of orange.

2. In a separate large mixing bowl, combine the flour, baking powder, cinnamon, cloves, cocoa, crushed chocolate chips, and walnuts.

3. Add the egg mixture to the flour mixture and mix well, using the low speed of the mixer.

4. Place the dough on a wooden board and softly knead. The dough may be sticky; if so, oil your hands lightly.

5. Break off pieces of dough about the size of a large walnut. Place on cookie sheets about 1 inch apart.

6. Bake in a preheated 350°F oven for about 20 minutes on the middle rack. Remove when slightly browned and let cool.

7. Frost cookies all around to keep soft. Place on waxed paper to dry.

FROSTING

½ cup unsweetened cocoa powder (Hershey's preferred)

2 cups confectioners' sugar

1 teaspoon oil of orange

1 teaspoon melted butter

Mix all the ingredients together. If the frosting is too thin, add more sugar.

ITALIAN TOTO COOKIES

YIELD: 3–4 DOZEN

These cookies are also called too too or tatto cookies. The addition of cloves gives them a unique flavor that distinguishes them from your ordinary Italian cookie, especially when combined with cinnamon and orange flavoring. Though the recipe seems long, the ingredients are readily available and the directions are very easy. It is always important when baking to have all ingredients at room temperature.

4 cups flour, sifted

4 teaspoons baking powder

5 teaspoons unsweetened cocoa powder

1 teaspoon ground cloves

½ teaspoon cinnamon

3 eggs, well beaten

1 cup milk

¾ cup vegetable oil

½ cup granulated sugar

½ cup brown sugar

1 teaspoon oil of orange or orange extract

1 teaspoon vanilla extract

1 cup coarsely crushed walnuts

¼ cup miniature chocolate chips

½ cup maraschino cherries in jar, drained and chopped (optional)

1. In a large bowl, combine sifted flour, baking powder, unsweetened cocoa, cloves, and cinnamon. Mix well.

2. In a separate bowl, add beaten eggs, milk, oil, white and brown sugars, orange oil, and vanilla. Mix well.

3. Add egg mixture to flour mixture and mix thoroughly. Dough will be fairly thick and sticky.

4. Add crushed nuts and chocolate chips. If desired, add drained, chopped cherries.

5. Turn dough onto a floured board and knead until you can handle well, using more flour if needed.

6. Wet hands with oil or dust with flour. Break off pieces of dough and roll into size of large walnuts.

7. Place on a greased cookie sheet, 1 inch apart, and bake for 15–20 minutes in a preheated 350°F oven. Let cool.

8. Spread frosting on cooled cookies and place on waxed paper to dry.

FROSTING

2 tablespoons melted butter

2 cups confectioners' sugar

1 heaping tablespoon unsweetened cocoa powder

½ teaspoon oil of orange or orange flavoring

1 teaspoon vanilla extract

2 tablespoons milk or black coffee

Mix ingredients well until smooth enough to spread. If mixture is too dry, add more milk or black coffee. If too soft, add more flour.

ITALIAN SESAME SEED COOKIES

YIELD: 2½ DOZEN LARGE OR 3½ DOZEN SMALL COOKIES

This is my wonderful tried-and-true recipe that has been handed down from generation to generation. It was given to us by one of the former owners of a pastry shop that once was noted for having the best Italian pastries in our neighborhood. The shop is closed now, but these cookies are one of its legacies.

1 cup melted butter or margarine, cooled

1 cup sugar

2 eggs, well beaten

2 tablespoons milk, plus additional for coating

1 teaspoon vanilla extract

3 teaspoons baking powder

3½–4 cups unbleached flour (King Arthur preferred)

Sesame seeds

1. Preheat oven to 375°F.

2. With an electric mixer on medium speed, cream melted butter and sugar.

3. Add 2 well-beaten eggs and mix.

4. Add milk, vanilla, and baking powder and mix well.

5. Add enough flour as needed. Mix until dough is soft and pliable, but not sticky.

6. Remove from bowl and knead gently, adding more flour if needed. Cover and allow to rest 15 minutes.

7. Pour some milk in a deep bowl and put sesame seeds in a wide bowl.

8. Break off dough pieces the size of walnuts and roll in the palms of your hands.

9. Roll dough pieces in milk first, then in seeds, covering generously all over.

10. Place on a greased cookie sheet, then flatten slightly. Cookies should have a short and wide rectangular shape for a better appearance after cooking.

11. Bake in the preheated oven for about 15 minutes or until lightly browned. Use middle rack, so bottoms of cookies will not burn.

ALMOND RICCIARELLI COOKIES

CRESCENT-SHAPED ALMOND COOKIES

YIELD: 2½ DOZEN

This recipe was donated by one of the lovely ladies who devoted many hours of volunteer work to the North End Union. Her name was never recorded, but her recipe will be remembered and enjoyed. These cookies are also known as Anise Tea Cookies.

2½ cups sifted all-purpose flour

½ teaspoon salt

¼ cup chopped pecans, walnuts, or other nuts

1 tablespoon anise flavoring, or 1 tablespoon aniseeds

⅔ cup vegetable oil

⅔ cup confectioners' sugar, plus more for dusting

3 tablespoons orange juice

2 teaspoons vanilla extract

1. Preheat oven to 350°F.

2. In a large bowl, combine sifted flour, salt, nuts, anise flavoring, and vegetable oil. Using an electric mixer, slowly beat these ingredients until well blended.

3. In a small bowl or blender, combine confectioners' sugar, orange juice, and vanilla. Mix briefly, then add to flour mixture. Beat on low speed until well blended. The mixture should be rather crumbly and a little on the dry side. If necessary, add more orange juice until dough is handleable but not moist.

4. Shape into small balls, squeezing slightly with the palms of your hands.

5. Put on an ungreased cookie sheet and press dough slightly with your fingers to form a half-moon or crescent shape about 1½ inches long. Space cookies a couple of inches apart.

6. Bake until lightly browned, about 20 minutes.

7. Remove from oven and, while still warm, roll cookies in confectioners' sugar.

8. Cool and store in a covered container.

PIGNOLI COOKIES

YIELD: 2½ DOZEN

This traditional recipe is especially popular at Christmastime and Easter. To make it you will need almond paste and pignoli nuts, which you'll find in a gourmet or specialty store. Grease your cookie sheets, and be sure to remove the cookies from the oven before the nuts burn.

1 pound pignoli nuts, left whole

1 (8-ounce) can almond paste

2 egg whites, slightly beaten

1 teaspoon lemon extract

½ cup granulated sugar

½ cup confectioners' sugar

¼ cup all-purpose flour

Pinch of salt

1. Preheat oven to 300°F.

2. Lightly grease 2 cookie sheets.

3. Put pignoli nuts in a small bowl.

4. In a medium bowl, blend the almond paste, using an electric mixer, until smooth. Add the egg whites and lemon extract and beat until well blended and smooth.

5. Sift the 2 sugars and flour with salt.

6. Slowly add sugar and flour mixture to almond and egg mixture, mixing on slow speed. The dough should be slightly sticky.

7. Using wet hands, form dough into walnut-shaped balls.

8. Flattening slightly, press dough into pignoli nuts (on one side of the cookie only). Place 1 inch apart on greased baking sheets, pignoli nuts on top.

9. Bake for 20–25 minutes or until golden brown.

10. Cool completely and store in a cookie canister.

RICOTTA COOKIES

YIELD: 3 DOZEN

These cookies are a nice surprise because they have the rich taste of butter, but the ricotta makes them light.

1 stick (½ cup) butter, at room temperature

¼ cup ricotta cheese

1 teaspoon vanilla extract

1 cup sugar

1 egg

2 cups sifted flour

½ teaspoon baking soda

½ teaspoon salt

1. Blend the butter with the ricotta until creamy. Add the vanilla and mix well.

2. Gradually add the sugar, beating until well blended. Add the egg and mix well.

3. Slowly stir in the flour, baking soda, and salt, blending well.

4. Drop the batter from a teaspoon onto a greased baking sheet.

5. Bake in a preheated 350°F oven for 10 minutes.

6. Using a spatula, transfer cookies to a serving platter. They will keep for several weeks if stored in a covered container.

EASTER TREATS

Easter was always my favorite holiday when I was growing up in the North End. The subject on everyone's minds was food (and, of course, church). Everyone bragged about how they made the best ricotta pie or pizzagiena or zeppole. The windows of every bakery displayed incredibly beautiful decorated breads filled with colorful dyed eggs. During that time of the year, Woolworth's department store used to sell live baby chicks. I loved them so much that I always bought one or two. I kept them in a cardboard box and took good care of them, feeding and cleaning their boxes every day. Then, several weeks later when they had grown large, our family would enjoy a fresh organic chicken dinner!

PIZZELLE

YIELD: ABOUT 32 PIZZELLE

These thin, crisp, waffle-like cookies, which measure about 4½ inches across, can be eaten plain, dusted with confectioners' sugar, or sandwiched with ham, chocolate ganache, Nutella, or even ice cream. While the pizzelle are still warm, they can be wrapped around a rod to form a tube shape and then filled like cannoli. Other options for flavorings include almond extract, liqueur, citrus rind, or spices such as cinnamon, ginger, and nutmeg. You need a pizzelle iron to make these cookies (a modern electric one will do).

1¾ cups all-purpose flour

2 teaspoons baking powder

3 large eggs

¾ cup sugar

1 stick (½ cup) butter or margarine, melted

½ tablespoon vanilla extract

1½ teaspoons anise flavoring or oil

Confectioners' sugar (optional)

1. Preheat the pizzelle iron according to directions. Spray once all over with cooking spray.

2. In a bowl, whisk together the flour and baking powder. Set aside.

3. In a large bowl, using a mixer on medium speed, lightly beat the eggs well, then add sugar, melted butter, vanilla, and anise flavoring.

4. On slow speed, gradually add the dry ingredients until smooth, occasionally scraping the sides of the bowl with a rubber spatula. If too loose and runny, add more flour as needed. Let mixture sit for at least 15 minutes.

5. Using a finger, spoon 1 rounded tablespoon (or 1 teaspoon if necessary) of batter into the center of the pizzelle iron grid. Cover and cook until light golden brown, about 45 seconds—do not lift the cover during baking (though it can be checked after 25 seconds). If batter overlaps the grill while cooking, trim cookie edges with scissors.

6. When done, lift the cover and loosen the pizzelle with a fork or spatula. A plastic fork is good for a nonstick surface. Continue with remaining batter.

7. Transfer to paper dishes or a wire rack to cool completely. When cool, sprinkle with confectioners' sugar, if desired.

8. Cookies can be stacked in a tightly covered container (do not crowd, to prevent breakage) and stored at room temperature for up to 2 weeks or in the freezer for up to 3 months.

When finished, wipe the iron grill with a paper towel. Leave top part up and do not put away until absolutely cooled. Do not wash.

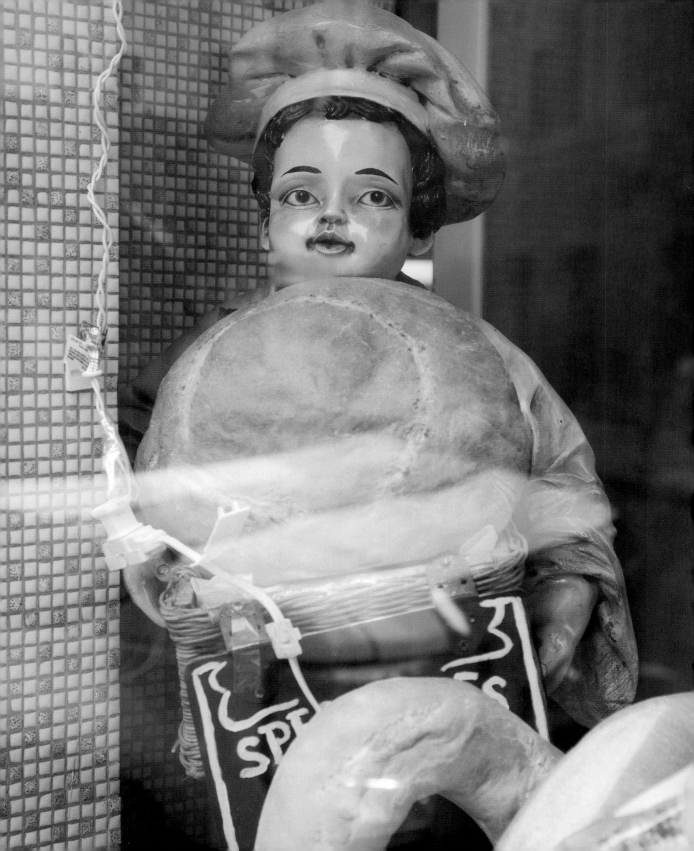

OSSO DEI MORTE

BONES OF THE DEAD

YIELD: 2–3 DOZEN COOKIES

Osso dei Morte is a pastry shaped to resemble a large broad bean. In the old days in Italy, the bean was looked upon as a funeral offering, and it was thought that the souls of the dead were enclosed in it. Versions of the recipe are found in various regions of Italy; this one is a favorite.

¼ **pound blanched almonds**

½ **cup sugar**

2 cups flour

½ **teaspoon ground cloves (optional)**

2⅓ **tablespoons butter, softened**

1 egg

Lemon or vanilla extract or brandy

Flour for dusting

1 egg yolk, beaten

1. Preheat oven to 300°F.

2. Pound the almonds in a mortar with the sugar until they resemble small grains of rice.

3. Put the flour in a large bowl and, with a fork, gradually stir in the ground cloves (if using), butter, and egg.

4. Add the almond and sugar mixture to the flour mixture. Combine well. Add enough lemon or vanilla extract or brandy to make a smooth dough.

5. Put dough on a lightly floured board and knead gently. Roll out thickly and cut the dough into thick strips with a sharp knife. Cut each strip diagonally into small pieces.

6. With your hands, flatten the pieces into the shape of favas, or large broad beans. Put them on a buttered sheet pan and sprinkle with a little flour. Brush with the beaten egg yolk.

7. Bake until the cookies are an even golden color, about 5 minutes. Watch carefully, because they bake quickly.

TORTONI

SERVES 12

This is a good recipe, but one that requires careful attention. Take your time, and you will be pleased with the result.

6 egg yolks

Pinch of salt

3 tablespoons warm water

¾ cup sugar

¼ cup water

1 tablespoon vanilla extract

3 tablespoons sherry

1 pint heavy cream

½ cup chopped almonds

1. Combine the egg yolks, salt, and warm water in the top of a double boiler. Over boiling water, beat until the yolks are light and lemon colored. Set aside.

2. Boil the sugar and ¼ cup water over medium heat, stirring constantly, until the syrup spins a thread from the end of a spoon.

3. Cool the syrup slightly, then beat it into the egg yolks, beating rapidly and constantly. Cook over hot (not boiling) water, stirring constantly, until thick, about 8 minutes. Remove from heat and cool to room temperature.

4. Add the vanilla and sherry and let the mixture cool some more.

5. Beat the cream until it is thick but not stiff. Stir the cream into the custard. Pour into 12 fluted paper cups.

6. Sprinkle the tops with the chopped almonds. Put the cups in the freezer.

7. Freeze until firm, about 3 hours, or for a few days. If desired, tortoni may be frozen in ice cube trays and served in sherbet glasses.

BISCUIT TORTONI

SERVES 6

Here is another tortoni recipe, but one that uses different ingredients. It makes a very elegant company dessert.

½ cup crushed Italian macaroons (without almonds)

½ cup crushed toasted almonds

¼ cup confectioners' sugar

2 cups heavy cream

3 tablespoons rum

6 maraschino cherries for garnish

1. Mix together the crushed macaroons, three-fourths of the almonds, confectioners' sugar, and 1 cup cream.

2. Whip the second cup of cream until it is stiff. Fold it into the macaroon mixture, alternating with the rum.

3. Spoon into 6 small paper cups and freeze. After 2 hours, sprinkle the tops with the remaining crushed almonds. Place a maraschino cherry in the center of each cup. Return the desserts to the freezer until serving time.

ZABAGLIONE

SERVES 6

Serve this in pretty dessert glasses as the perfect ending for an elegant meal or for a special dinner party.

4 egg yolks

¼ cup sugar

¾ cup port or marsala wine

Pinch of cinnamon

1. Beat the yolks until they are light and lemon colored. Gradually add the sugar, beating constantly. Add the wine and beat well.

2. Pour into the top of a double boiler and cook over hot (not boiling) water until thick, beating constantly with a rotary beater.

3. Pour into dessert dishes, sprinkle with cinnamon, and serve. Or chill and serve as a sauce over fruit.

MONTE BIANCO

CHESTNUT PUREE WITH A MOUNTAIN OF WHIPPED CREAM

SERVES 4–6

In Italy the month of November first starts with prayers for the dead and for the souls in purgatory. It is also a time for visiting the graves of loved ones. Coincidentally, the first chestnut harvest begins in November. Chestnut dishes are traditional and seasonal. They are used for stuffings, mashed as a side dish, or incorporated into sweet puffs, cakes, and creams. Monte Bianco is a favorite holiday dessert.

1 (1-pound) can chestnut puree, or fresh blanched and ground chestnuts (see page 353)

½ cup whole milk

1 cup plus 1 teaspoon sugar

1 teaspoon rum flavoring

1 tablespoon butter

1½ teaspoons vanilla extract

½ pint cold heavy cream

Grated chocolate for garnish (optional)

1. In the upper part of a double boiler, thoroughly heat chestnut puree over boiling water.

2. In a medium saucepan on low heat, warm milk, 1 cup sugar, rum flavoring, butter, and 1 teaspoon vanilla, stirring until sugar is dissolved.

3. Add the heated chestnut puree, stirring lightly with a wire whisk.

4. Remove mixture from heat, spoon into a glass serving bowl, and chill.

5. To serve, whip the cold cream, 1 teaspoon sugar, and remaining ½ teaspoon vanilla until stiff peaks form. Just before serving, pile it in a mountain shape in the center of the chestnut puree. You may add a few shavings of grated chocolate on top.

6. Present the Monte Bianco at the table in the mound, then spoon it into dessert cups for people to eat.

TARTUFI CIOCCOLATO

CHOCOLATE TRUFFLES

SERVES 6

This ice-cream dessert is a favorite in the cafes of Rome. For this recipe, you will need the richest chocolate ice cream available. Colored, fluted paper cups add flair to this exciting dessert.

6 maraschino cherries, well drained

6 large scoops of rich chocolate ice cream

2 cups shaved pure bittersweet chocolate

¾ cup heavy cream, whipped

1. Embed a cherry in the center of each ice-cream scoop.

2. Place shaved chocolate in a small bowl.

3. Thickly coat each scoop of ice cream with the shaved chocolate. Reserve some chocolate for garnish.

4. Place each ice-cream ball in a fluted paper cup. Set on a small, shallow plate and freeze until solid.

5. Serve each one on a small, decorative dessert dish and swirl some whipped cream over the top. Garnish top of whipped cream with some shaved chocolate.

Keep the bittersweet chocolate in the refrigerator to help you shave it neatly. A clean cheese shaver works well for this procedure.

BRANDIED CHERRIES

YIELD: 2 QUARTS

These cherries must be stored for a month before using. This can be helpful if you are making them for a holiday when you will be busy with other things.

2 pounds bing cherries

2 cups brandy

2 cups sugar

1 cup water

1. Wash the cherries and cut off half of each stem.

2. Place the cherries in 2 sterilized quart jars and cover them with the brandy. Cover the jars, but do not seal. Let stand overnight.

3. Boil the sugar and water together for 10 minutes. Skim the surface and cool.

4. Drain the brandy from the cherries and add it to the syrup. Stir well. Pour the liquid back into the jars over the cherries. Seal tightly and store in a cool, dark cupboard.

BRANDIED CHESTNUTS

YIELD: 1 QUART

Chestnuts must be blanched and shelled before they can be used. There are many ways to blanch them. This is an easy one: Cut slits in each nut before putting them in a pan and covering them with water. Boil gently until tender, about 30 minutes. Drain, then remove shells and skins. Chestnuts prepared this way are easily pureed or mashed. Brandied chestnuts must be stored for a month before using them.

1¼ cups sugar

1 cup water

1 pound chestnuts, blanched and shelled

1 cup brandy

1. Boil the sugar and water in a small saucepan for 10 minutes. Skim the surface.

2. Put the peeled chestnuts in a bowl and pour the hot syrup over them. Cover and let stand overnight.

3. The next day, drain the syrup from the chestnuts and combine it with the brandy in a saucepan. Bring to a boil.

4. Put the chestnuts in a hot, sterilized quart jar or 2 pint jars and pour the boiling syrup over them. Seal tightly and store in a cool, dark cupboard.

GRANITA DI LIMONE

LEMON ICE

SERVES 4

Children will enjoy this lemon ice. It is also used as an after-dinner refreshment or as a cooling palate cleanser between the courses of a heavy meal.

1 envelope unflavored gelatin

¼ cup cold water

4 cups water

1 cup sugar

Juice of 3 lemons

4 lemon slices for garnish

1. Soften the gelatin in ¼ cup cold water.

2. In a large saucepan, boil the 4 cups water and sugar for 5 minutes. Remove from the heat and add the lemon juice.

3. Add the softened gelatin to the syrup, stirring until dissolved.

4. Pour into a shallow pan and freeze until almost firm, about 2–3 hours. Transfer to the refrigerator for 20–30 minutes before serving to allow the ice to soften a little. To serve, scoop into individual bowls and garnish with a slice of lemon.

LEMON
SLUSH

Small 1.50
Large 2.00

GELATO

ITALIAN SHERBET

SERVES 4

Another nice cooling dessert. This gelato is more like ice cream than the granita.

2 cups water

2 cups sugar

Pinch of salt

1 cup freshly squeezed lemon juice

Grated rind of 1 lemon

2 egg whites

1. Boil the water, sugar, and salt for 5 minutes over medium heat.

2. Strain the lemon juice into the sugar syrup. Add the grated lemon rind. Cool.

3. Beat the egg whites until stiff but not dry. Fold them gently into the cooled syrup.

4. Pour into a shallow pan, cover with waxed paper, and freeze until firm, about 3 hours.

BUDINO DI AMARETTI

MACAROON PUDDING

SERVES 4

This recipe was given to me by the chef of a restaurant in Italy. The addition of macaroon cookie crumbs gives this pudding an especially light, delicate texture.

4 or 5 macaroon cookies

3 ounces unsweetened chocolate

3 cups whole milk

4 eggs, slightly beaten

½ cup sugar

Butter

Whipped cream

Maraschino cherries for garnish

1. Put macaroon cookies in a plastic bag and crush with a rolling pin until fine.

2. Heat chocolate and milk in a small saucepan, using low heat.

3. When chocolate is melted, beat with a small whisk until smooth. Remove from heat.

4. Beat eggs and sugar together until well blended. Slowly add egg mixture to hot chocolate mixture and stir constantly and vigorously with a whisk until completely smooth.

5. Return pan to stove and cook until thick, stirring constantly for 10 minutes.

6. Turn off heat, add macaroon crumbs to pan, and beat with whisk until smooth and shiny. Cool slightly.

7. Pour pudding into a buttered 1-quart baking dish. Refrigerate for at least 3 hours before serving.

8. Top with whipped cream and cherry garnish.

FRUIT AND WINE D'ITALIA

SERVES 6

This heavenly mixture of fruits and wine is a great dessert when you need something light to pick you up. Serve it alone or with fresh whipped cream. (Whip 1 pint of cold heavy cream with 1 cup confectioners' sugar in a well-chilled bowl. Add a drop or two of vanilla or anise flavoring. Refrigerate immediately until needed.)

¼ cup golden seedless raisins

White wine

Small bunch seedless red grapes

1 apple, peeled and chopped

1 orange, peeled and segmented

1 pear, chopped

½ cup maraschino cherries, halved

3–4 dates, cut in pieces

Juice of half lemon

2 heaping tablespoons sugar

¼ cup maraschino liqueur

1 banana, peeled and sliced

Whipped cream (optional)

Maraschino cherries for garnish

1. Soak the raisins in enough white wine to cover.

2. Drop the loose red grapes in a large bowl. Add the chopped apple, orange segments, chopped pear, maraschino cherries, and dates.

3. Pour the raisins with wine into the large bowl. Add the lemon juice, sugar, and maraschino liqueur.

4. Stir gently using a big spoon. Chill for at least 30 minutes.

5. Just before serving, add the sliced banana and stir gently.

6. Place in sherbet glasses with some of the syrup. Top each serving with whipped cream, if using, and a single maraschino cherry.

You may add or substitute melon, strawberries, peaches, or any fruit in season.

BAKED STUFFED FIGS

SERVES 6

This Roman recipe is a healthy snack. Use as an alternative to sugar candy.

12 dried figs, stems snipped

⅓ cup finely chopped almonds or walnuts

1 tablespoon ground cinnamon

1 tablespoon ground mace

1 cup warm water

¾ cup honey

2 tablespoons lemon juice

1. Cover the figs with warm water and let sit until soft, about 30 minutes. Drain.

2. Preheat oven to 350°F.

3. Combine the nuts, cinnamon, and mace. Cut a slit in each fig to form a pocket and gently squeeze a little nut mixture inside each pocket.

4. Arrange stuffed figs in a single layer in a baking pan to fit. Combine the warm water, honey, and lemon juice and drizzle over figs.

5. Cover the pan with foil and bake until tender, about 20 minutes, or until a light caramel sauce has formed on the bottom of the pan. Be careful not to burn the sauce and figs.

NONNA'S SWEET
EASTER EGG BREAD BASKETS

YIELD: 8 LARGE BASKETS
(OR YOU CAN ALSO DIVIDE DOUGH FURTHER TO MAKE 16 SMALL BASKETS)

This is a recipe that I take particular pride in making, especially in my cooking classes. My students really enjoy sculpting baskets of different sizes. They can't wait to take them home and show off their creations to friends and family members. Don't forget to boil the eggs in advance.

BREAD

½ **cup lukewarm water**

1 **cup plus 1 teaspoon sugar**

2 **packages dry granular yeast**

1 **cup milk**

1 **teaspoon salt**

¼ **cup butter or margarine**

3 **eggs, beaten**

6–7 **cups unbleached flour
(King Arthur preferred)**

1 **(4-ounce) jar maraschino cherries,
drained and chopped**

8 **hard-boiled eggs, dyed in different colors**

Multicolored candies

1. In a small bowl, mix ½ cup lukewarm water with 1 teaspoon sugar and, using your fingers, dissolve sugar. Add yeast to water and dissolve, using fingers. Let rest until bubbly and foamy, about 10 minutes.

2. In a small saucepan, heat milk, salt, butter, and 1 cup sugar. Stir over low heat until butter is melted and mixture is warm. (Be sure mixture is not hot when added to the beaten eggs or the eggs will cook.)

3. Place milk mixture and beaten eggs in a large bowl. Beat together with a wire whisk, then beat in 2 cups flour, the yeast mixture, and chopped cherries. Mix well until smooth.

4. Add remaining flour and mix well with hands. Turn dough onto a floured wooden board.

5. Gently knead dough for about 8–10 minutes until smooth, using floured hands (dough will be sticky because of the cherries).

6. Return dough to greased large bowl, cover with plastic, and allow to rest 1½ hours.

7. When double in size, punch down and divide into 9 equal parts. Eight parts will be for the baskets and 1 part will make the basket handles.

8. Twist 8 parts into a spiral shape, form spirals into circles, and knot ends to form a nest.

9. Put nests on a greased baking sheet and press a dyed egg into each one.

10. Break off 16 pieces of dough from the last of the 9 parts, allowing 2 small pieces for each dough basket (dough will rise considerably).

11. Slightly roll each piece of dough and make a thin cross shape with the 2 pieces of rolled dough. Place one of the 8 cross-pieces over each dough basket, leaving some of the egg in each basket exposed.

12. Tuck cross ends under each basket and pinch together to secure.

13. Place baking sheet in a warm place and allow baskets to rise until double in size (about 1 hour).

14. Bake in a preheated 350°F oven for 20 minutes.

15. Remove from oven and place each basket on a rack to cool.

16. While still warm, spoon glaze (recipe below) over each baked basket and sprinkle immediately with multicolored candies.

GLAZE

3 tablespoons soft butter

3 cups sifted confectioners' sugar

5 tablespoons milk

¾ teaspoon vanilla extract

Combine all the ingredients, stirring with a large spoon until smooth. Use immediately.

INDEX

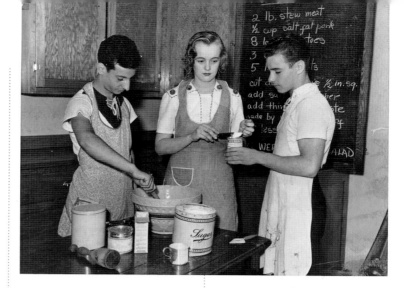

ABOUT THE AUTHOR

Marguerite DiMino Buonopane is a former restaurant chef-owner and host of the legendary luncheons at the old North End Union, a nonprofit community settlement house. For thirty years she taught cooking classes in the North End, and she writes for the magazines *Scene* and *On-Tray*.